DISTRICT X
Mr. M

007-85

DISTRIC

David Hine
writer

David Yardin, Lan Medina
& Mike Perkins
pencilers

Alejandro Sicat
& Drew Hennessy
with Avalon Studios
inkers

CTX Mr. M

colorists
Avalon's Andy Troy, Dan Kemp & David Kemp

letters
**Richard Starkings & Comicraft's Rob Steen
& Albert Deschesne**

cover art
Steve McNiven

assistant editors
Sean Ryan, Stephanie Moore & Cory Sedlmeier

editor
Mike Marts

collections editor
Jeff Youngquist

assistant editor
Jennifer Grünwald

book designer
Carrie Beadle

creative director
Tom Marvelli

editor in chief
Joe Quesada

publisher
Dan Buckley

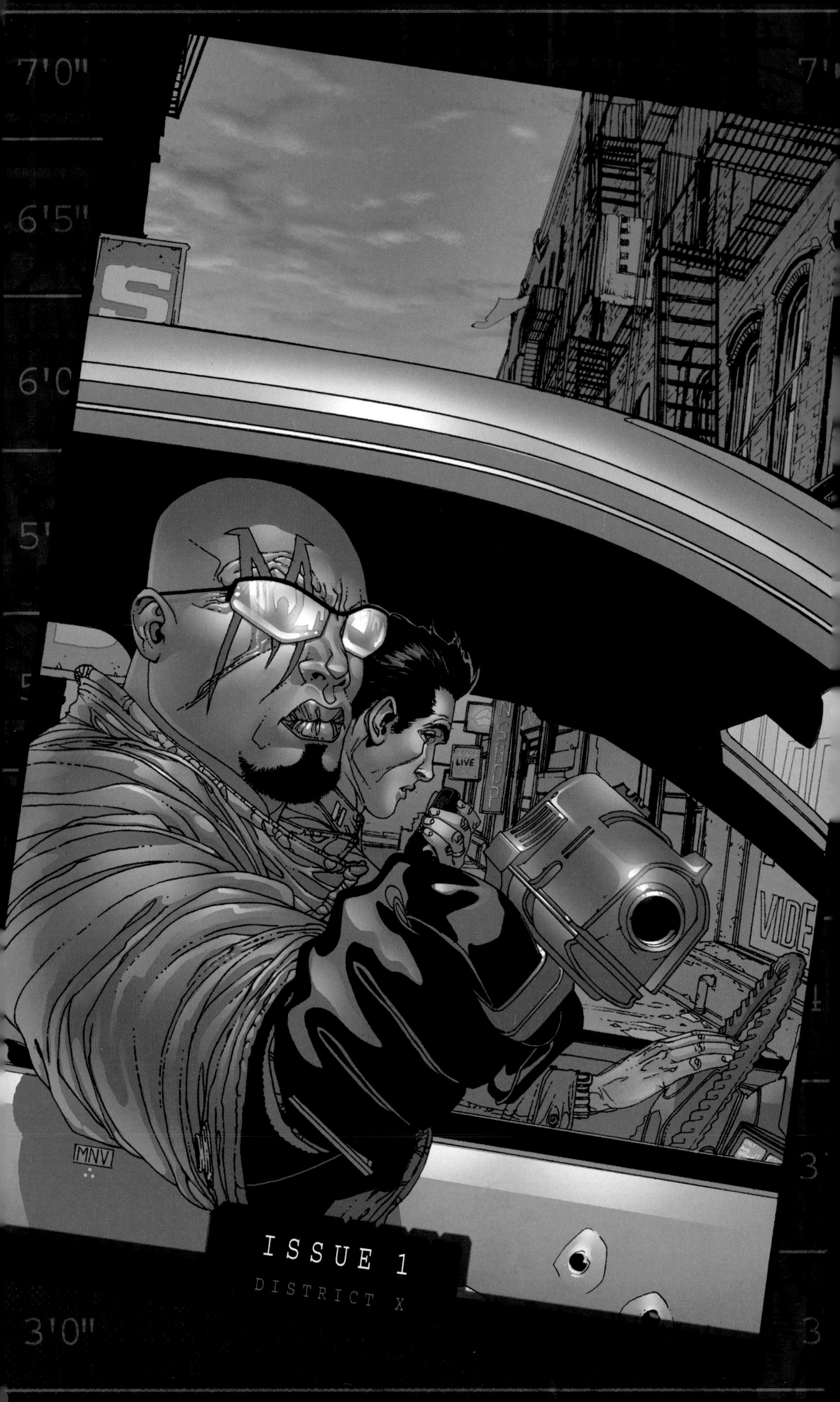
7'0"
6'5"
6'0
LIVE
MNV
ISSUE 1
DISTRICT X
3'0"

DISTRICT X ▾ MR. M 1 OF 6

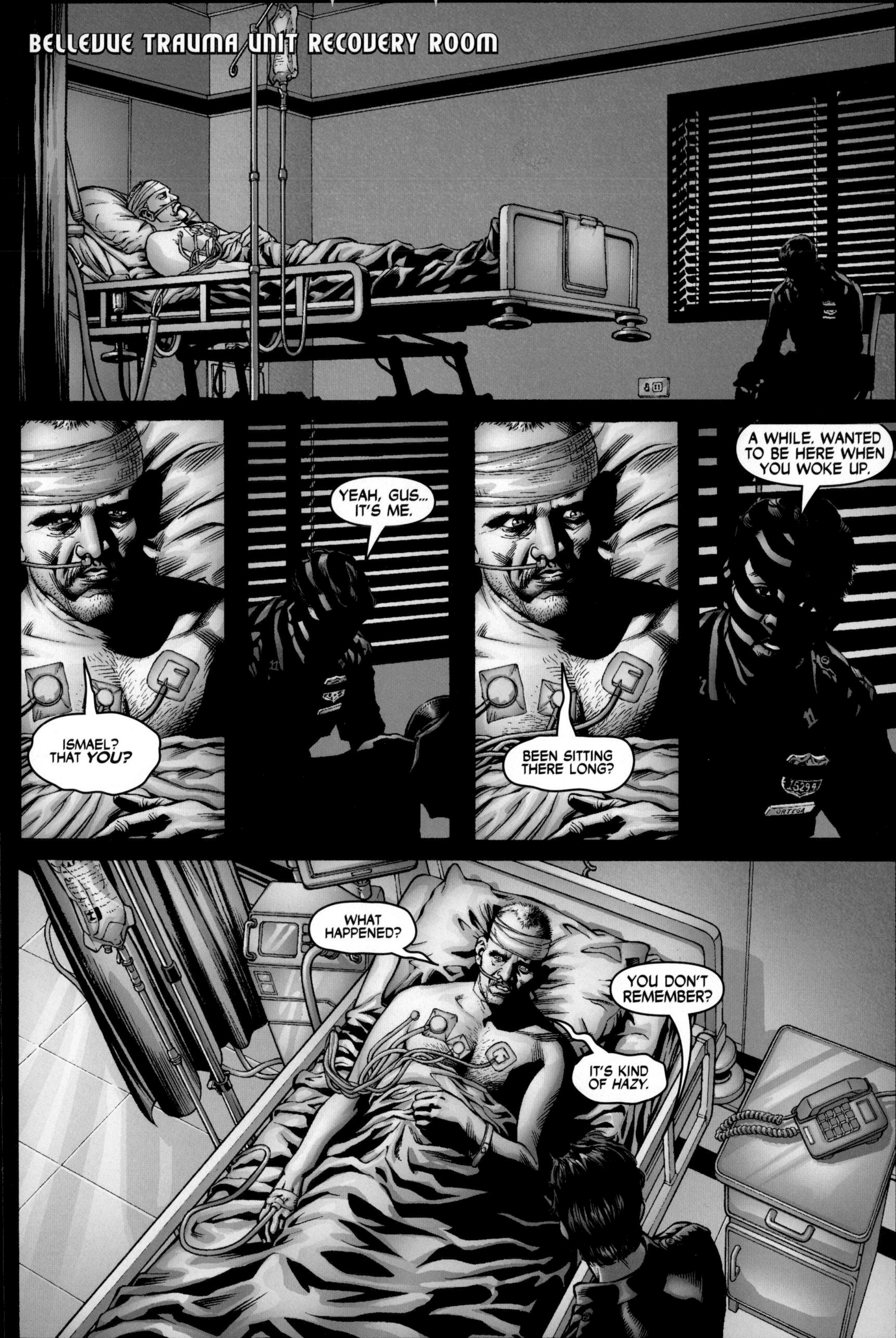
BELLEVUE TRAUMA UNIT RECOVERY ROOM
ISMAEL? THAT *YOU*?
YEAH, GUS... IT'S ME.
BEEN SITTING THERE LONG?
A WHILE. WANTED TO BE HERE WHEN YOU WOKE UP.
15294
ORTEGA
WHAT HAPPENED?
YOU DON'T REMEMBER?
IT'S KIND OF *HAZY*.

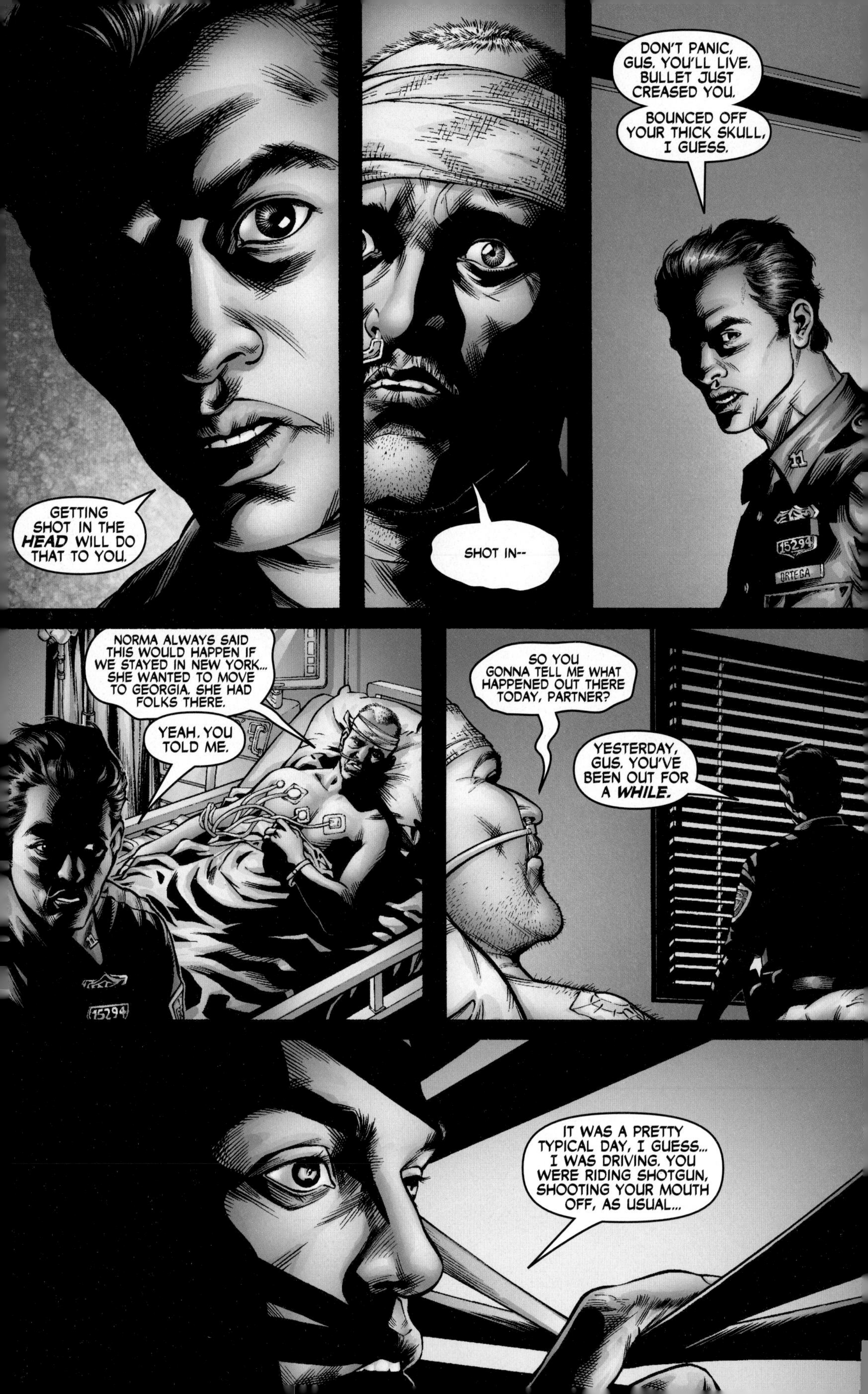
GETTING SHOT IN THE HEAD WILL DO THAT TO YOU.
SHOT IN--
DON'T PANIC, GUS. YOU'LL LIVE. BULLET JUST CREASED YOU.
BOUNCED OFF YOUR THICK SKULL, I GUESS.
15294
ORTEGA
NORMA ALWAYS SAID THIS WOULD HAPPEN IF WE STAYED IN NEW YORK... SHE WANTED TO MOVE TO GEORGIA. SHE HAD FOLKS THERE.
YEAH. YOU TOLD ME.
15294
SO YOU GONNA TELL ME WHAT HAPPENED OUT THERE TODAY, PARTNER?
YESTERDAY, GUS. YOU'VE BEEN OUT FOR A WHILE.
IT WAS A PRETTY TYPICAL DAY, I GUESS... I WAS DRIVING. YOU WERE RIDING SHOTGUN, SHOOTING YOUR MOUTH OFF, AS USUAL...

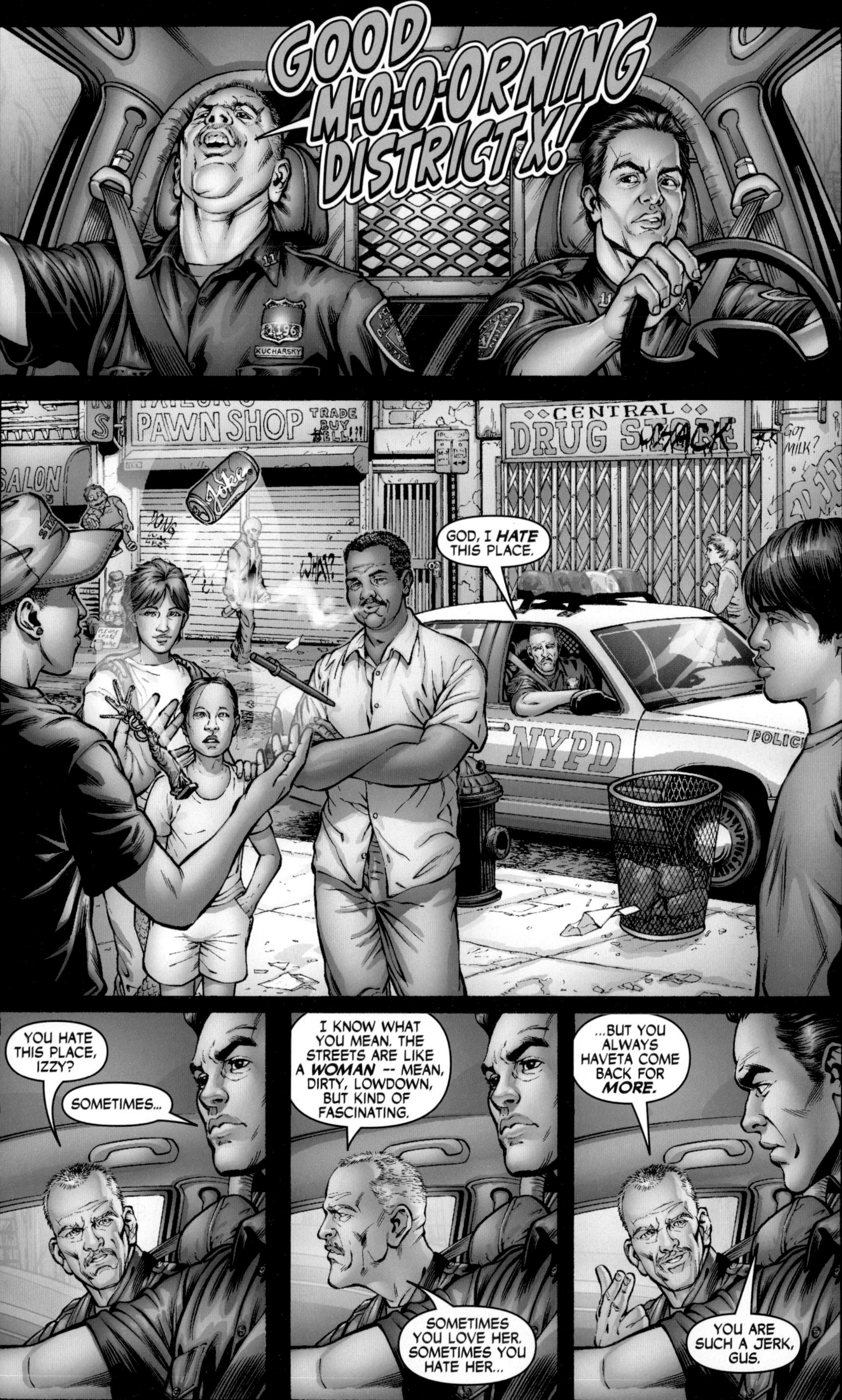
GOOD M-O-O-ORNING DISTRICT X!
KUCHARSKY
1196
PAWN SHOP
TRADE BUY SELL!!!
SALON
CENTRAL DRUG STORE
GOT MILK?
GOD, I HATE THIS PLACE.
NYPD
POLICE
YOU HATE THIS PLACE, IZZY?
SOMETIMES...
I KNOW WHAT YOU MEAN. THE STREETS ARE LIKE A WOMAN -- MEAN, DIRTY, LOWDOWN, BUT KIND OF FASCINATING.
SOMETIMES YOU LOVE HER. SOMETIMES YOU HATE HER...
...BUT YOU ALWAYS HAVETA COME BACK FOR MORE.
YOU ARE SUCH A JERK, GUS.

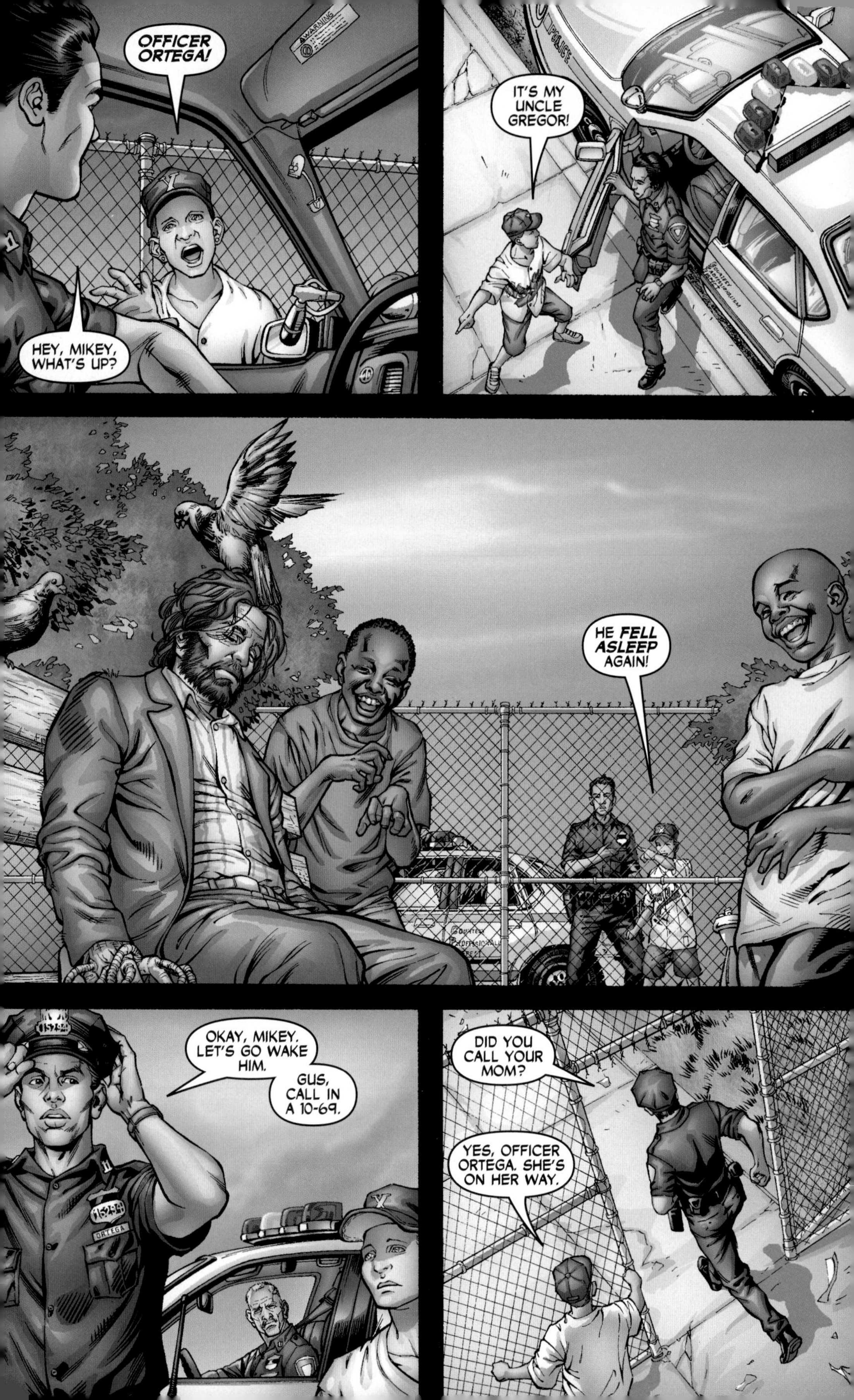
OFFICER ORTEGA!
HEY, MIKEY, WHAT'S UP?
IT'S MY UNCLE GREGOR!
HE FELL ASLEEP AGAIN!
OKAY, MIKEY. LET'S GO WAKE HIM.
GUS, CALL IN A 10-69.
DID YOU CALL YOUR MOM?
YES, OFFICER ORTEGA. SHE'S ON HER WAY.

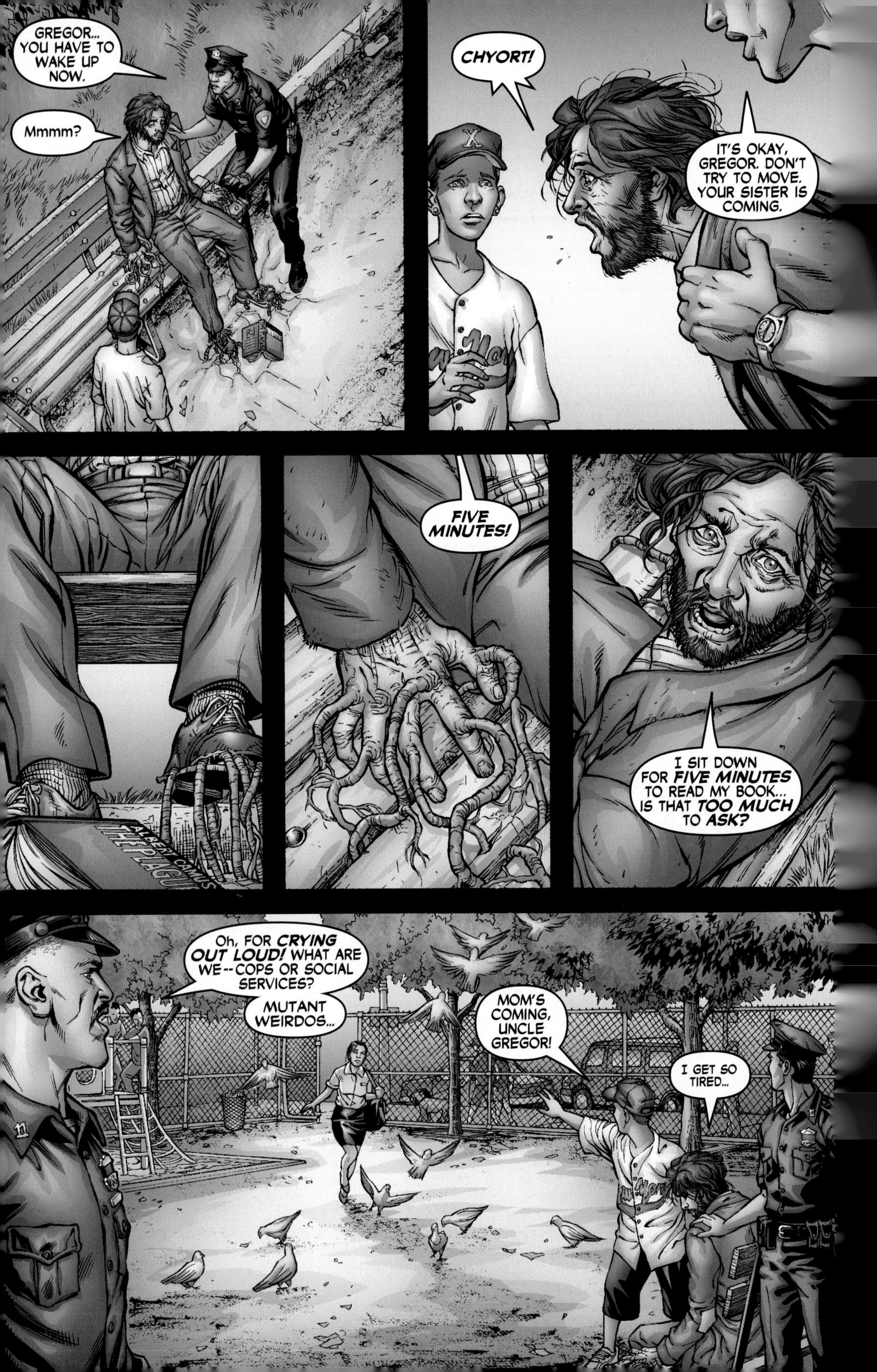
GREGOR... YOU HAVE TO WAKE UP NOW.
Mmmm?
CHYORT!
IT'S OKAY, GREGOR. DON'T TRY TO MOVE. YOUR SISTER IS COMING.
FIVE MINUTES!
I SIT DOWN FOR FIVE MINUTES TO READ MY BOOK... IS THAT TOO MUCH TO ASK?
Oh, FOR CRYING OUT LOUD! WHAT ARE WE--COPS OR SOCIAL SERVICES?
MUTANT WEIRDOS...
MOM'S COMING, UNCLE GREGOR!
I GET SO TIRED...

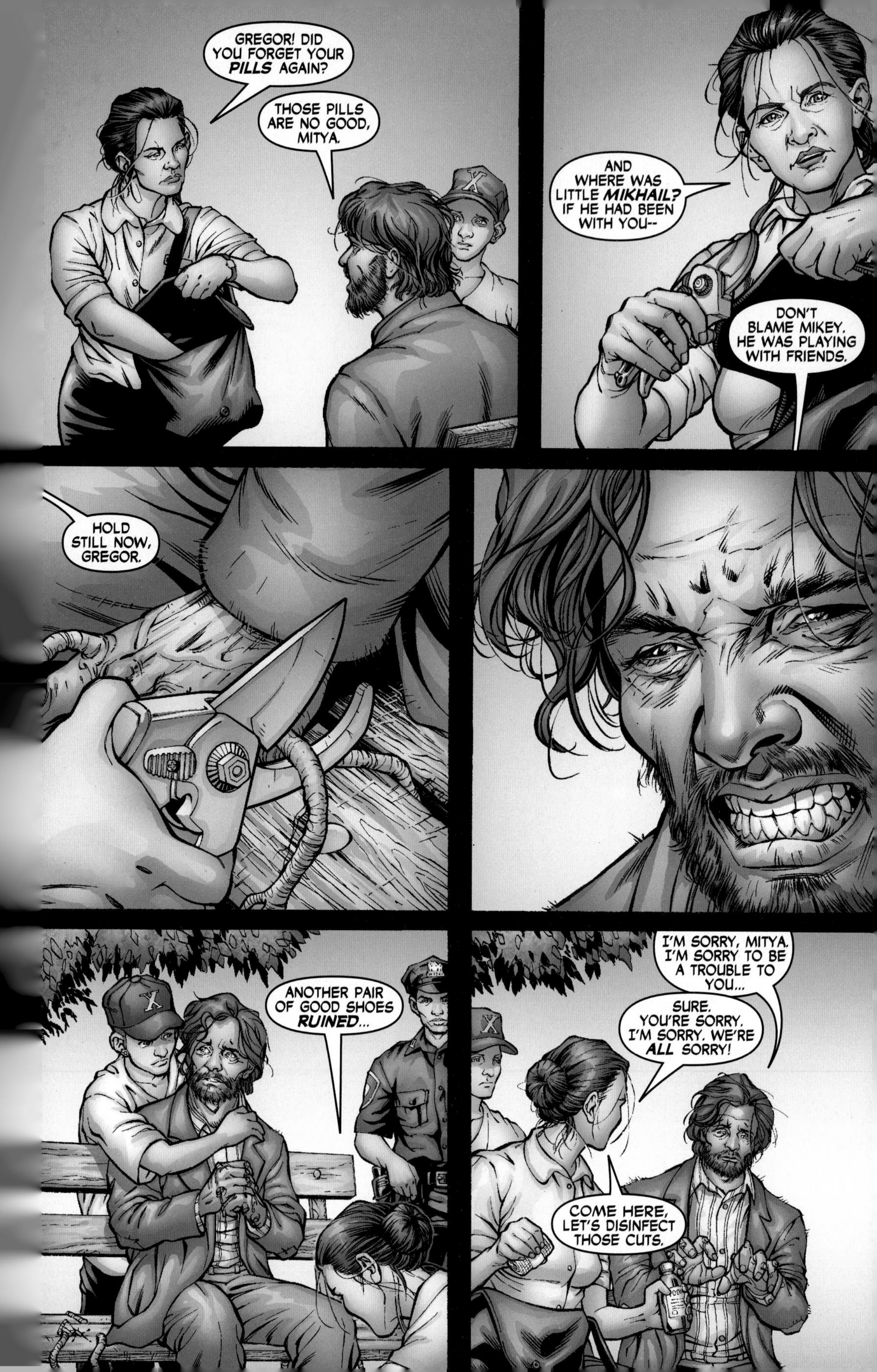
GREGOR! DID YOU FORGET YOUR PILLS AGAIN?
THOSE PILLS ARE NO GOOD, MITYA.
AND WHERE WAS LITTLE MIKHAIL? IF HE HAD BEEN WITH YOU--
DON'T BLAME MIKEY. HE WAS PLAYING WITH FRIENDS.
HOLD STILL NOW, GREGOR.
ANOTHER PAIR OF GOOD SHOES RUINED...
I'M SORRY, MITYA. I'M SORRY TO BE A TROUBLE TO YOU...
SURE. YOU'RE SORRY. I'M SORRY. WE'RE ALL SORRY!
COME HERE, LET'S DISINFECT THOSE CUTS.

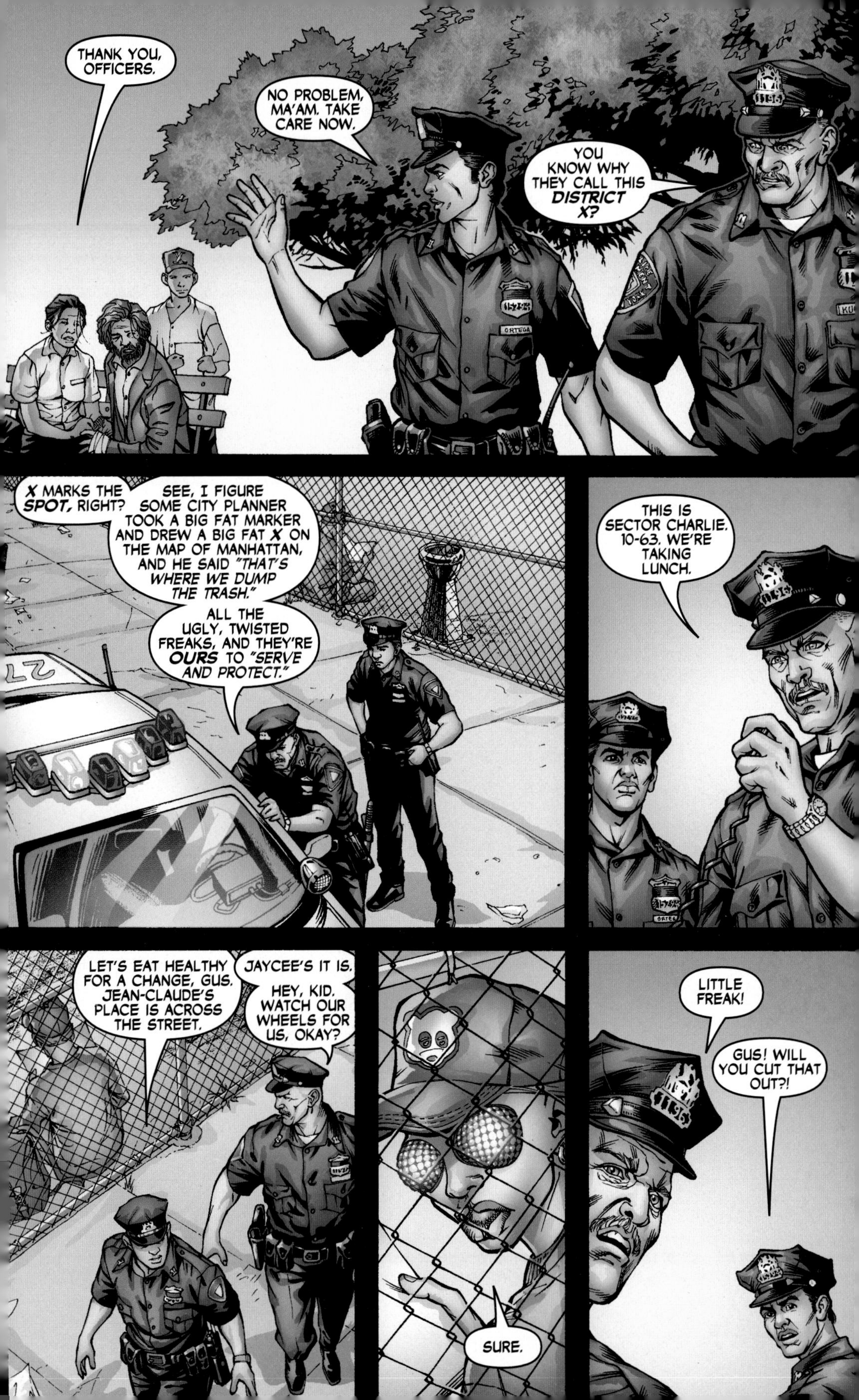
THANK YOU, OFFICERS.
NO PROBLEM, MA'AM. TAKE CARE NOW.
YOU KNOW WHY THEY CALL THIS DISTRICT X?
X MARKS THE SPOT, RIGHT?
SEE, I FIGURE SOME CITY PLANNER TOOK A BIG FAT MARKER AND DREW A BIG FAT X ON THE MAP OF MANHATTAN, AND HE SAID "THAT'S WHERE WE DUMP THE TRASH."
ALL THE UGLY, TWISTED FREAKS, AND THEY'RE OURS TO "SERVE AND PROTECT."
THIS IS SECTOR CHARLIE. 10-63. WE'RE TAKING LUNCH.
LET'S EAT HEALTHY FOR A CHANGE, GUS. JEAN-CLAUDE'S PLACE IS ACROSS THE STREET.
JAYCEE'S IT IS.
HEY, KID. WATCH OUR WHEELS FOR US, OKAY?
SURE.
LITTLE FREAK!
GUS! WILL YOU CUT THAT OUT?!

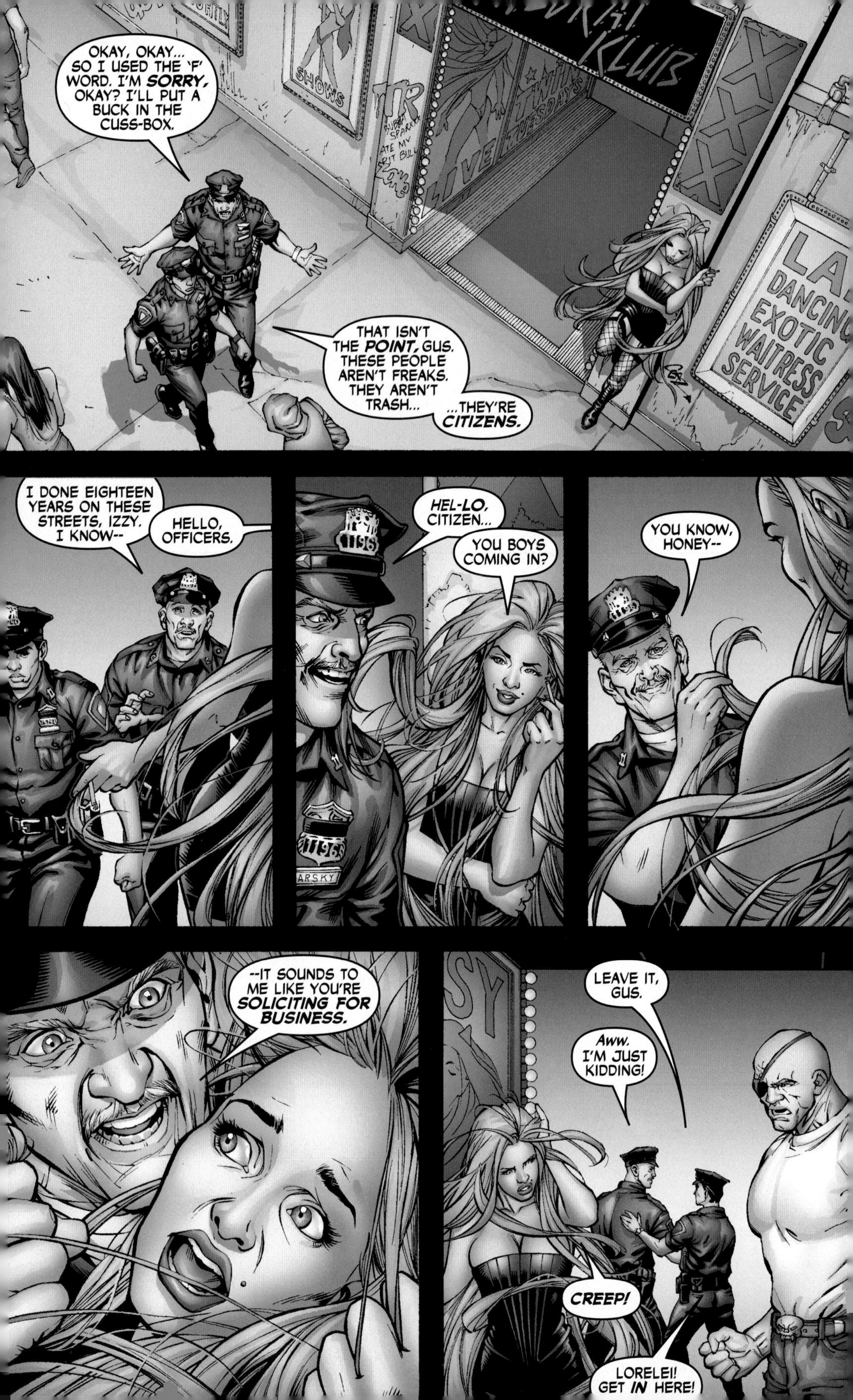

KLUB
SHOWS
LIVE
TWIN TUESDAYS
OKAY, OKAY... SO I USED THE 'F' WORD. I'M **SORRY,** OKAY? I'LL PUT A BUCK IN THE CUSS-BOX.
THAT ISN'T THE **POINT,** GUS. THESE PEOPLE AREN'T FREAKS. THEY AREN'T TRASH...
...THEY'RE **CITIZENS.**
DANCING EXOTIC WAITRESS SERVICE
I DONE EIGHTEEN YEARS ON THESE STREETS, IZZY. I KNOW--
HELLO, OFFICERS.
HEL-LO, CITIZEN...
YOU BOYS COMING IN?
YOU KNOW, HONEY--
--IT SOUNDS TO ME LIKE YOU'RE **SOLICITING FOR BUSINESS.**
LEAVE IT, GUS.
AWW. I'M JUST KIDDING!
CREEP!
LORELEI! GET **IN** HERE!

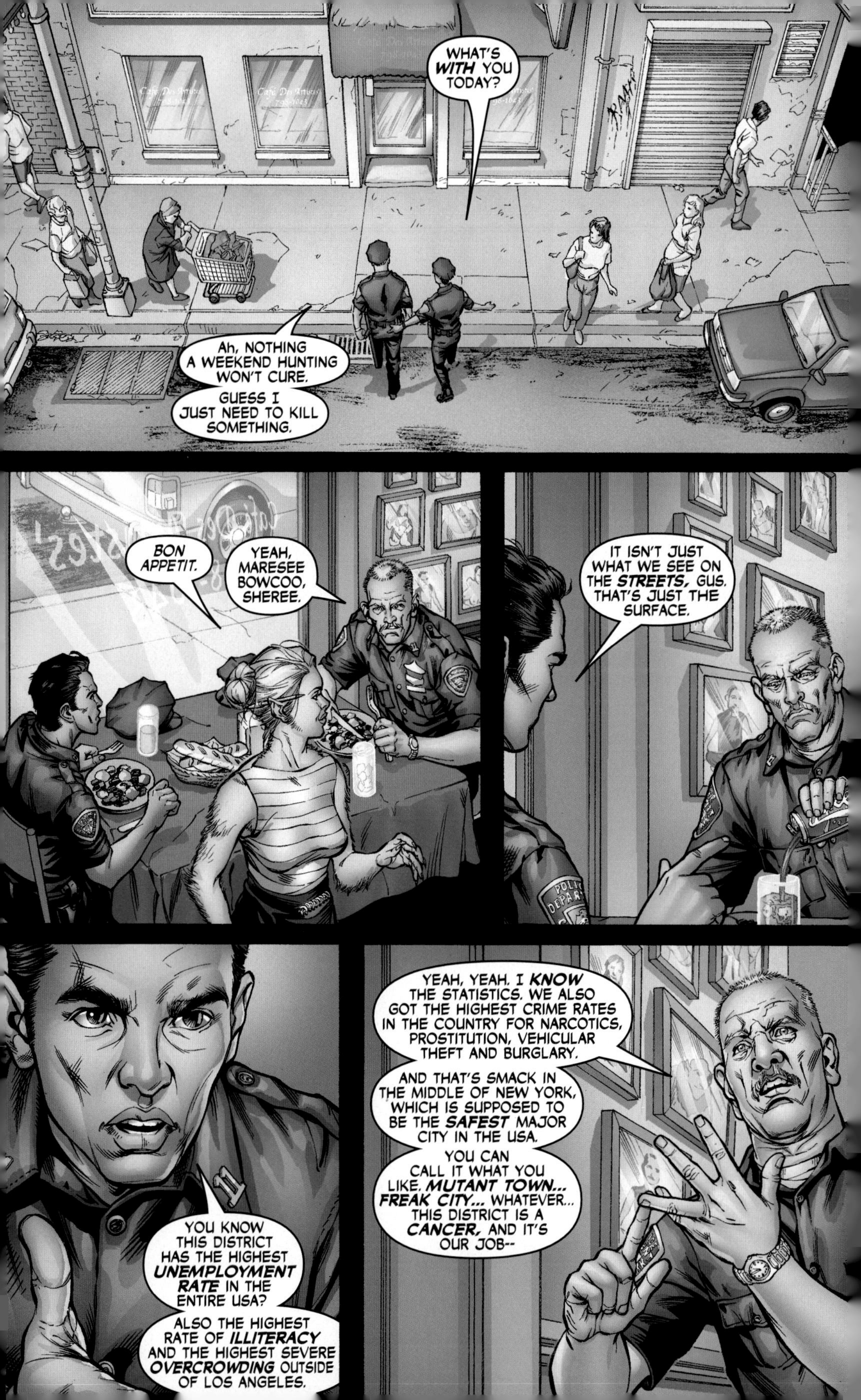

WHAT'S WITH YOU TODAY?
Ah, NOTHING A WEEKEND HUNTING WON'T CURE.
GUESS I JUST NEED TO KILL SOMETHING.
BON APPETIT.
YEAH, MARESEE BOWCOO, SHEREE.
IT ISN'T JUST WHAT WE SEE ON THE STREETS, GUS. THAT'S JUST THE SURFACE.
YOU KNOW THIS DISTRICT HAS THE HIGHEST UNEMPLOYMENT RATE IN THE ENTIRE USA?
ALSO THE HIGHEST RATE OF ILLITERACY AND THE HIGHEST SEVERE OVERCROWDING OUTSIDE OF LOS ANGELES.
YEAH, YEAH. I KNOW THE STATISTICS. WE ALSO GOT THE HIGHEST CRIME RATES IN THE COUNTRY FOR NARCOTICS, PROSTITUTION, VEHICULAR THEFT AND BURGLARY.
AND THAT'S SMACK IN THE MIDDLE OF NEW YORK, WHICH IS SUPPOSED TO BE THE SAFEST MAJOR CITY IN THE USA.
YOU CAN CALL IT WHAT YOU LIKE. MUTANT TOWN... FREAK CITY... WHATEVER... THIS DISTRICT IS A CANCER, AND IT'S OUR JOB--

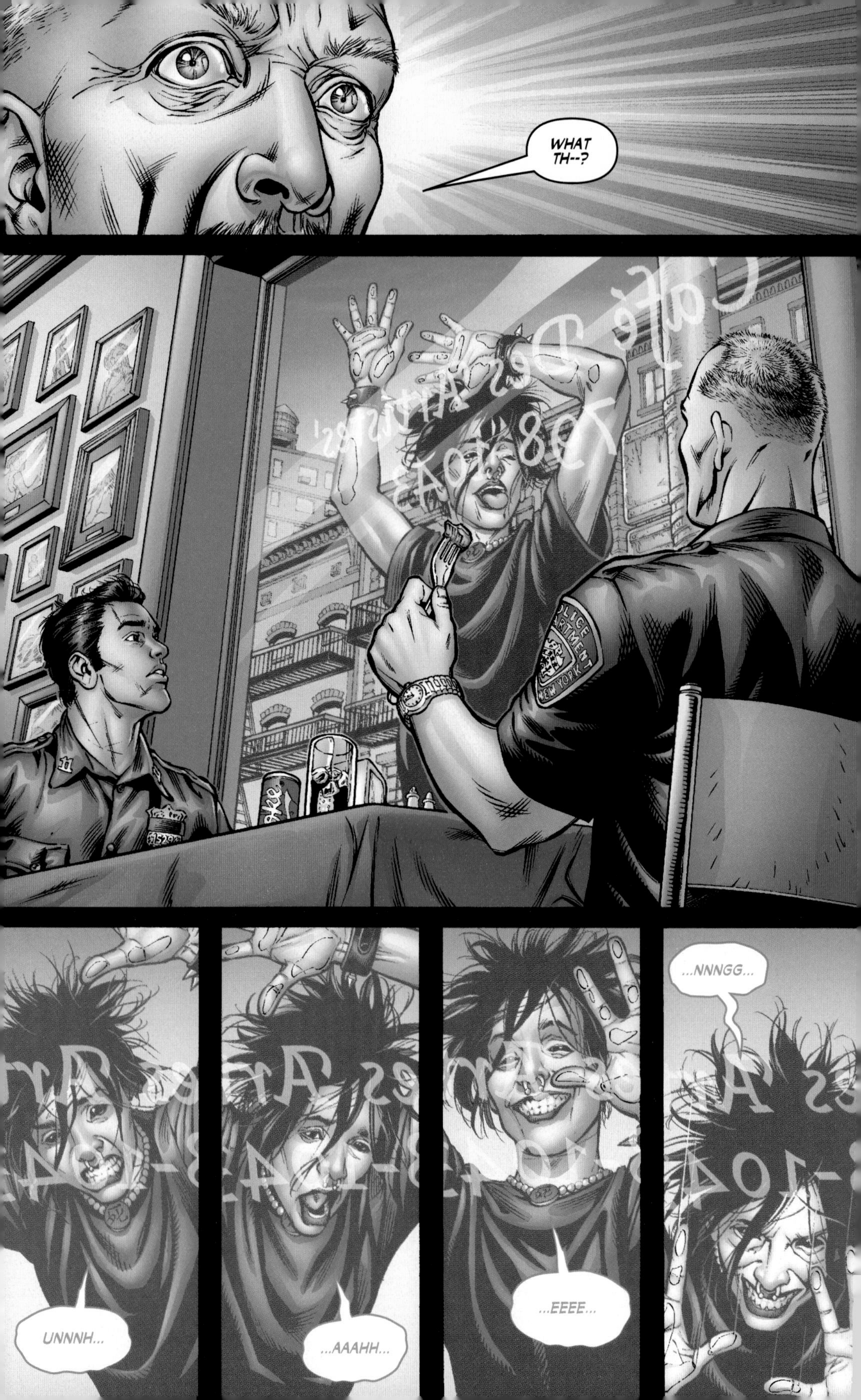
WHAT TH--?
UNNNH...
...AAAHH...
...EEEE...
...NNNGG...

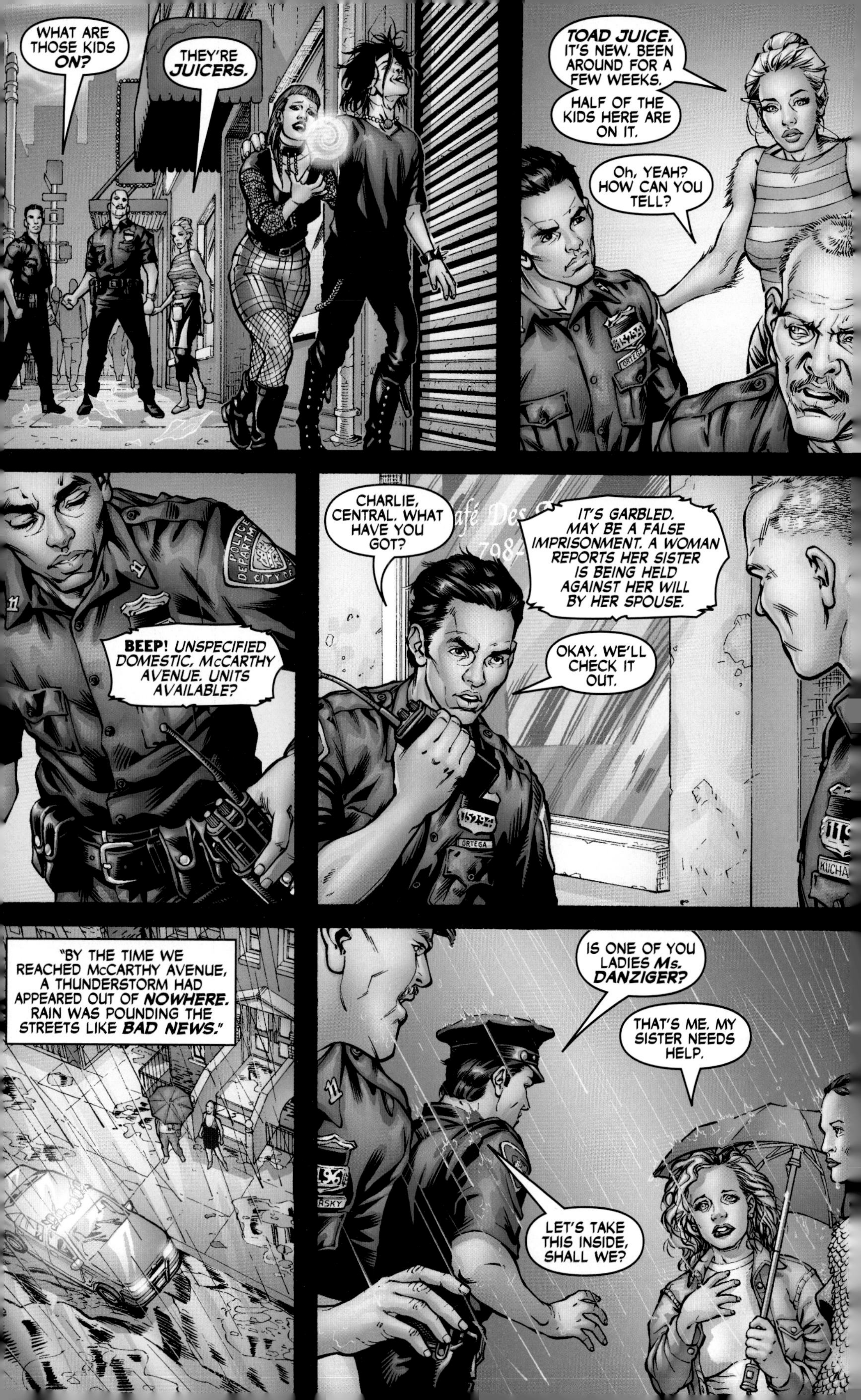
WHAT ARE THOSE KIDS ON?
THEY'RE JUICERS.
TOAD JUICE. IT'S NEW. BEEN AROUND FOR A FEW WEEKS.
HALF OF THE KIDS HERE ARE ON IT.
Oh, YEAH? HOW CAN YOU TELL?
BEEP! UNSPECIFIED DOMESTIC, McCARTHY AVENUE. UNITS AVAILABLE?
CHARLIE, CENTRAL. WHAT HAVE YOU GOT?
IT'S GARBLED. MAY BE A FALSE IMPRISONMENT. A WOMAN REPORTS HER SISTER IS BEING HELD AGAINST HER WILL BY HER SPOUSE.
OKAY. WE'LL CHECK IT OUT.
"BY THE TIME WE REACHED McCARTHY AVENUE, A THUNDERSTORM HAD APPEARED OUT OF NOWHERE. RAIN WAS POUNDING THE STREETS LIKE BAD NEWS."
IS ONE OF YOU LADIES Ms. DANZIGER?
THAT'S ME. MY SISTER NEEDS HELP.
LET'S TAKE THIS INSIDE, SHALL WE?

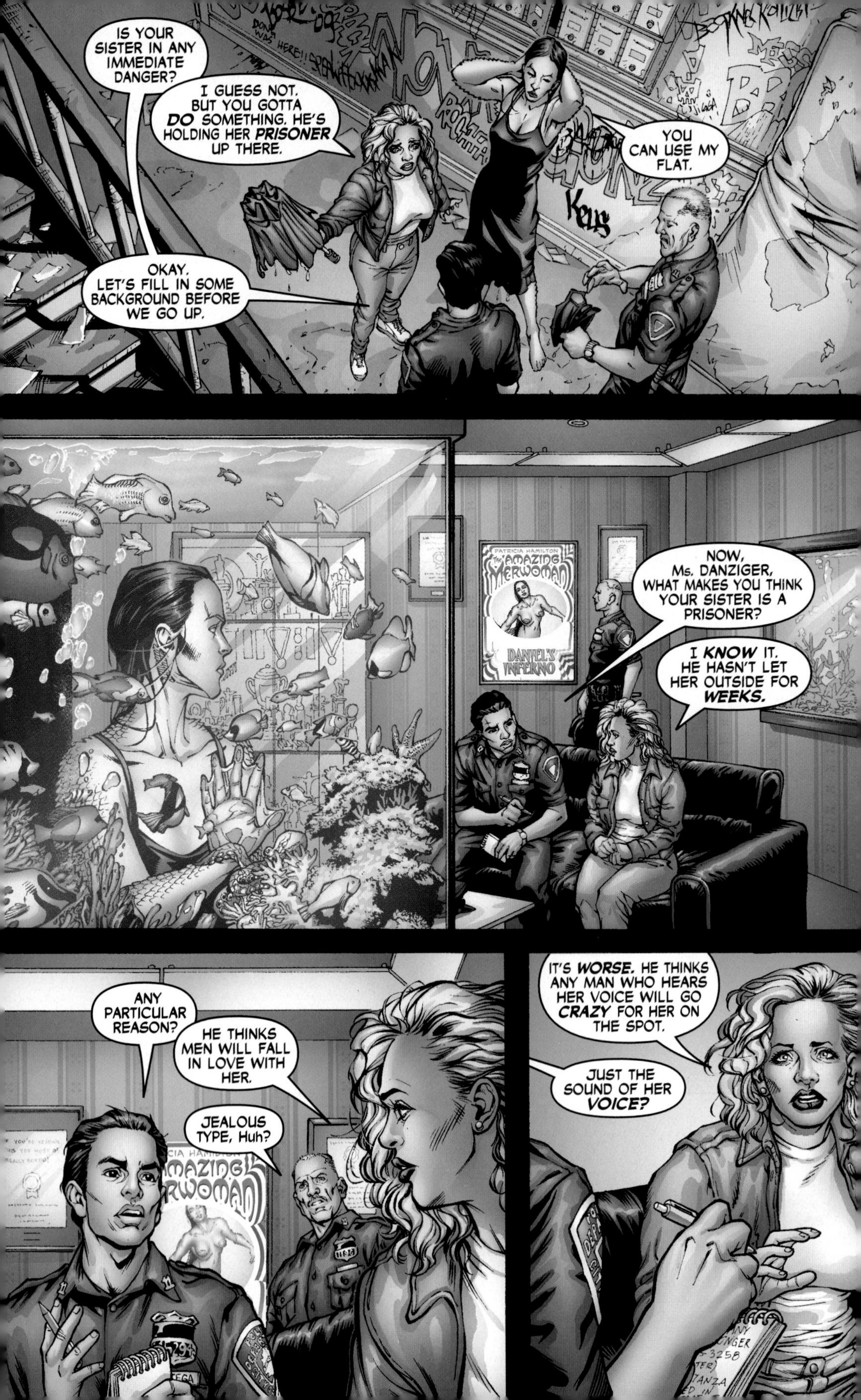

IS YOUR SISTER IN ANY IMMEDIATE DANGER?
I GUESS NOT. BUT YOU GOTTA DO SOMETHING. HE'S HOLDING HER PRISONER UP THERE.
YOU CAN USE MY FLAT.
OKAY. LET'S FILL IN SOME BACKGROUND BEFORE WE GO UP.
PATRICIA HAMILTON The AMAZING MERWOMAN DANIEL'S INFERNO
NOW, Ms. DANZIGER, WHAT MAKES YOU THINK YOUR SISTER IS A PRISONER?
I KNOW IT. HE HASN'T LET HER OUTSIDE FOR WEEKS.
ANY PARTICULAR REASON?
HE THINKS MEN WILL FALL IN LOVE WITH HER.
JEALOUS TYPE, Huh?
IT'S WORSE. HE THINKS ANY MAN WHO HEARS HER VOICE WILL GO CRAZY FOR HER ON THE SPOT.
JUST THE SOUND OF HER VOICE?

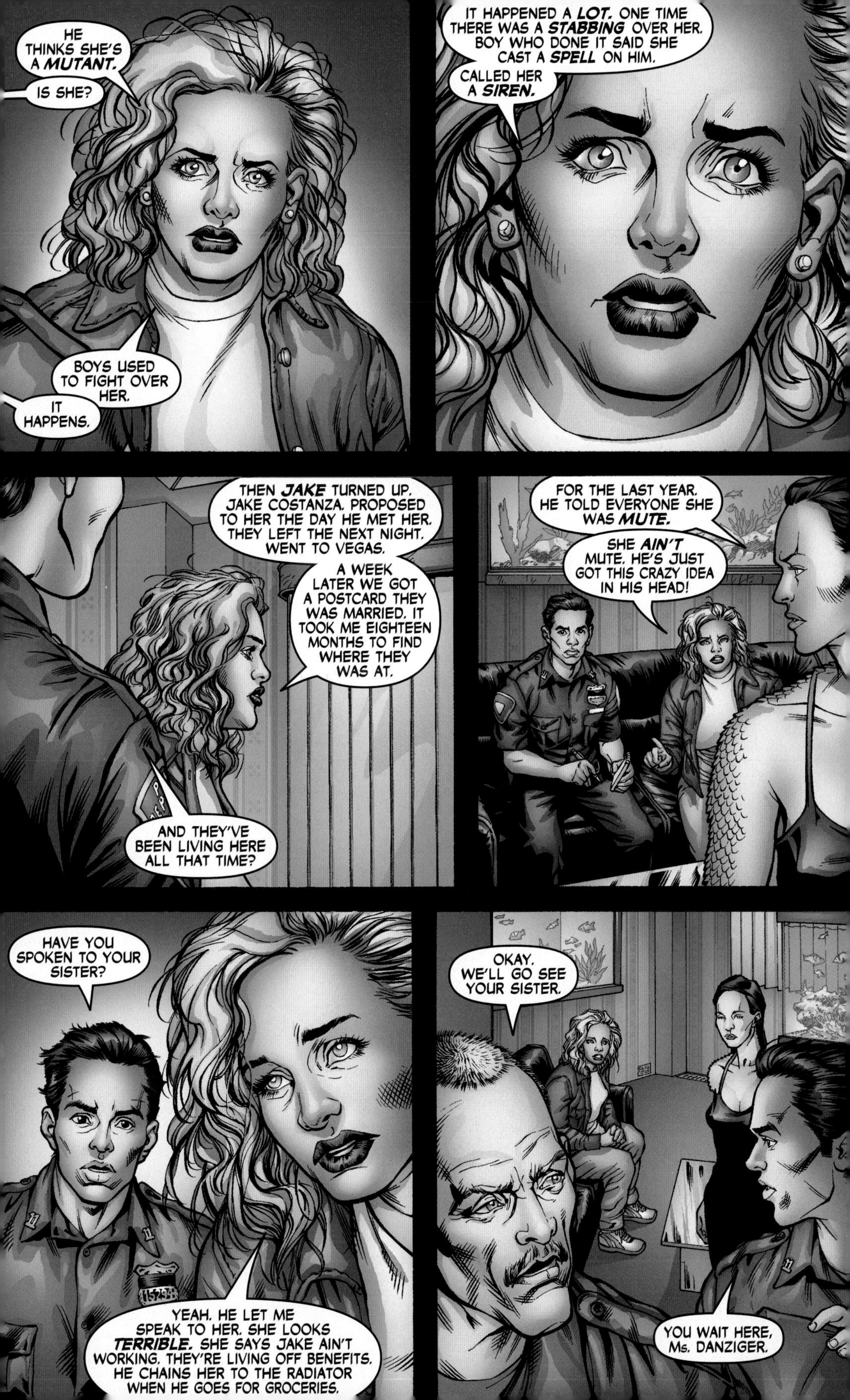
HE THINKS SHE'S A MUTANT.
IS SHE?
BOYS USED TO FIGHT OVER HER.
IT HAPPENS.
IT HAPPENED A LOT. ONE TIME THERE WAS A STABBING OVER HER. BOY WHO DONE IT SAID SHE CAST A SPELL ON HIM.
CALLED HER A SIREN.
THEN JAKE TURNED UP. JAKE COSTANZA. PROPOSED TO HER THE DAY HE MET HER. THEY LEFT THE NEXT NIGHT. WENT TO VEGAS.
A WEEK LATER WE GOT A POSTCARD THEY WAS MARRIED. IT TOOK ME EIGHTEEN MONTHS TO FIND WHERE THEY WAS AT.
AND THEY'VE BEEN LIVING HERE ALL THAT TIME?
FOR THE LAST YEAR. HE TOLD EVERYONE SHE WAS MUTE.
SHE AIN'T MUTE. HE'S JUST GOT THIS CRAZY IDEA IN HIS HEAD!
HAVE YOU SPOKEN TO YOUR SISTER?
YEAH. HE LET ME SPEAK TO HER. SHE LOOKS TERRIBLE. SHE SAYS JAKE AIN'T WORKING. THEY'RE LIVING OFF BENEFITS. HE CHAINS HER TO THE RADIATOR WHEN HE GOES FOR GROCERIES.
OKAY. WE'LL GO SEE YOUR SISTER.
YOU WAIT HERE, Ms. DANZIGER.

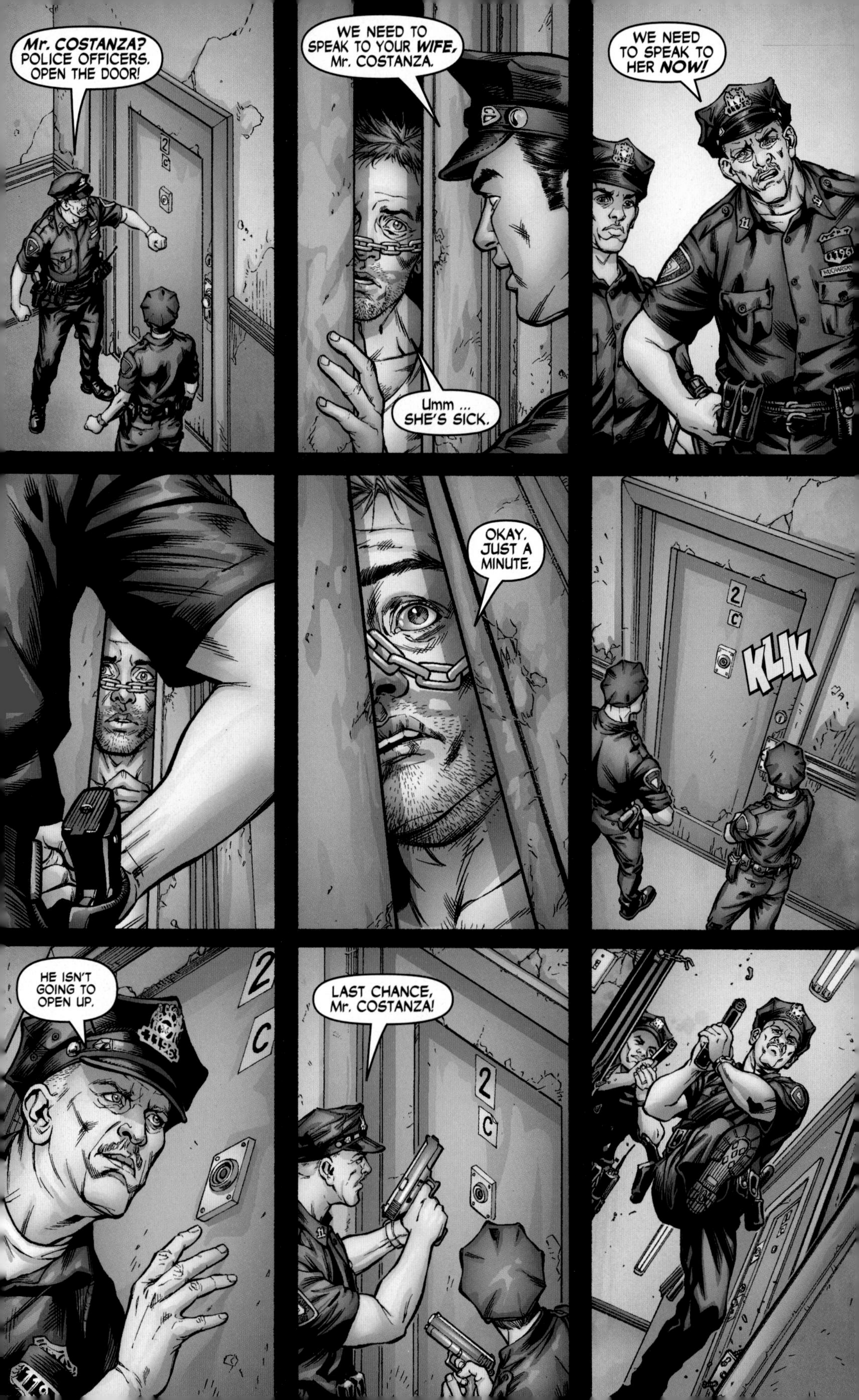
Mr. COSTANZA? POLICE OFFICERS. OPEN THE DOOR!
WE NEED TO SPEAK TO YOUR WIFE, Mr. COSTANZA.
Umm ... SHE'S SICK.
WE NEED TO SPEAK TO HER NOW!
OKAY, JUST A MINUTE.
KLIK
HE ISN'T GOING TO OPEN UP.
LAST CHANCE, Mr. COSTANZA!

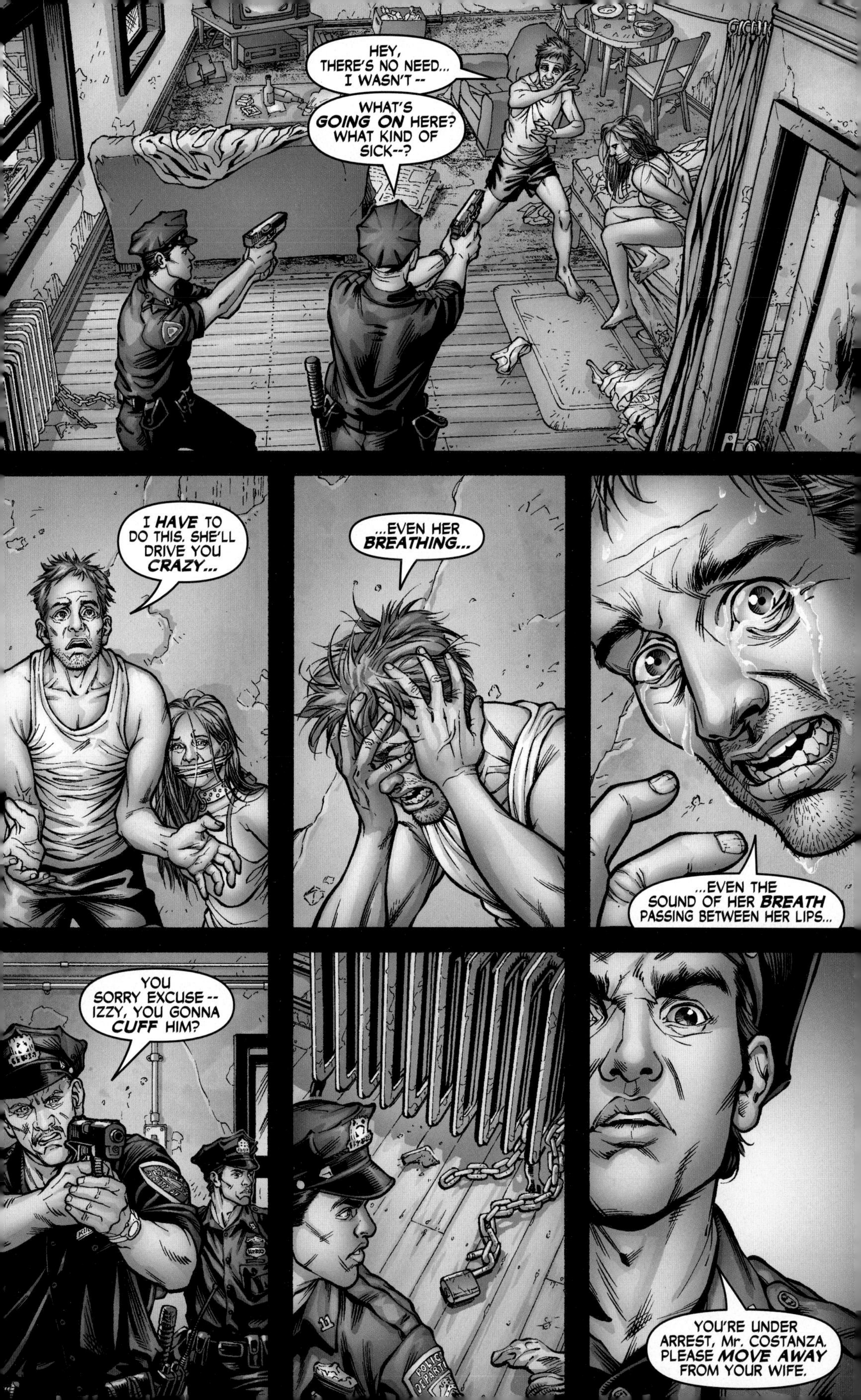

HEY, THERE'S NO NEED... I WASN'T --
WHAT'S GOING ON HERE? WHAT KIND OF SICK--?
I HAVE TO DO THIS. SHE'LL DRIVE YOU CRAZY...
...EVEN HER BREATHING...
...EVEN THE SOUND OF HER BREATH PASSING BETWEEN HER LIPS...
YOU SORRY EXCUSE -- IZZY, YOU GONNA CUFF HIM?
YOU'RE UNDER ARREST, Mr. COSTANZA. PLEASE MOVE AWAY FROM YOUR WIFE.

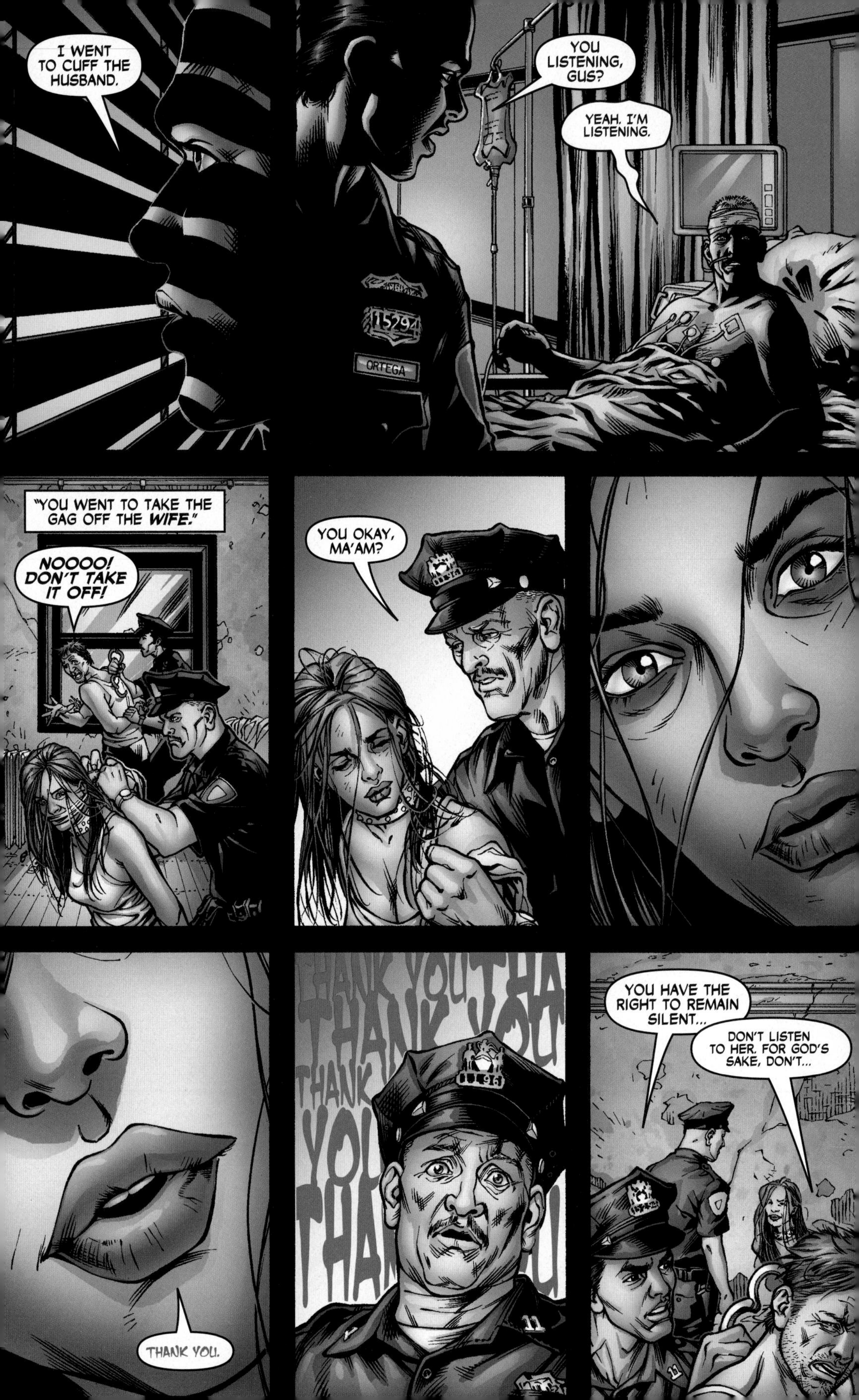
I WENT TO CUFF THE HUSBAND.
YOU LISTENING, GUS?
YEAH. I'M LISTENING.
15294
ORTEGA
"YOU WENT TO TAKE THE GAG OFF THE *WIFE*."
NOOOO! DON'T TAKE IT OFF!
YOU OKAY, MA'AM?
THANK YOU.
THANK YOU THA
THANK YOU
THANK
YOU
THAN
YOU HAVE THE RIGHT TO REMAIN SILENT...
DON'T LISTEN TO HER. FOR GOD'S SAKE, DON'T...

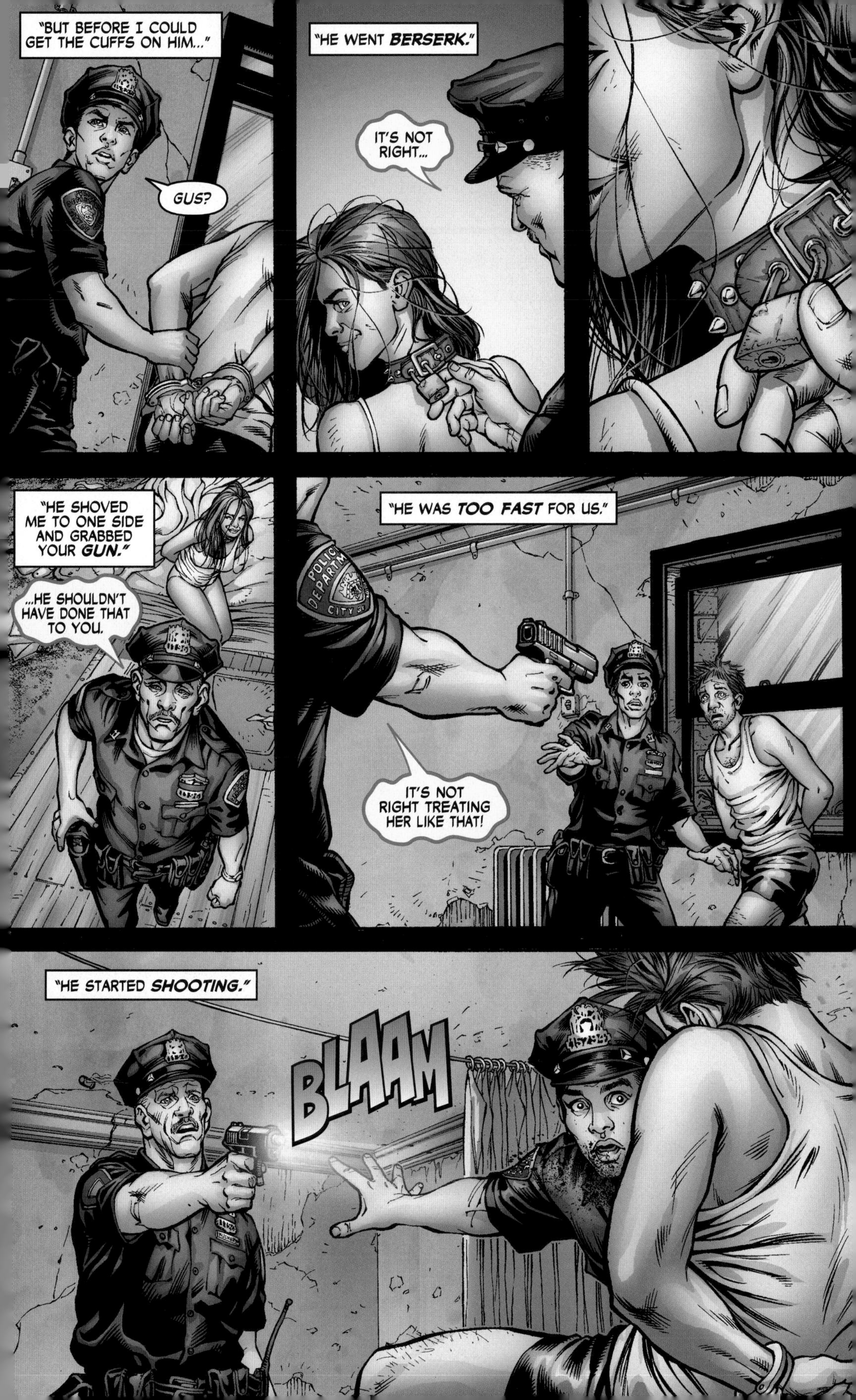
"BUT BEFORE I COULD GET THE CUFFS ON HIM..."
GUS?
"HE WENT BERSERK."
IT'S NOT RIGHT...
"HE SHOVED ME TO ONE SIDE AND GRABBED YOUR GUN."
...HE SHOULDN'T HAVE DONE THAT TO YOU.
"HE WAS TOO FAST FOR US."
IT'S NOT RIGHT TREATING HER LIKE THAT!
"HE STARTED SHOOTING."
BLAAM

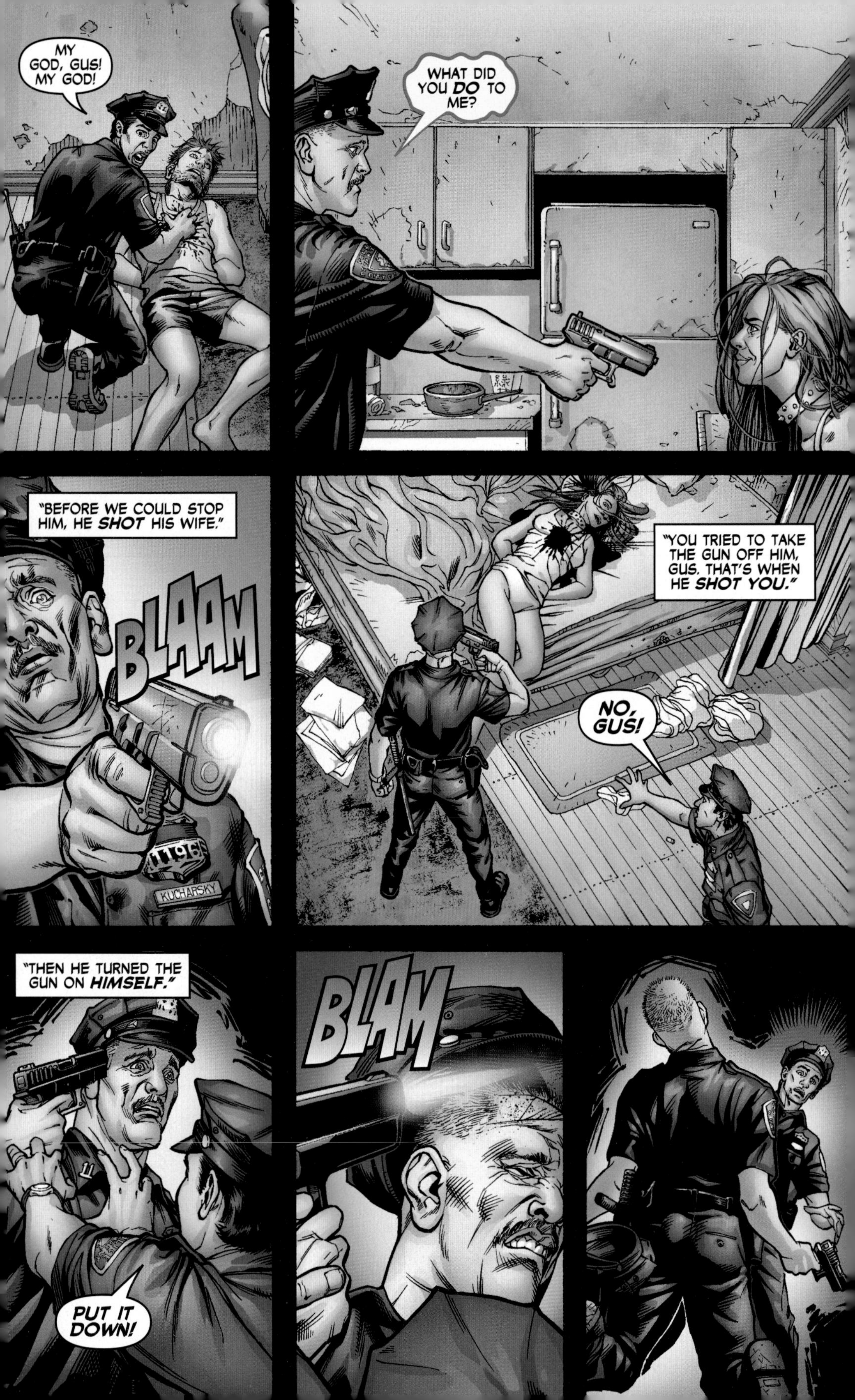
MY GOD, GUS! MY GOD!
WHAT DID YOU DO TO ME?
"BEFORE WE COULD STOP HIM, HE SHOT HIS WIFE."
BLAAM
1196
KUCHARSKY
"YOU TRIED TO TAKE THE GUN OFF HIM, GUS. THAT'S WHEN HE SHOT YOU."
NO, GUS!
"THEN HE TURNED THE GUN ON HIMSELF."
PUT IT DOWN!
BLAM

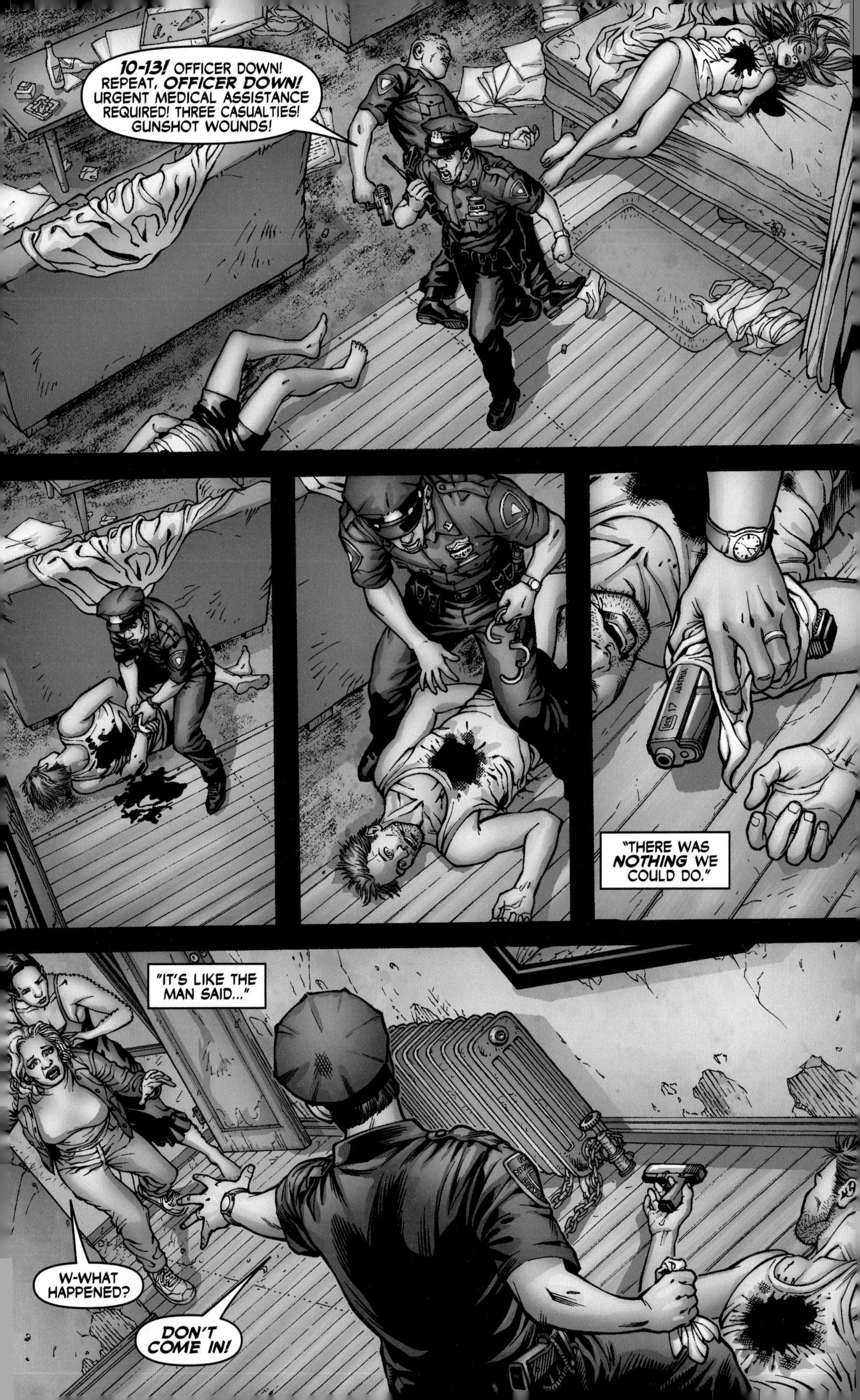
10-13! OFFICER DOWN! REPEAT, OFFICER DOWN! URGENT MEDICAL ASSISTANCE REQUIRED! THREE CASUALTIES! GUNSHOT WOUNDS!
"THERE WAS NOTHING WE COULD DO."
"IT'S LIKE THE MAN SAID..."
W-WHAT HAPPENED?
DON'T COME IN!

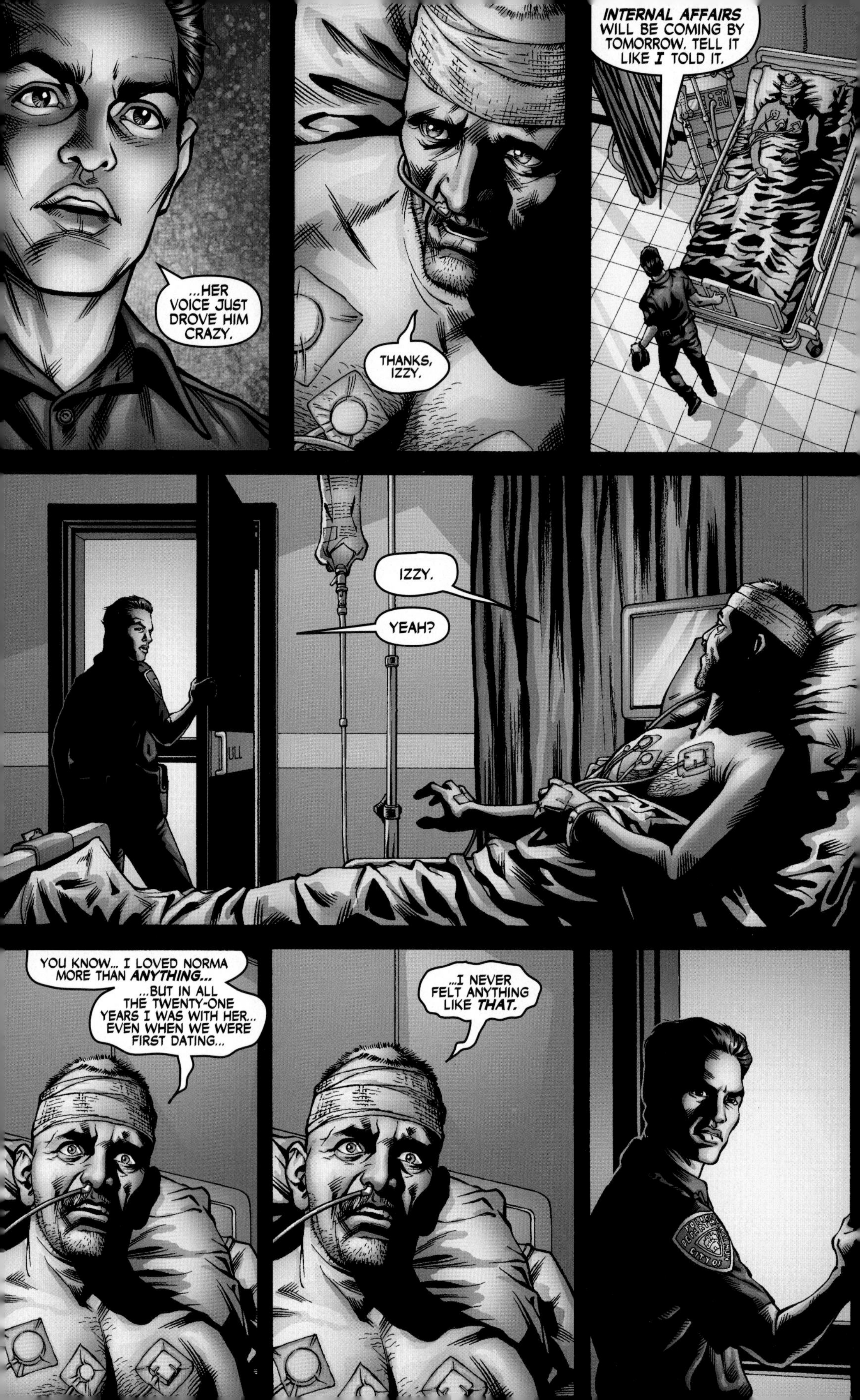
...HER VOICE JUST DROVE HIM CRAZY.
THANKS, IZZY.
INTERNAL AFFAIRS WILL BE COMING BY TOMORROW. TELL IT LIKE I TOLD IT.
IZZY.
YEAH?
YOU KNOW... I LOVED NORMA MORE THAN ANYTHING...
...BUT IN ALL THE TWENTY-ONE YEARS I WAS WITH HER... EVEN WHEN WE WERE FIRST DATING...
...I NEVER FELT ANYTHING LIKE THAT.

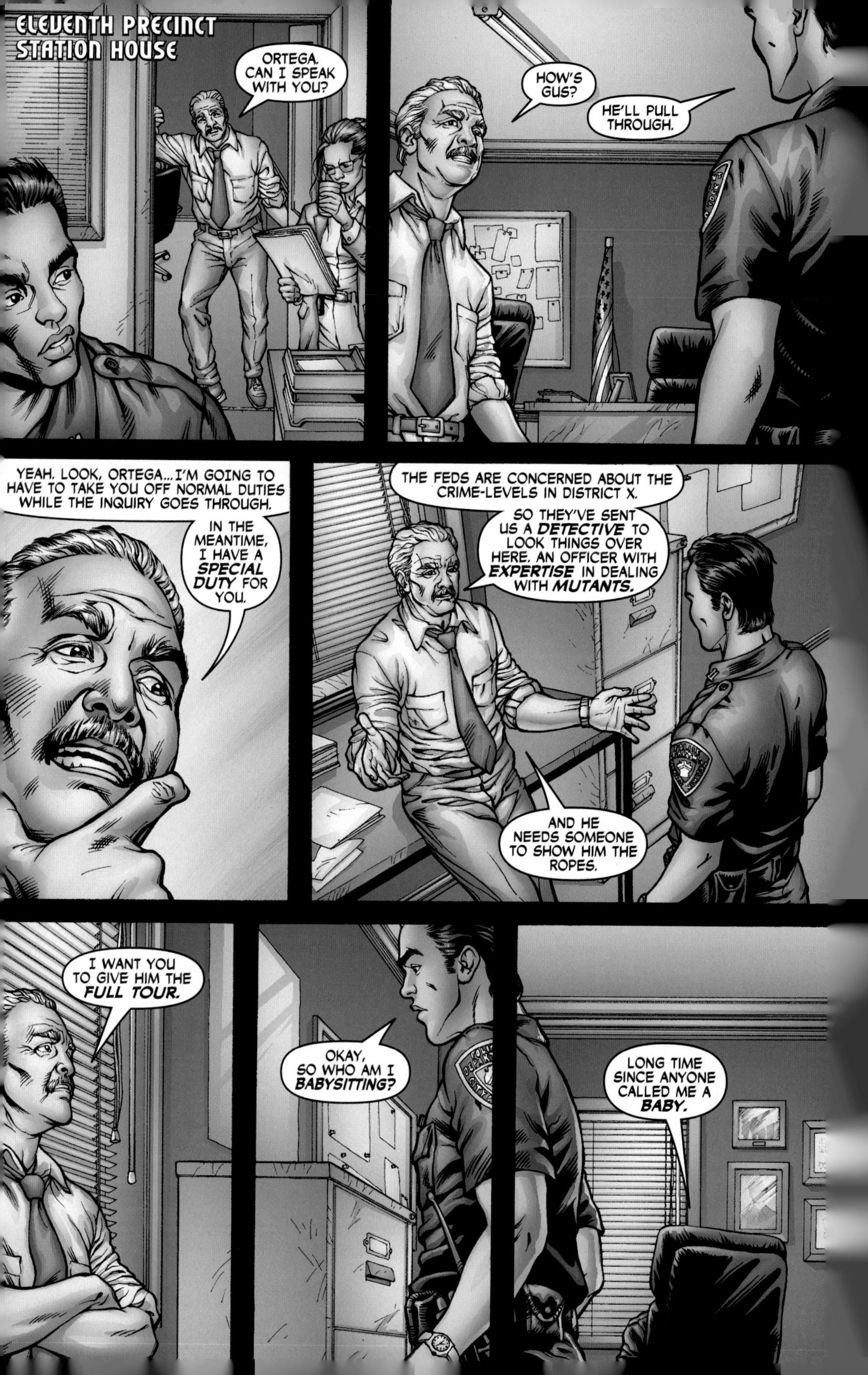
ELEVENTH PRECINCT STATION HOUSE
ORTEGA, CAN I SPEAK WITH YOU?
HOW'S GUS?
HE'LL PULL THROUGH.
YEAH. LOOK, ORTEGA... I'M GOING TO HAVE TO TAKE YOU OFF NORMAL DUTIES WHILE THE INQUIRY GOES THROUGH.
IN THE MEANTIME, I HAVE A SPECIAL DUTY FOR YOU.
THE FEDS ARE CONCERNED ABOUT THE CRIME-LEVELS IN DISTRICT X.
SO THEY'VE SENT US A DETECTIVE TO LOOK THINGS OVER HERE. AN OFFICER WITH EXPERTISE IN DEALING WITH MUTANTS.
AND HE NEEDS SOMEONE TO SHOW HIM THE ROPES.
I WANT YOU TO GIVE HIM THE FULL TOUR.
OKAY, SO WHO AM I BABYSITTING?
LONG TIME SINCE ANYONE CALLED ME A BABY.

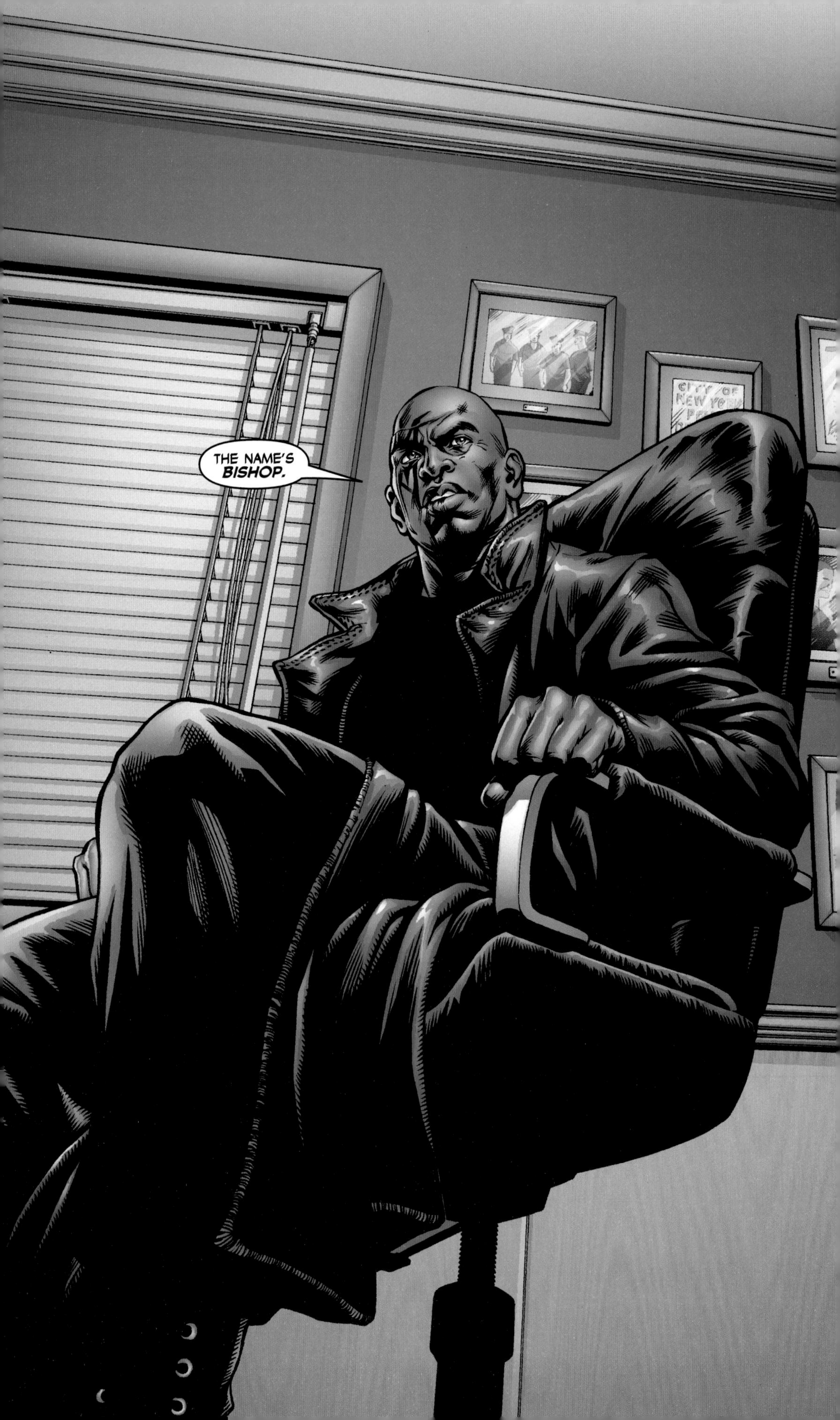
THE NAME'S BISHOP.

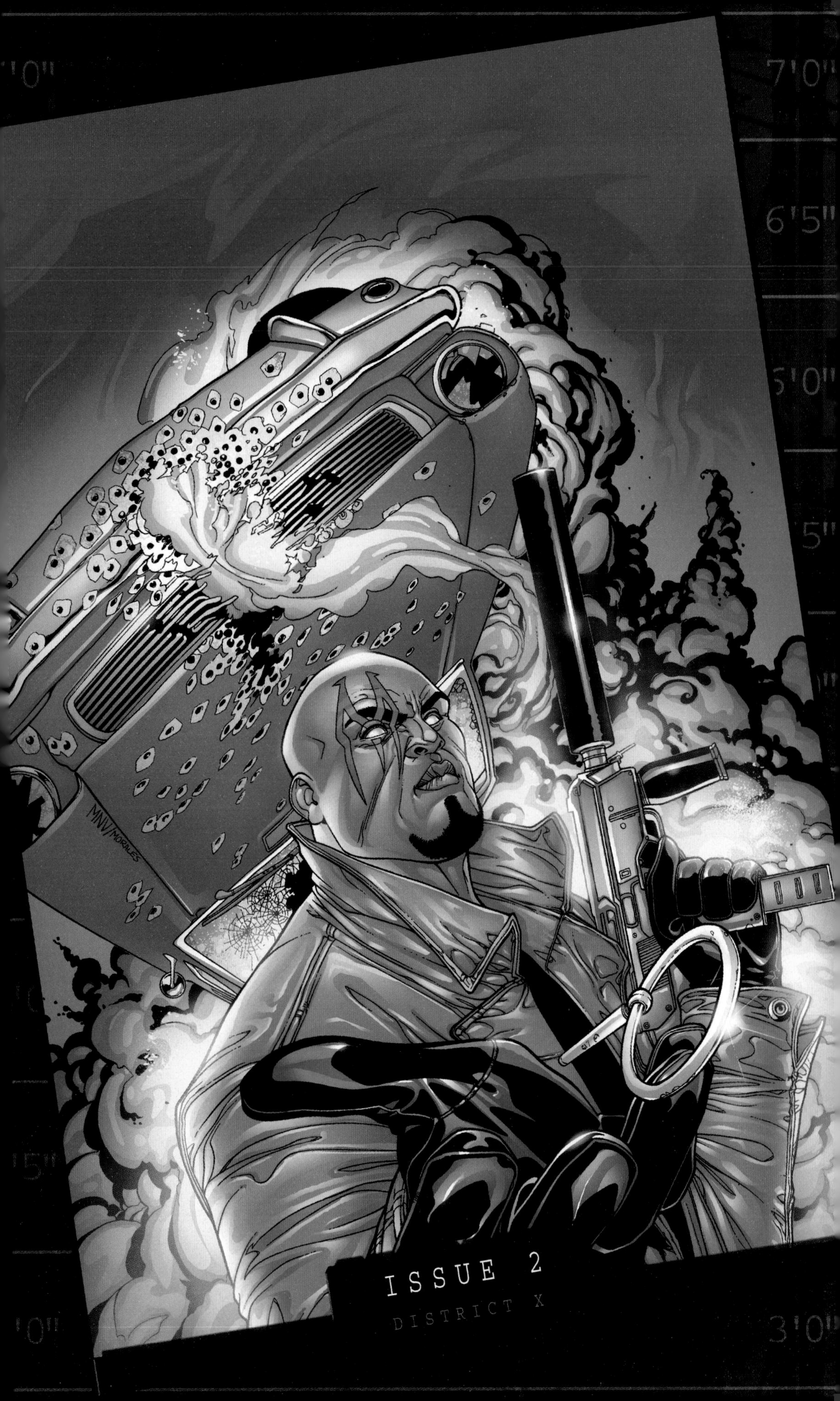
7'0"
6'5"
MNV/MORALES
3'0"

ISSUE 2

DISTRICT X

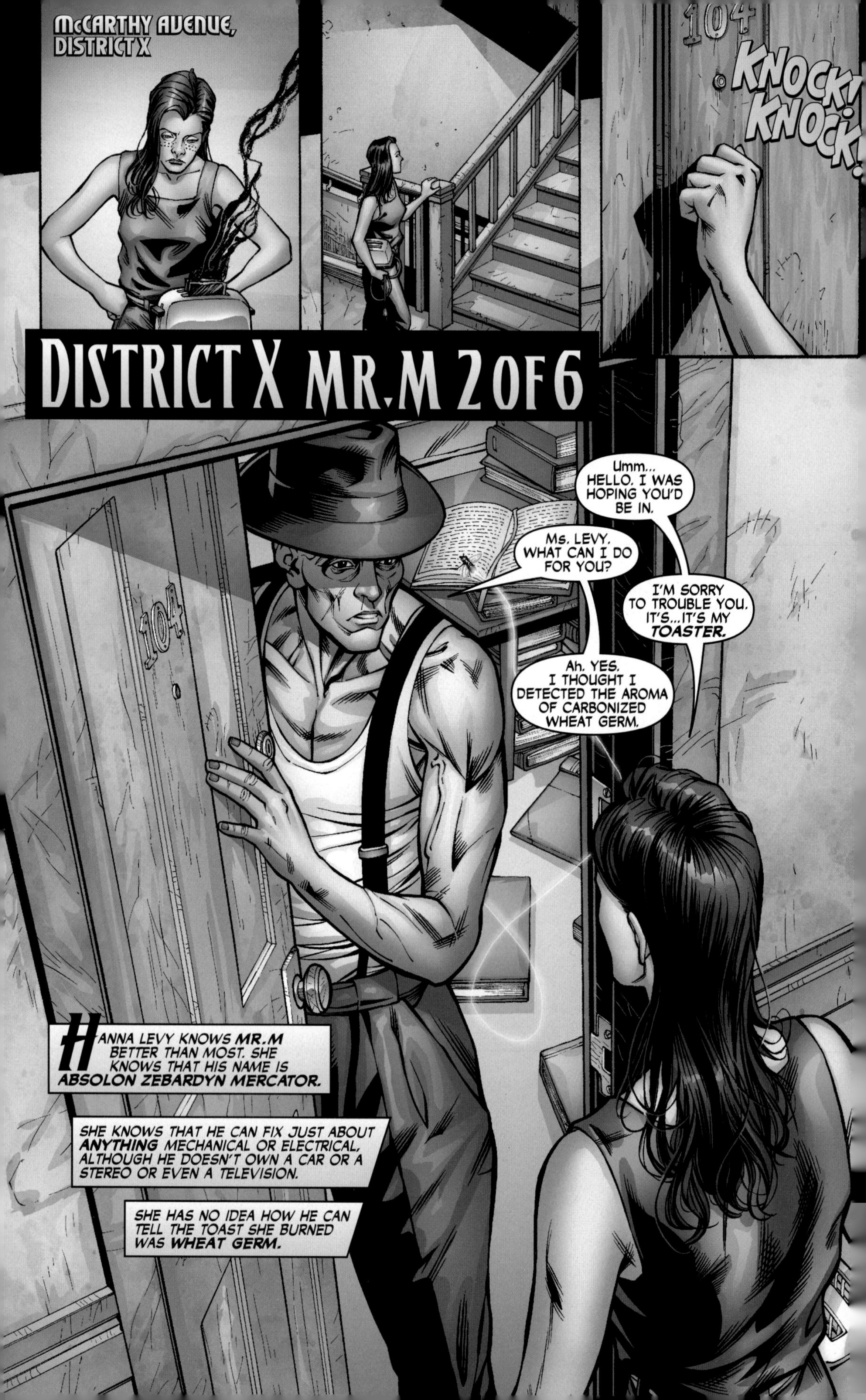
McCARTHY AVENUE, DISTRICT X
KNOCK! KNOCK!
DISTRICT X MR. M 2 OF 6
Umm... HELLO. I WAS HOPING YOU'D BE IN.
Ms. LEVY. WHAT CAN I DO FOR YOU?
I'M SORRY TO TROUBLE YOU. IT'S...IT'S MY TOASTER.
Ah. YES. I THOUGHT I DETECTED THE AROMA OF CARBONIZED WHEAT GERM.
HANNA LEVY KNOWS MR. M BETTER THAN MOST. SHE KNOWS THAT HIS NAME IS ABSOLON ZEBARDYN MERCATOR.
SHE KNOWS THAT HE CAN FIX JUST ABOUT ANYTHING MECHANICAL OR ELECTRICAL, ALTHOUGH HE DOESN'T OWN A CAR OR A STEREO OR EVEN A TELEVISION.
SHE HAS NO IDEA HOW HE CAN TELL THE TOAST SHE BURNED WAS WHEAT GERM.

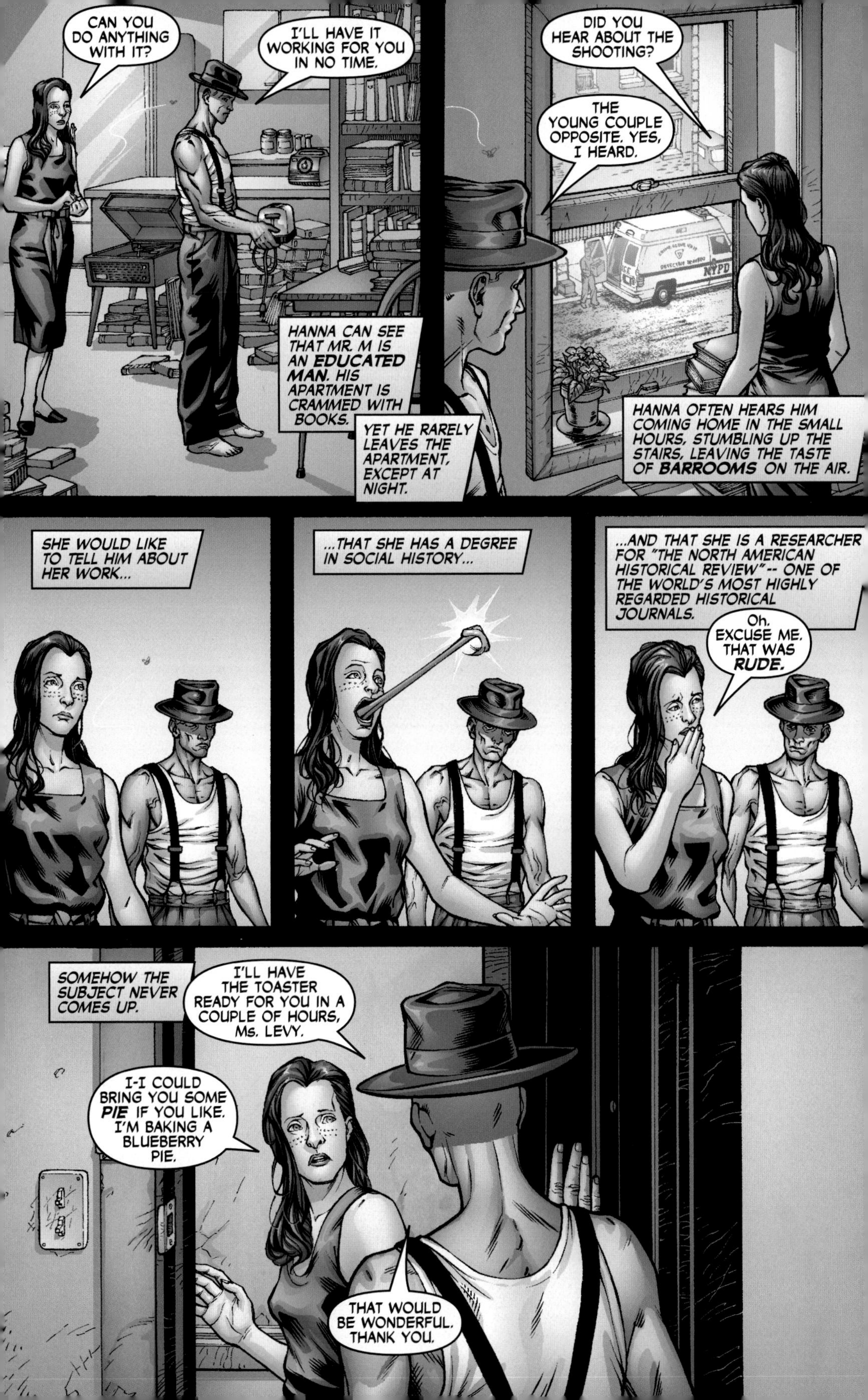
CAN YOU DO ANYTHING WITH IT?
I'LL HAVE IT WORKING FOR YOU IN NO TIME.
HANNA CAN SEE THAT MR. M IS AN **EDUCATED MAN**. HIS APARTMENT IS CRAMMED WITH BOOKS.
YET HE RARELY LEAVES THE APARTMENT, EXCEPT AT NIGHT.
DID YOU HEAR ABOUT THE SHOOTING?
THE YOUNG COUPLE OPPOSITE. YES, I HEARD.
NYPD
HANNA OFTEN HEARS HIM COMING HOME IN THE SMALL HOURS, STUMBLING UP THE STAIRS, LEAVING THE TASTE OF **BARROOMS** ON THE AIR.
SHE WOULD LIKE TO TELL HIM ABOUT HER WORK...
...THAT SHE HAS A DEGREE IN SOCIAL HISTORY...
...AND THAT SHE IS A RESEARCHER FOR "THE NORTH AMERICAN HISTORICAL REVIEW"-- ONE OF THE WORLD'S MOST HIGHLY REGARDED HISTORICAL JOURNALS.
Oh. EXCUSE ME. THAT WAS **RUDE.**
SOMEHOW THE SUBJECT NEVER COMES UP.
I'LL HAVE THE TOASTER READY FOR YOU IN A COUPLE OF HOURS, Ms. LEVY.
I-I COULD BRING YOU SOME **PIE** IF YOU LIKE. I'M BAKING A BLUEBERRY PIE.
THAT WOULD BE WONDERFUL. THANK YOU.

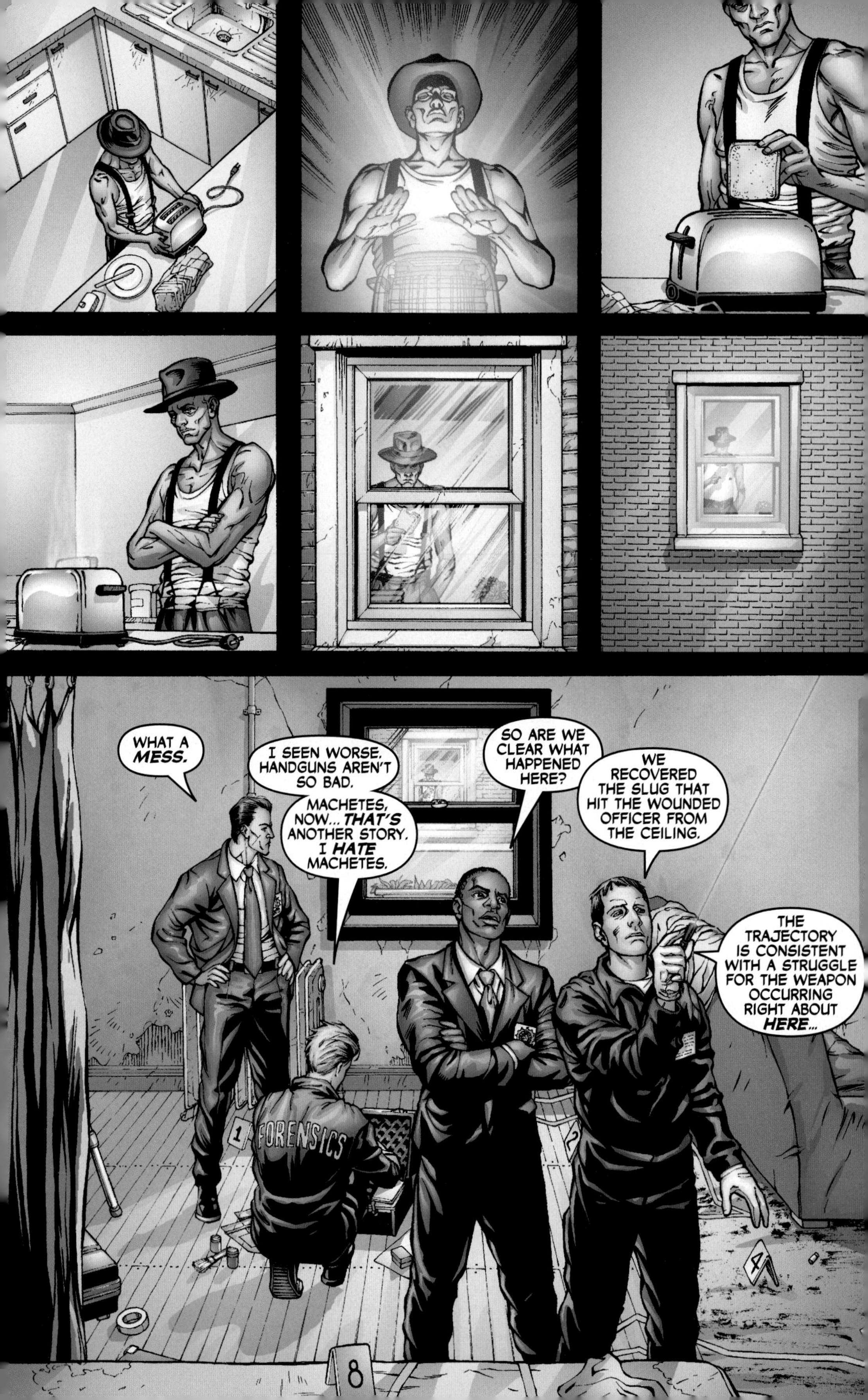
WHAT A *MESS.*
I SEEN WORSE. HANDGUNS AREN'T SO BAD.
MACHETES, NOW... *THAT'S* ANOTHER STORY. I *HATE* MACHETES.
SO ARE WE CLEAR WHAT HAPPENED HERE?
WE RECOVERED THE SLUG THAT HIT THE WOUNDED OFFICER FROM THE CEILING.
THE TRAJECTORY IS CONSISTENT WITH A STRUGGLE FOR THE WEAPON OCCURRING RIGHT ABOUT *HERE...*
FORENSICS
1
2
4
8

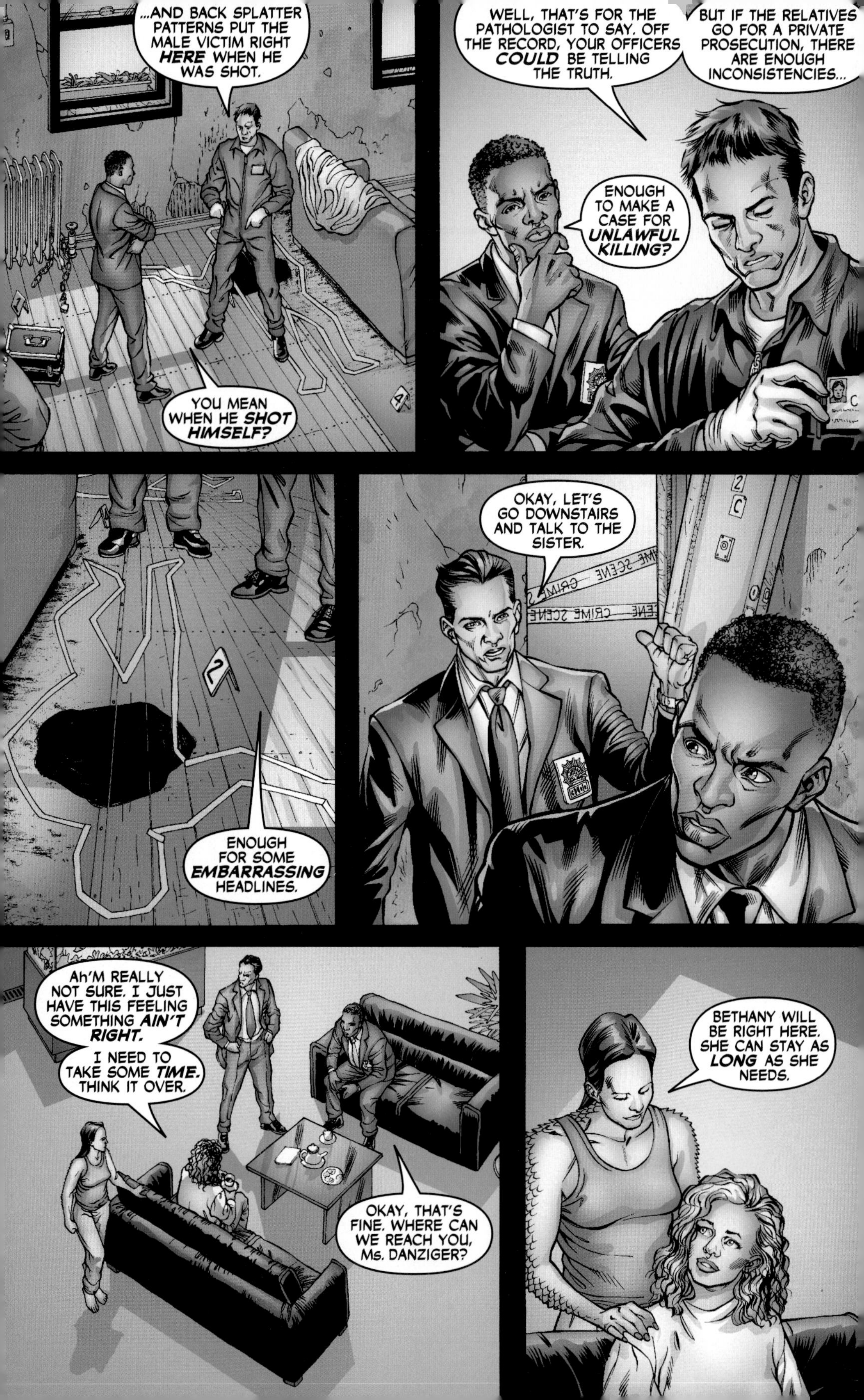
...AND BACK SPLATTER PATTERNS PUT THE MALE VICTIM RIGHT *HERE* WHEN HE WAS SHOT.
YOU MEAN WHEN HE *SHOT HIMSELF?*
WELL, THAT'S FOR THE PATHOLOGIST TO SAY. OFF THE RECORD, YOUR OFFICERS *COULD* BE TELLING THE TRUTH.
BUT IF THE RELATIVES GO FOR A PRIVATE PROSECUTION, THERE ARE ENOUGH INCONSISTENCIES...
ENOUGH TO MAKE A CASE FOR *UNLAWFUL KILLING?*
ENOUGH FOR SOME *EMBARRASSING* HEADLINES.
OKAY, LET'S GO DOWNSTAIRS AND TALK TO THE SISTER.
CRIME SCENE
Ah'M REALLY NOT SURE. I JUST HAVE THIS FEELING SOMETHING *AIN'T RIGHT.*
I NEED TO TAKE SOME *TIME.* THINK IT OVER.
OKAY, THAT'S FINE. WHERE CAN WE REACH YOU, Ms. DANZIGER?
BETHANY WILL BE RIGHT HERE. SHE CAN STAY AS *LONG* AS SHE NEEDS.

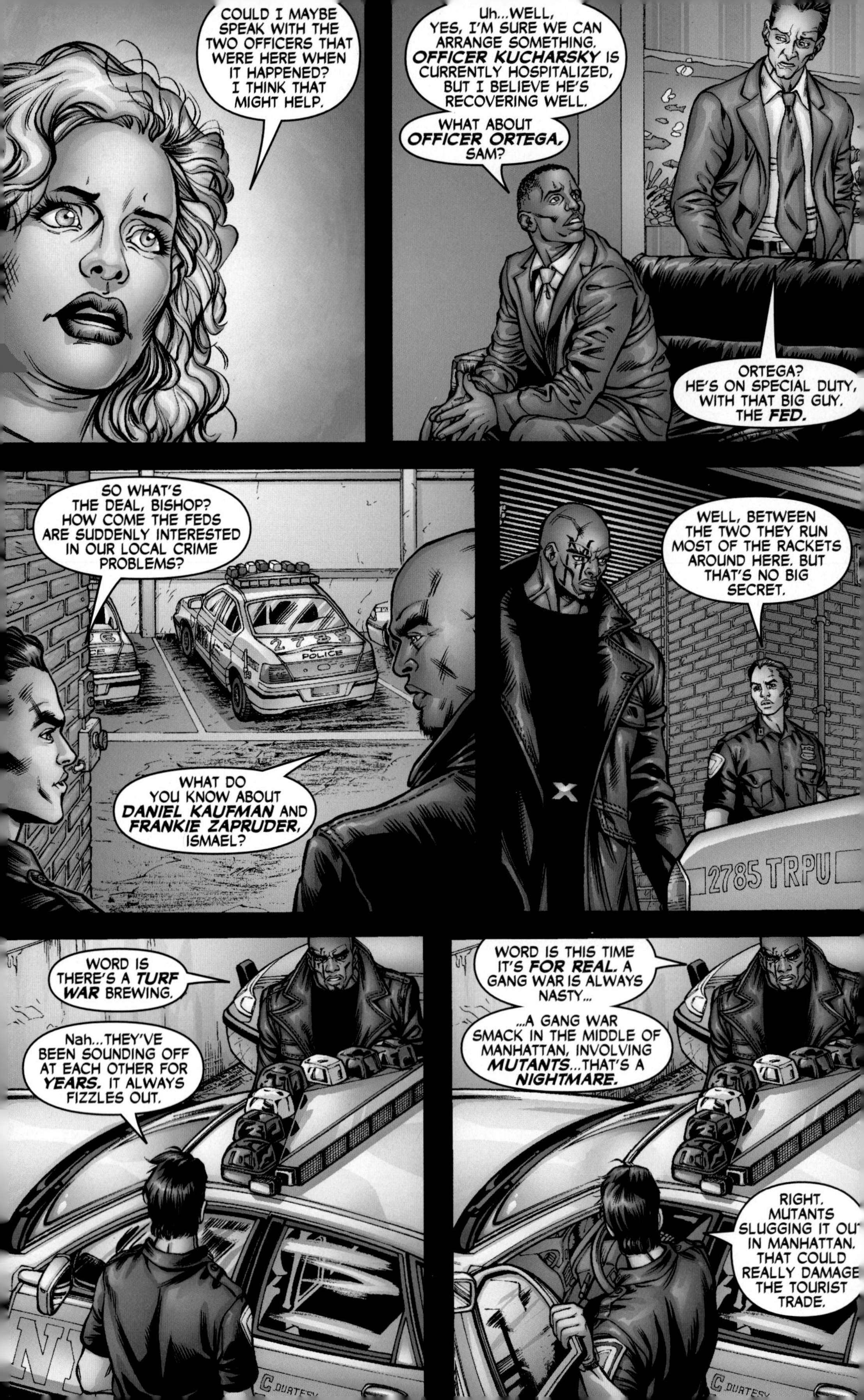
COULD I MAYBE SPEAK WITH THE TWO OFFICERS THAT WERE HERE WHEN IT HAPPENED? I THINK THAT MIGHT HELP.
Uh...WELL, YES, I'M SURE WE CAN ARRANGE SOMETHING. OFFICER KUCHARSKY IS CURRENTLY HOSPITALIZED, BUT I BELIEVE HE'S RECOVERING WELL.
WHAT ABOUT OFFICER ORTEGA, SAM?
ORTEGA? HE'S ON SPECIAL DUTY, WITH THAT BIG GUY. THE FED.
SO WHAT'S THE DEAL, BISHOP? HOW COME THE FEDS ARE SUDDENLY INTERESTED IN OUR LOCAL CRIME PROBLEMS?
WHAT DO YOU KNOW ABOUT DANIEL KAUFMAN AND FRANKIE ZAPRUDER, ISMAEL?
WELL, BETWEEN THE TWO THEY RUN MOST OF THE RACKETS AROUND HERE. BUT THAT'S NO BIG SECRET.
2785 TRPU
WORD IS THERE'S A TURF WAR BREWING.
Nah...THEY'VE BEEN SOUNDING OFF AT EACH OTHER FOR YEARS. IT ALWAYS FIZZLES OUT.
WORD IS THIS TIME IT'S FOR REAL. A GANG WAR IS ALWAYS NASTY...
...A GANG WAR SMACK IN THE MIDDLE OF MANHATTAN, INVOLVING MUTANTS...THAT'S A NIGHTMARE.
RIGHT. MUTANTS SLUGGING IT OU IN MANHATTAN. THAT COULD REALLY DAMAGE THE TOURIST TRADE.

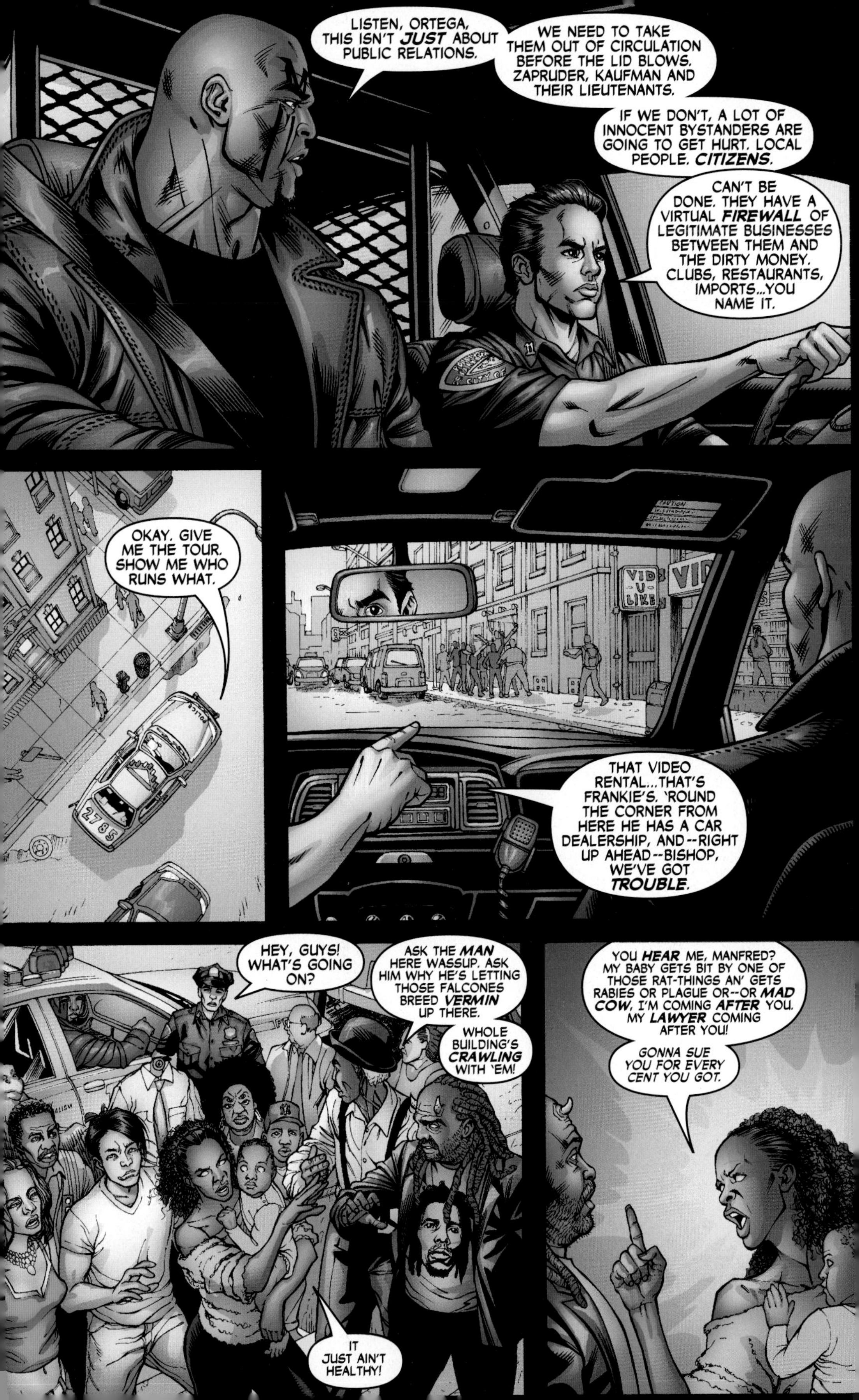
LISTEN, ORTEGA, THIS ISN'T *JUST* ABOUT PUBLIC RELATIONS.
WE NEED TO TAKE THEM OUT OF CIRCULATION BEFORE THE LID BLOWS. ZAPRUDER, KAUFMAN AND THEIR LIEUTENANTS.
IF WE DON'T, A LOT OF INNOCENT BYSTANDERS ARE GOING TO GET HURT. LOCAL PEOPLE. *CITIZENS*.
CAN'T BE DONE. THEY HAVE A VIRTUAL *FIREWALL* OF LEGITIMATE BUSINESSES BETWEEN THEM AND THE DIRTY MONEY. CLUBS, RESTAURANTS, IMPORTS...YOU NAME IT.
OKAY. GIVE ME THE TOUR. SHOW ME WHO RUNS WHAT.
VID U LIKE
THAT VIDEO RENTAL...THAT'S FRANKIE'S. 'ROUND THE CORNER FROM HERE HE HAS A CAR DEALERSHIP, AND--RIGHT UP AHEAD--BISHOP, WE'VE GOT *TROUBLE*.
HEY, GUYS! WHAT'S GOING ON?
ASK THE *MAN* HERE WASSUP. ASK HIM WHY HE'S LETTING THOSE FALCONES BREED *VERMIN* UP THERE.
WHOLE BUILDING'S *CRAWLING* WITH 'EM!
IT JUST AIN'T HEALTHY!
YOU *HEAR* ME, MANFRED? MY BABY GETS BIT BY ONE OF THOSE RAT-THINGS AN' GETS RABIES OR PLAGUE OR--OR *MAD COW*, I'M COMING *AFTER* YOU. MY *LAWYER* COMING AFTER YOU!
GONNA SUE YOU FOR EVERY CENT YOU GOT.

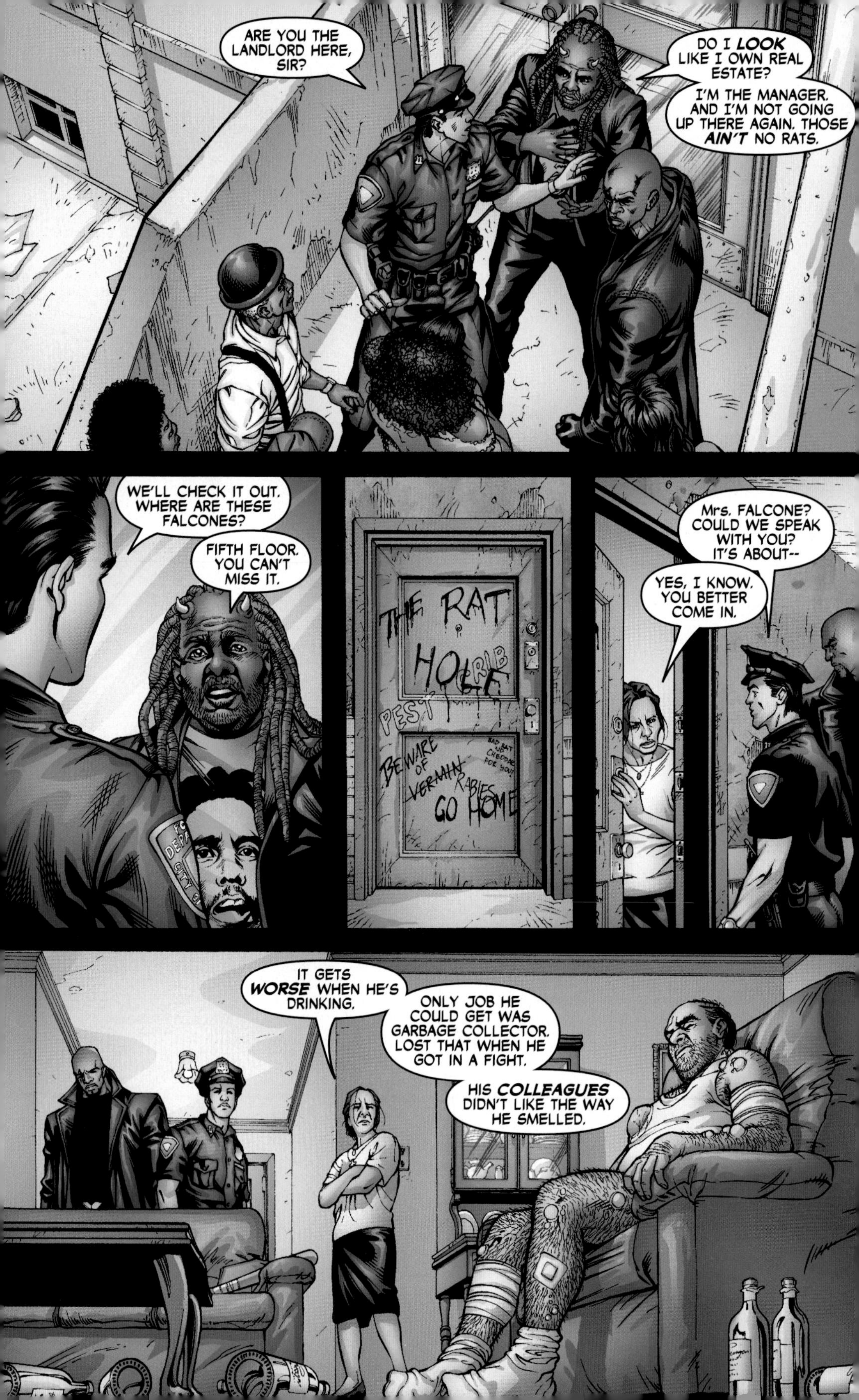
ARE YOU THE LANDLORD HERE, SIR?
DO I LOOK LIKE I OWN REAL ESTATE?
I'M THE MANAGER. AND I'M NOT GOING UP THERE AGAIN. THOSE AIN'T NO RATS.
WE'LL CHECK IT OUT. WHERE ARE THESE FALCONES?
FIFTH FLOOR. YOU CAN'T MISS IT.
THE RAT HOLE
CRIB
PEST
BEWARE OF VERMIN RABIES
BAD RAT NO CHEDDAR FOR YOU!
GO HOME
Mrs. FALCONE? COULD WE SPEAK WITH YOU? IT'S ABOUT--
YES, I KNOW. YOU BETTER COME IN.
IT GETS WORSE WHEN HE'S DRINKING.
ONLY JOB HE COULD GET WAS GARBAGE COLLECTOR. LOST THAT WHEN HE GOT IN A FIGHT.
HIS COLLEAGUES DIDN'T LIKE THE WAY HE SMELLED.

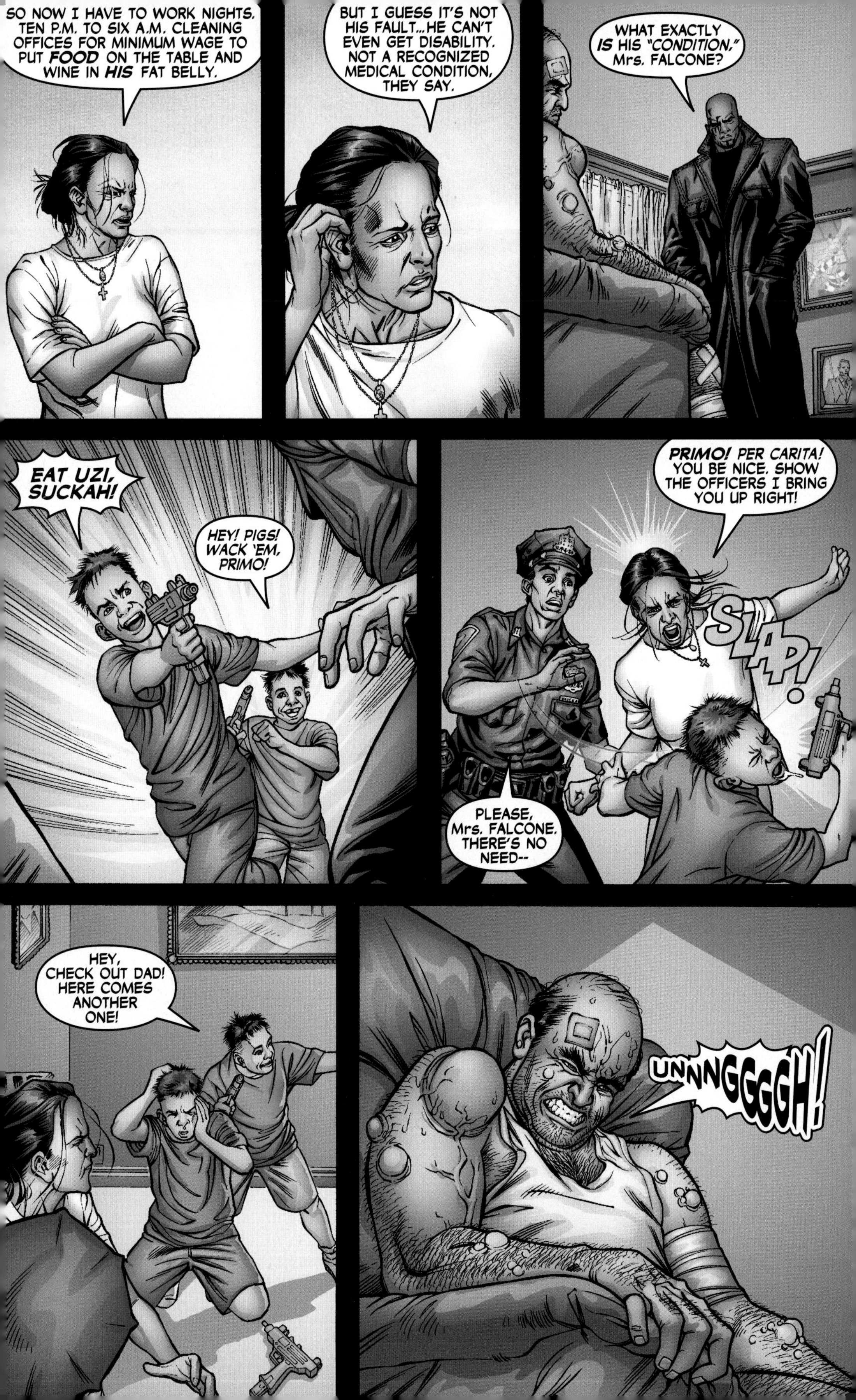
SO NOW I HAVE TO WORK NIGHTS. TEN P.M. TO SIX A.M. CLEANING OFFICES FOR MINIMUM WAGE TO PUT FOOD ON THE TABLE AND WINE IN HIS FAT BELLY.
BUT I GUESS IT'S NOT HIS FAULT...HE CAN'T EVEN GET DISABILITY. NOT A RECOGNIZED MEDICAL CONDITION, THEY SAY.
WHAT EXACTLY IS HIS "CONDITION," Mrs. FALCONE?
EAT UZI, SUCKAH!
HEY! PIGS! WACK 'EM, PRIMO!
PRIMO! PER CARITA! YOU BE NICE. SHOW THE OFFICERS I BRING YOU UP RIGHT!
SLAP!
PLEASE, Mrs. FALCONE. THERE'S NO NEED--
HEY, CHECK OUT DAD! HERE COMES ANOTHER ONE!
UNNNGGGGH!

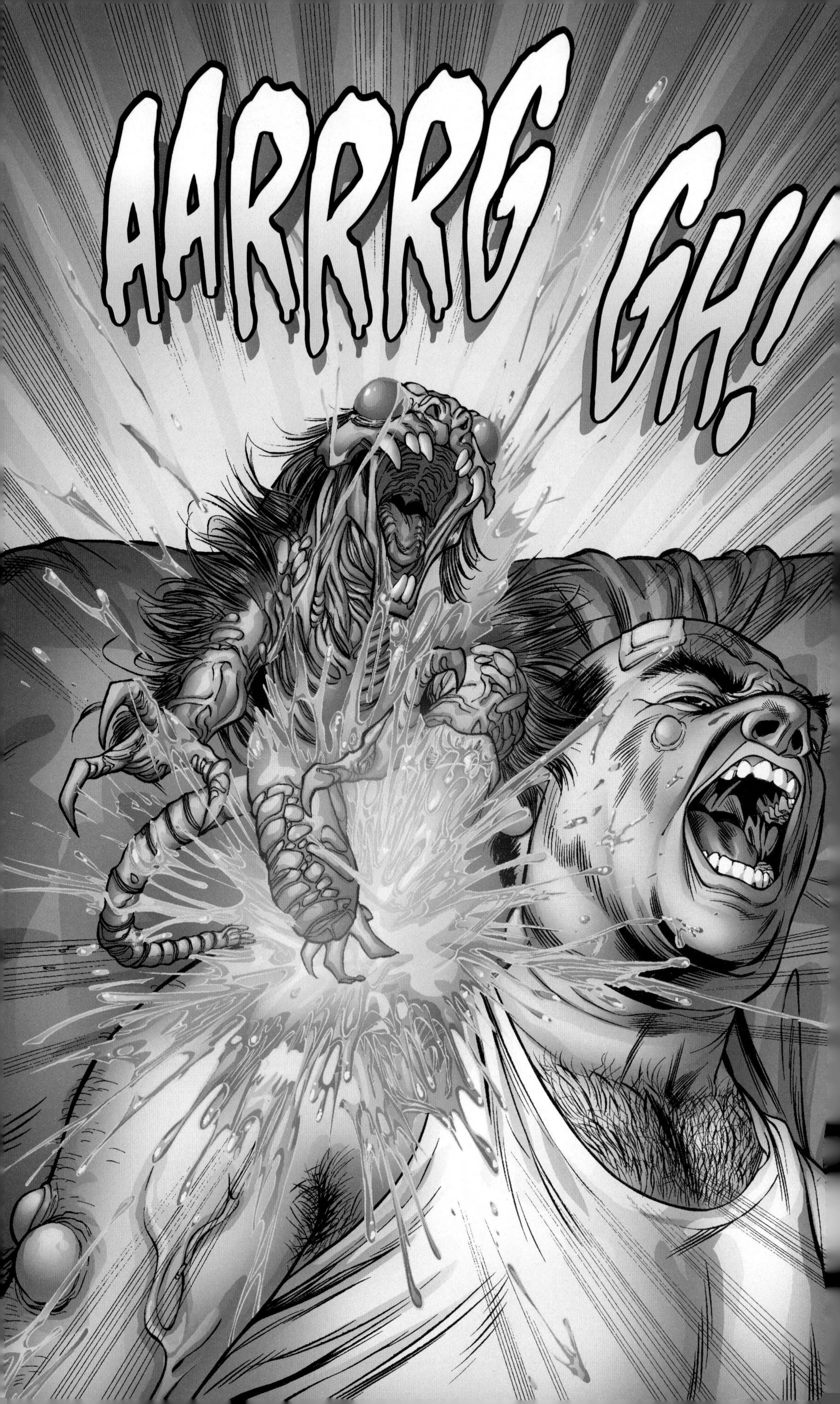
AARRRGGH!

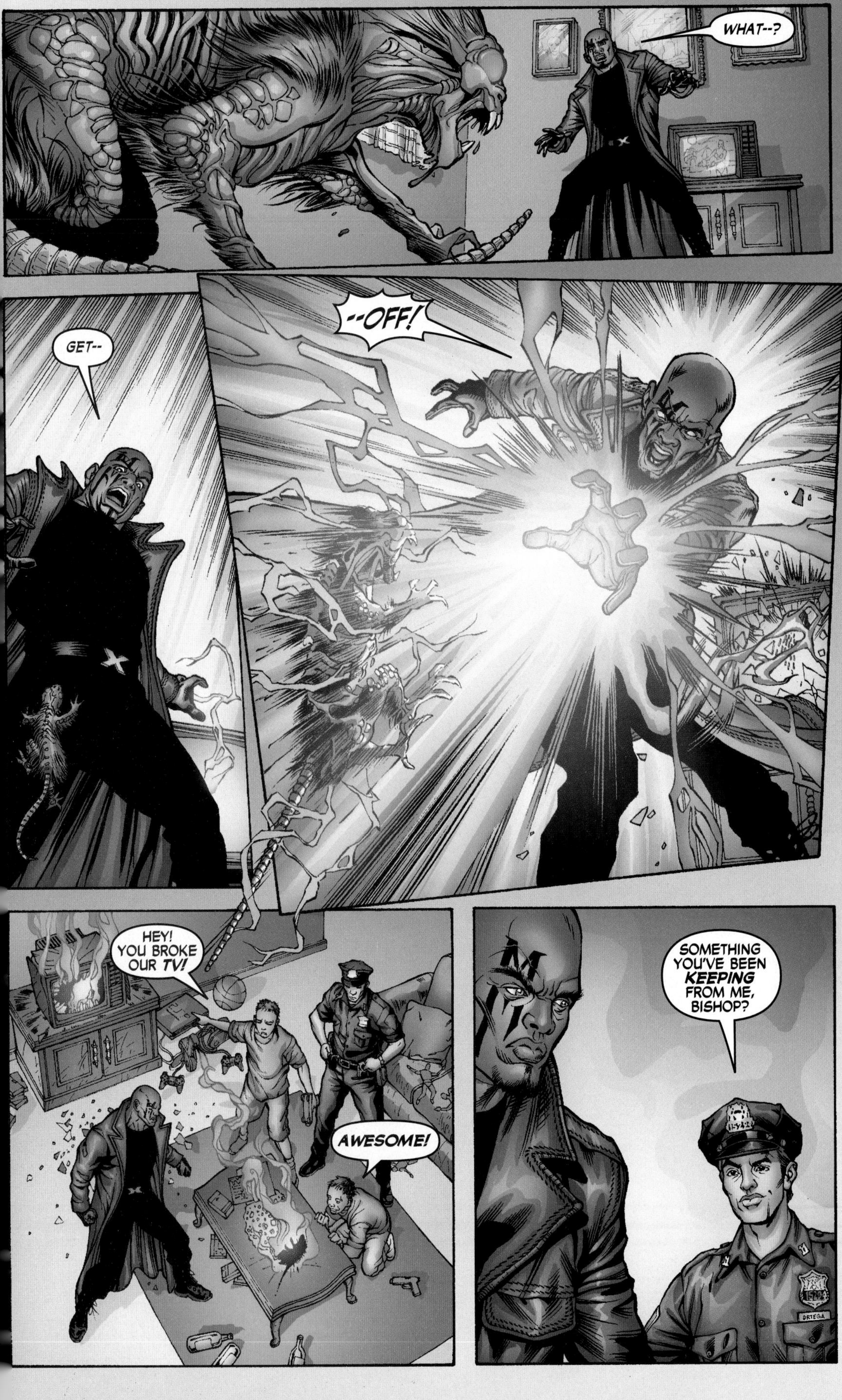
WHAT--?
GET--
--OFF!
HEY! YOU BROKE OUR TV!
AWESOME!
SOMETHING YOU'VE BEEN KEEPING FROM ME, BISHOP?

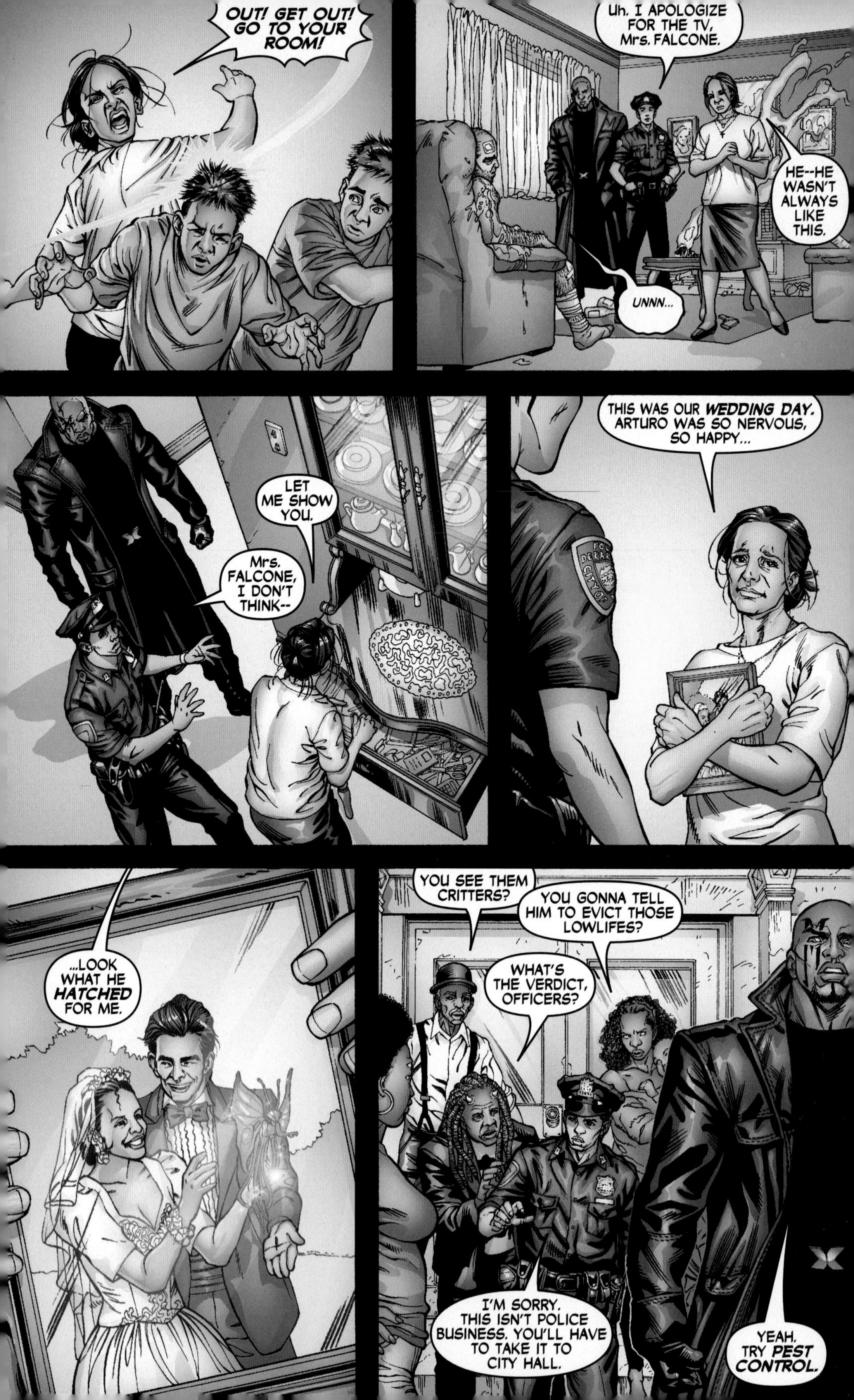
OUT! GET OUT! GO TO YOUR ROOM!
Uh. I APOLOGIZE FOR THE TV, Mrs. FALCONE.
HE--HE WASN'T ALWAYS LIKE THIS.
UNNN...
LET ME SHOW YOU.
Mrs. FALCONE, I DON'T THINK--
THIS WAS OUR WEDDING DAY. ARTURO WAS SO NERVOUS, SO HAPPY...
...LOOK WHAT HE HATCHED FOR ME.
YOU SEE THEM CRITTERS?
YOU GONNA TELL HIM TO EVICT THOSE LOWLIFES?
WHAT'S THE VERDICT, OFFICERS?
I'M SORRY. THIS ISN'T POLICE BUSINESS. YOU'LL HAVE TO TAKE IT TO CITY HALL.
YEAH. TRY PEST CONTROL.

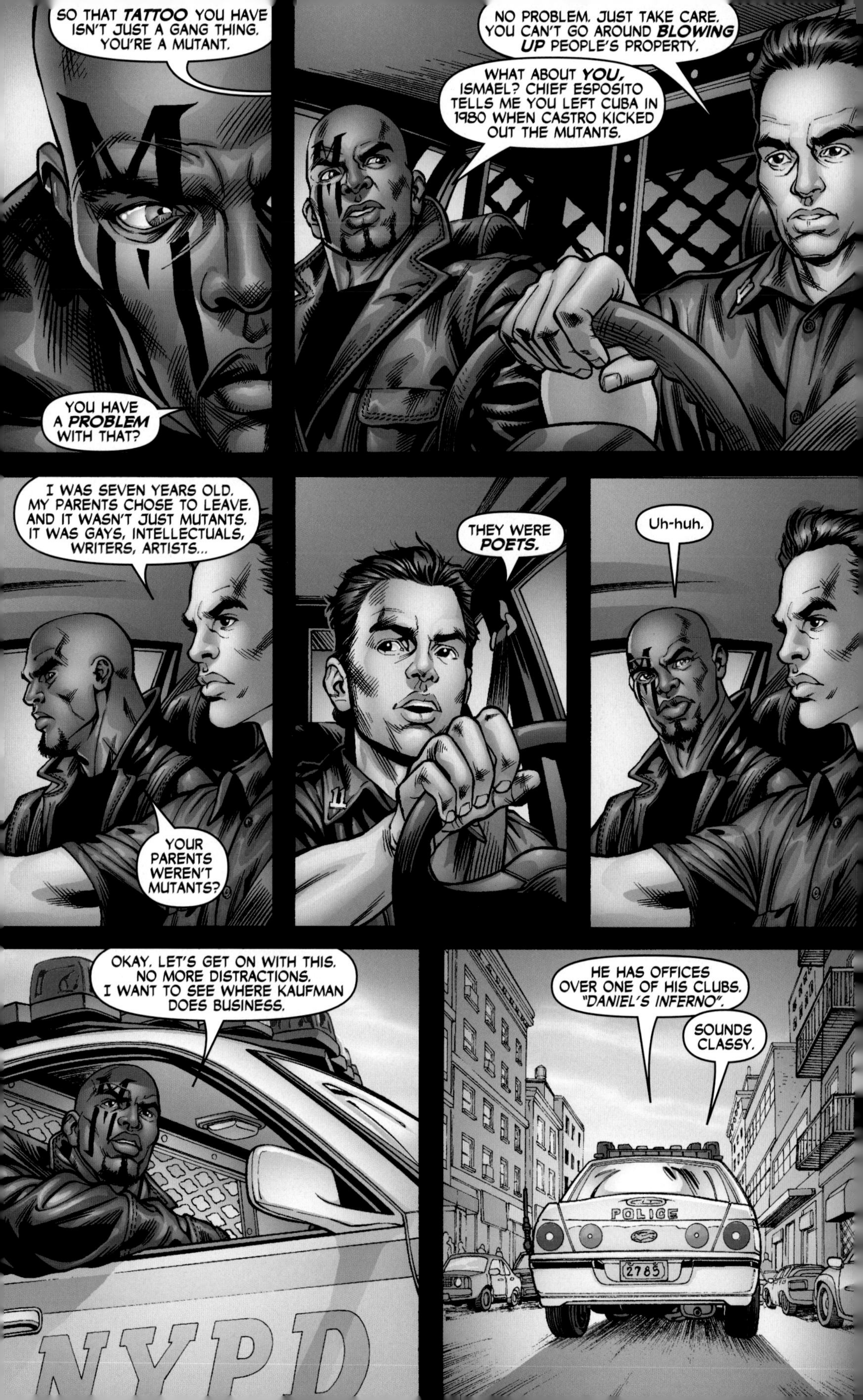
SO THAT TATTOO YOU HAVE ISN'T JUST A GANG THING. YOU'RE A MUTANT.
YOU HAVE A PROBLEM WITH THAT?
NO PROBLEM. JUST TAKE CARE. YOU CAN'T GO AROUND BLOWING UP PEOPLE'S PROPERTY.
WHAT ABOUT YOU, ISMAEL? CHIEF ESPOSITO TELLS ME YOU LEFT CUBA IN 1980 WHEN CASTRO KICKED OUT THE MUTANTS.
I WAS SEVEN YEARS OLD. MY PARENTS CHOSE TO LEAVE. AND IT WASN'T JUST MUTANTS. IT WAS GAYS, INTELLECTUALS, WRITERS, ARTISTS...
YOUR PARENTS WEREN'T MUTANTS?
THEY WERE POETS.
Uh-huh.
OKAY. LET'S GET ON WITH THIS. NO MORE DISTRACTIONS. I WANT TO SEE WHERE KAUFMAN DOES BUSINESS.
NYPD
HE HAS OFFICES OVER ONE OF HIS CLUBS. "DANIEL'S INFERNO".
SOUNDS CLASSY.
POLICE
2785

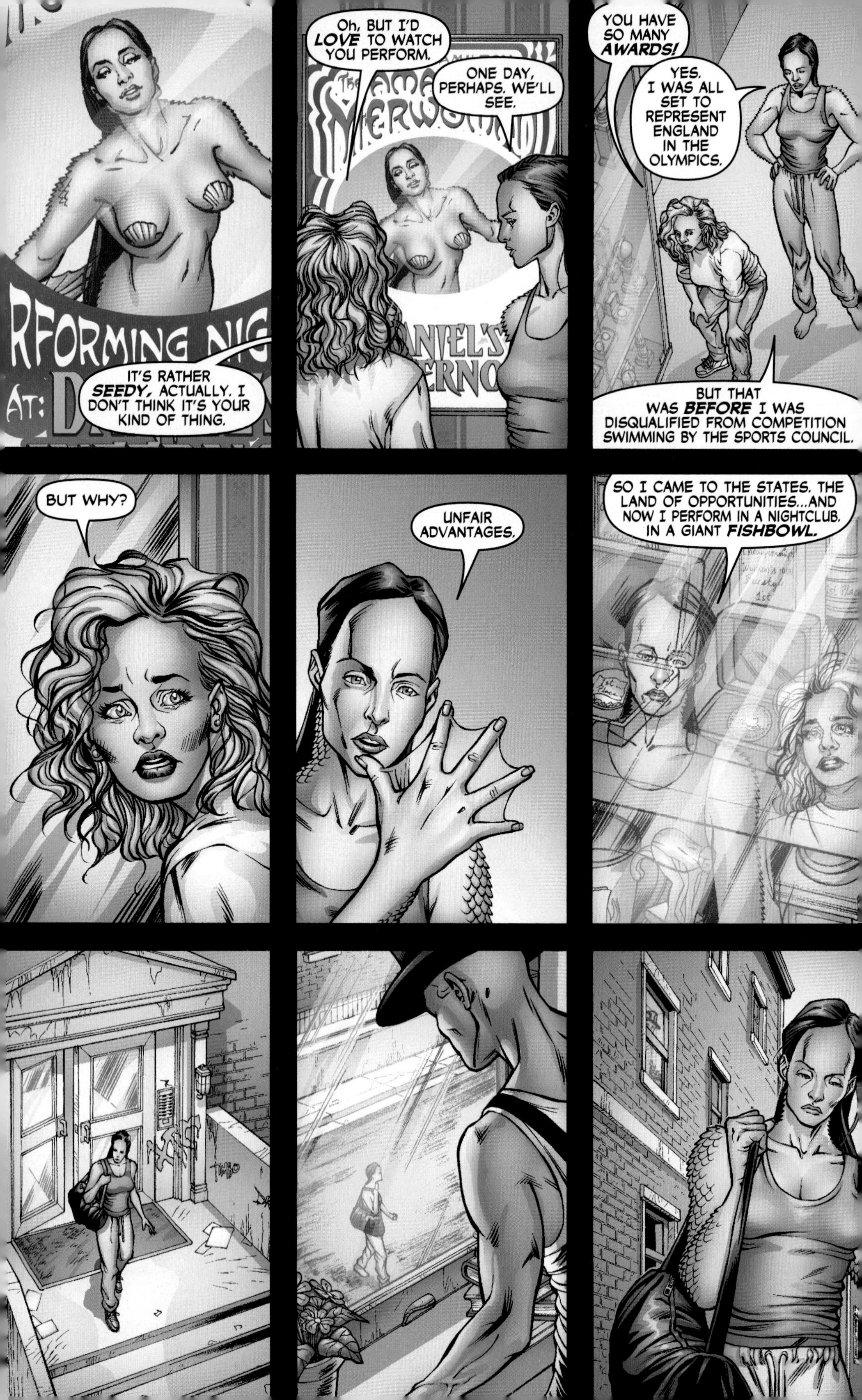
RFORMING NIG
AT:
IT'S RATHER SEEDY, ACTUALLY. I DON'T THINK IT'S YOUR KIND OF THING.
Oh, BUT I'D LOVE TO WATCH YOU PERFORM.
ONE DAY, PERHAPS. WE'LL SEE.
YOU HAVE SO MANY AWARDS!
YES. I WAS ALL SET TO REPRESENT ENGLAND IN THE OLYMPICS.
BUT THAT WAS BEFORE I WAS DISQUALIFIED FROM COMPETITION SWIMMING BY THE SPORTS COUNCIL.
BUT WHY?
UNFAIR ADVANTAGES.
SO I CAME TO THE STATES. THE LAND OF OPPORTUNITIES...AND NOW I PERFORM IN A NIGHTCLUB. IN A GIANT FISHBOWL.

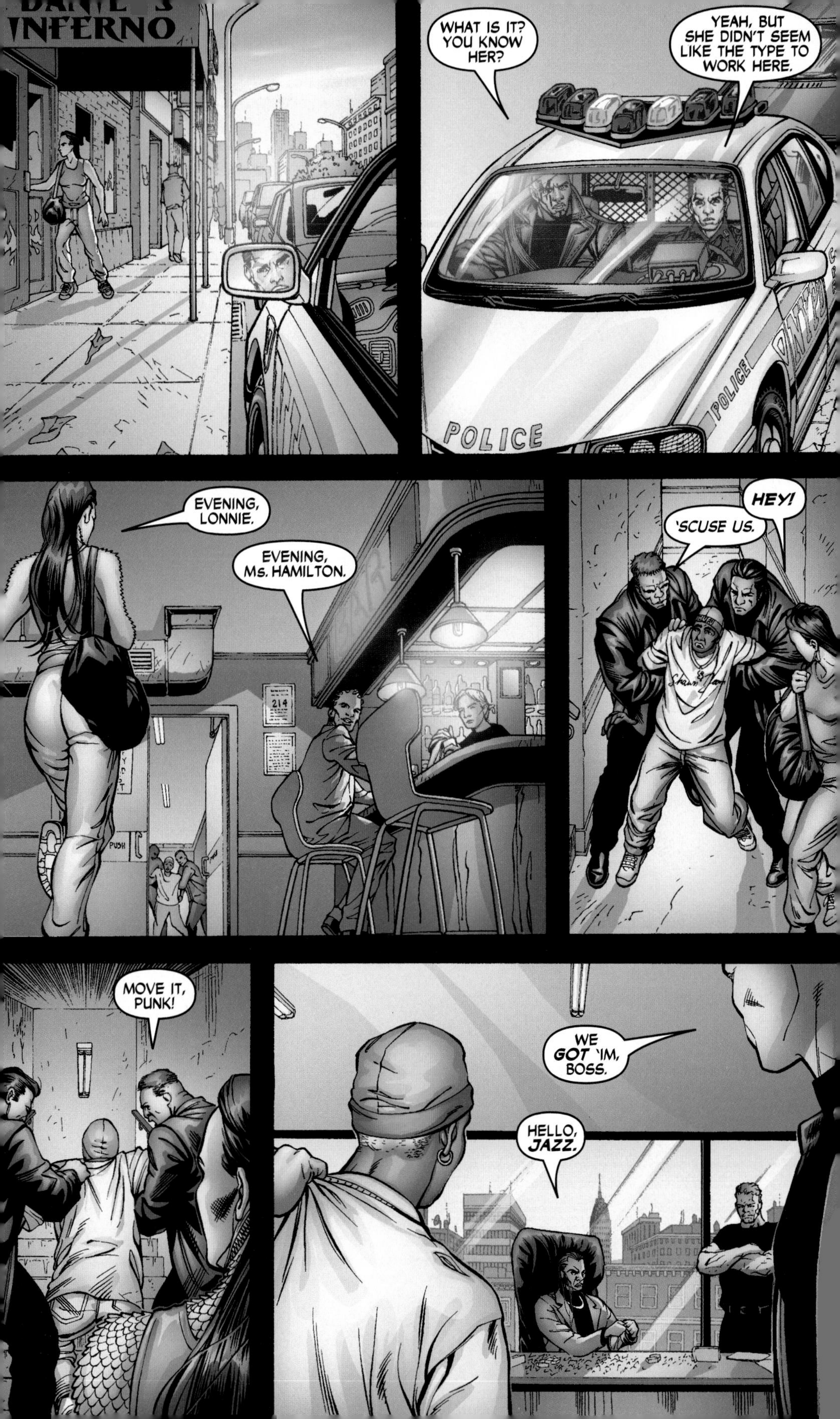
INFERNO
WHAT IS IT? YOU KNOW HER?
YEAH, BUT SHE DIDN'T SEEM LIKE THE TYPE TO WORK HERE.
POLICE
POLICE
EVENING, LONNIE.
EVENING, Ms. HAMILTON.
214
PUSH
HEY!
'SCUSE US.
MOVE IT, PUNK!
WE GOT 'IM, BOSS.
HELLO, JAZZ.

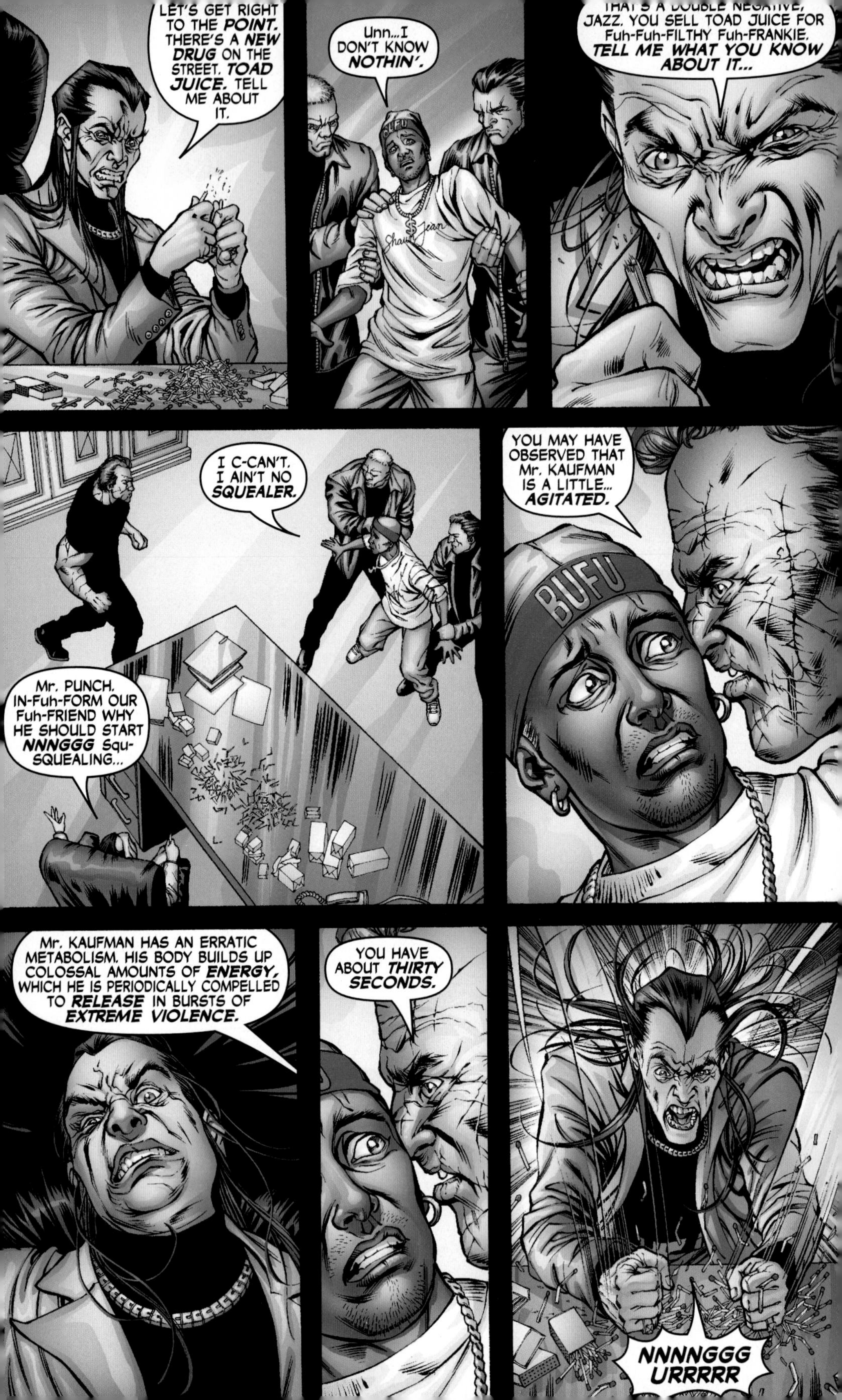
LET'S GET RIGHT TO THE POINT. THERE'S A NEW DRUG ON THE STREET. TOAD JUICE. TELL ME ABOUT IT.
Unn...I DON'T KNOW NOTHIN'.
BUFU
Shawn Jean
THAT'S A DOUBLE NEGATIVE, JAZZ. YOU SELL TOAD JUICE FOR Fuh-Fuh-FILTHY Fuh-FRANKIE. TELL ME WHAT YOU KNOW ABOUT IT...
I C-CAN'T. I AIN'T NO SQUEALER.
Mr. PUNCH. IN-Fuh-FORM OUR Fuh-FRIEND WHY HE SHOULD START NNNGGG Squ-SQUEALING...
YOU MAY HAVE OBSERVED THAT Mr. KAUFMAN IS A LITTLE... AGITATED.
BUFU
Mr. KAUFMAN HAS AN ERRATIC METABOLISM. HIS BODY BUILDS UP COLOSSAL AMOUNTS OF ENERGY, WHICH HE IS PERIODICALLY COMPELLED TO RELEASE IN BURSTS OF EXTREME VIOLENCE.
YOU HAVE ABOUT THIRTY SECONDS.
NNNNGGG URRRRR

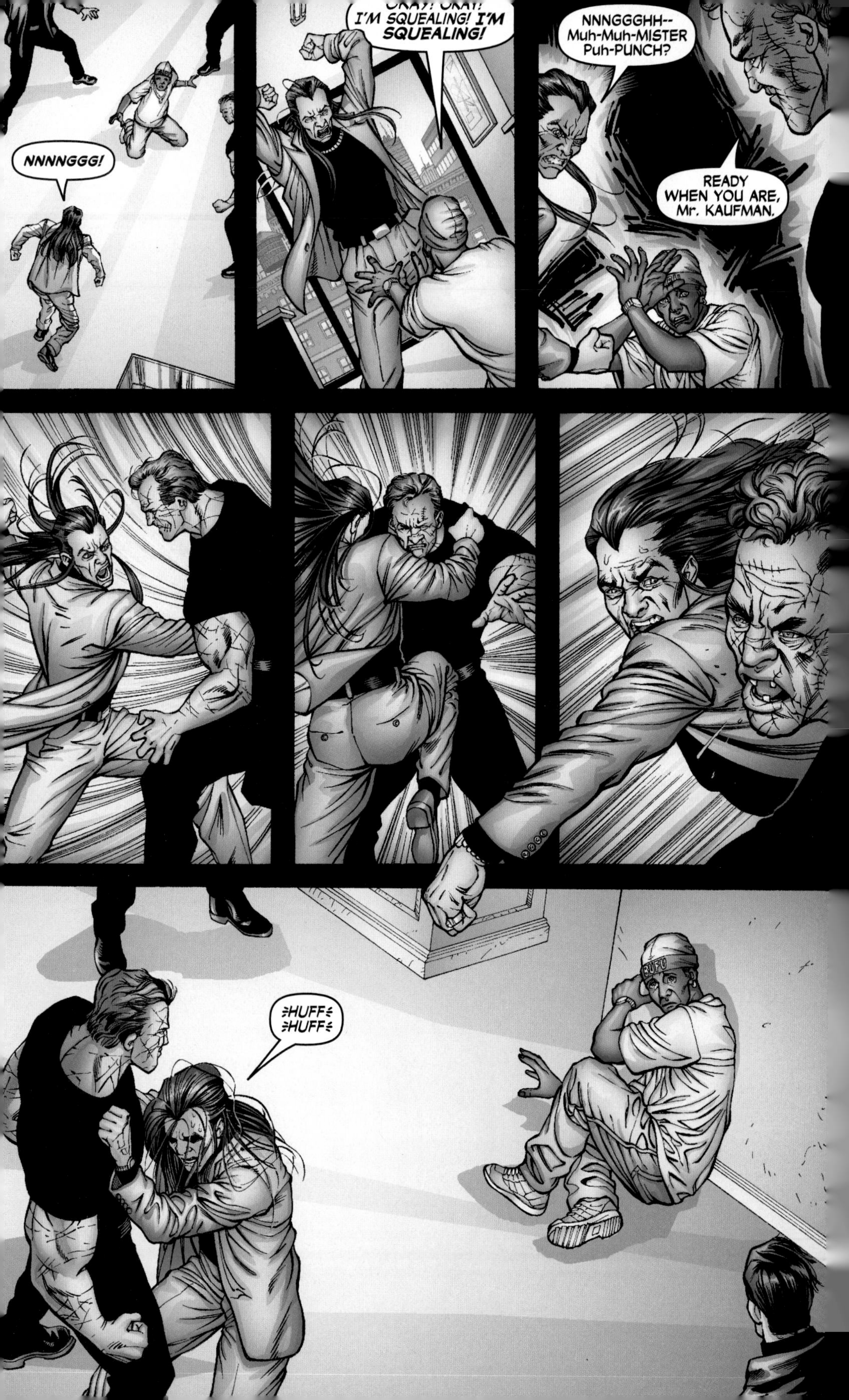
NNNNGGG!
I'M SQUEALING! I'M SQUEALING!
NNNGGGHH-- Muh-Muh-MISTER Puh-PUNCH?
READY WHEN YOU ARE, Mr. KAUFMAN.
HUFF HUFF

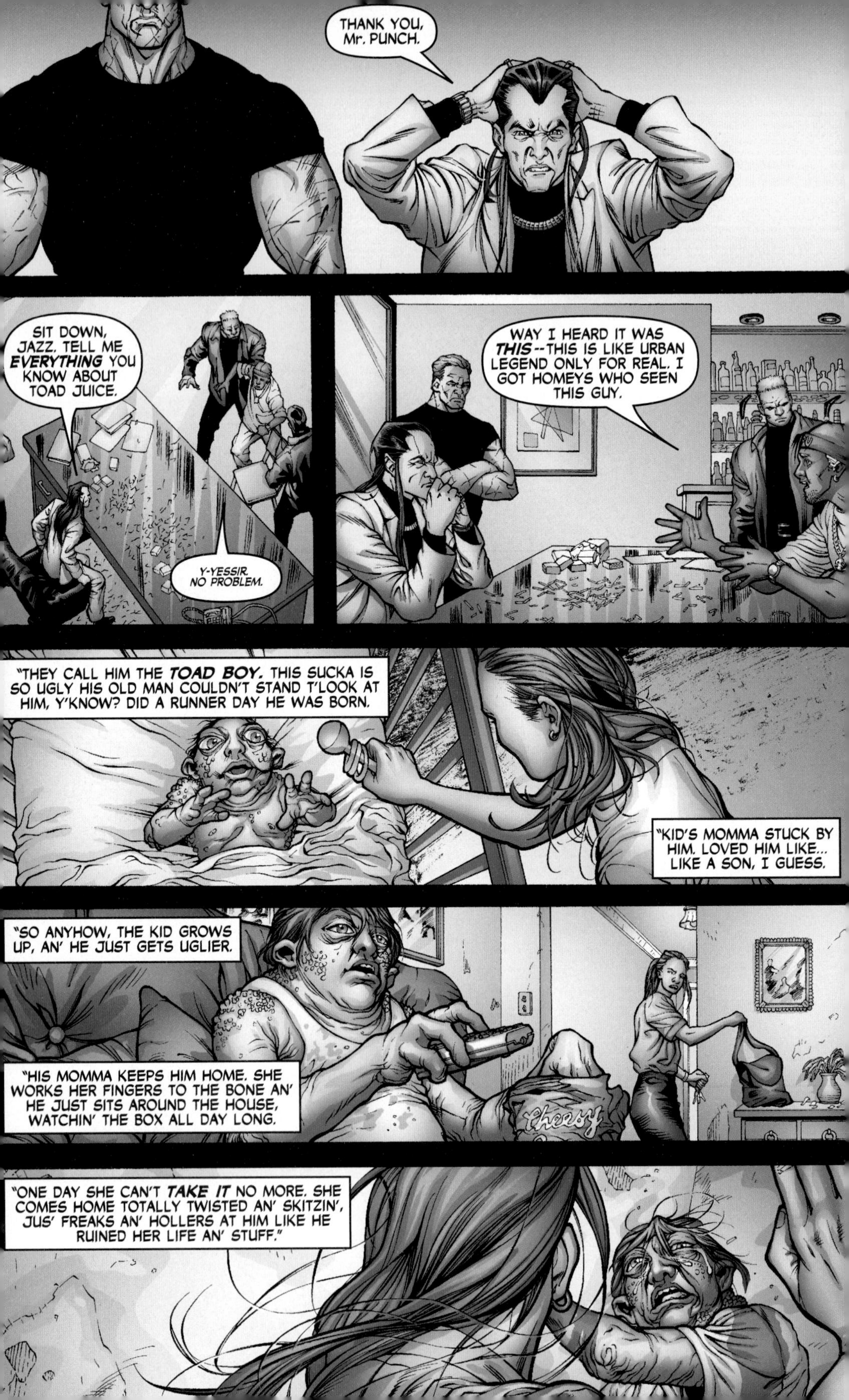
THANK YOU, Mr. PUNCH.
SIT DOWN, JAZZ. TELL ME EVERYTHING YOU KNOW ABOUT TOAD JUICE.
Y-YESSIR. NO PROBLEM.
WAY I HEARD IT WAS THIS--THIS IS LIKE URBAN LEGEND ONLY FOR REAL. I GOT HOMEYS WHO SEEN THIS GUY.
"THEY CALL HIM THE TOAD BOY. THIS SUCKA IS SO UGLY HIS OLD MAN COULDN'T STAND T'LOOK AT HIM, Y'KNOW? DID A RUNNER DAY HE WAS BORN.
"KID'S MOMMA STUCK BY HIM. LOVED HIM LIKE... LIKE A SON, I GUESS.
"SO ANYHOW, THE KID GROWS UP, AN' HE JUST GETS UGLIER.
"HIS MOMMA KEEPS HIM HOME. SHE WORKS HER FINGERS TO THE BONE AN' HE JUST SITS AROUND THE HOUSE, WATCHIN' THE BOX ALL DAY LONG.
"ONE DAY SHE CAN'T TAKE IT NO MORE. SHE COMES HOME TOTALLY TWISTED AN' SKITZIN', JUS' FREAKS AN' HOLLERS AT HIM LIKE HE RUINED HER LIFE AN' STUFF."

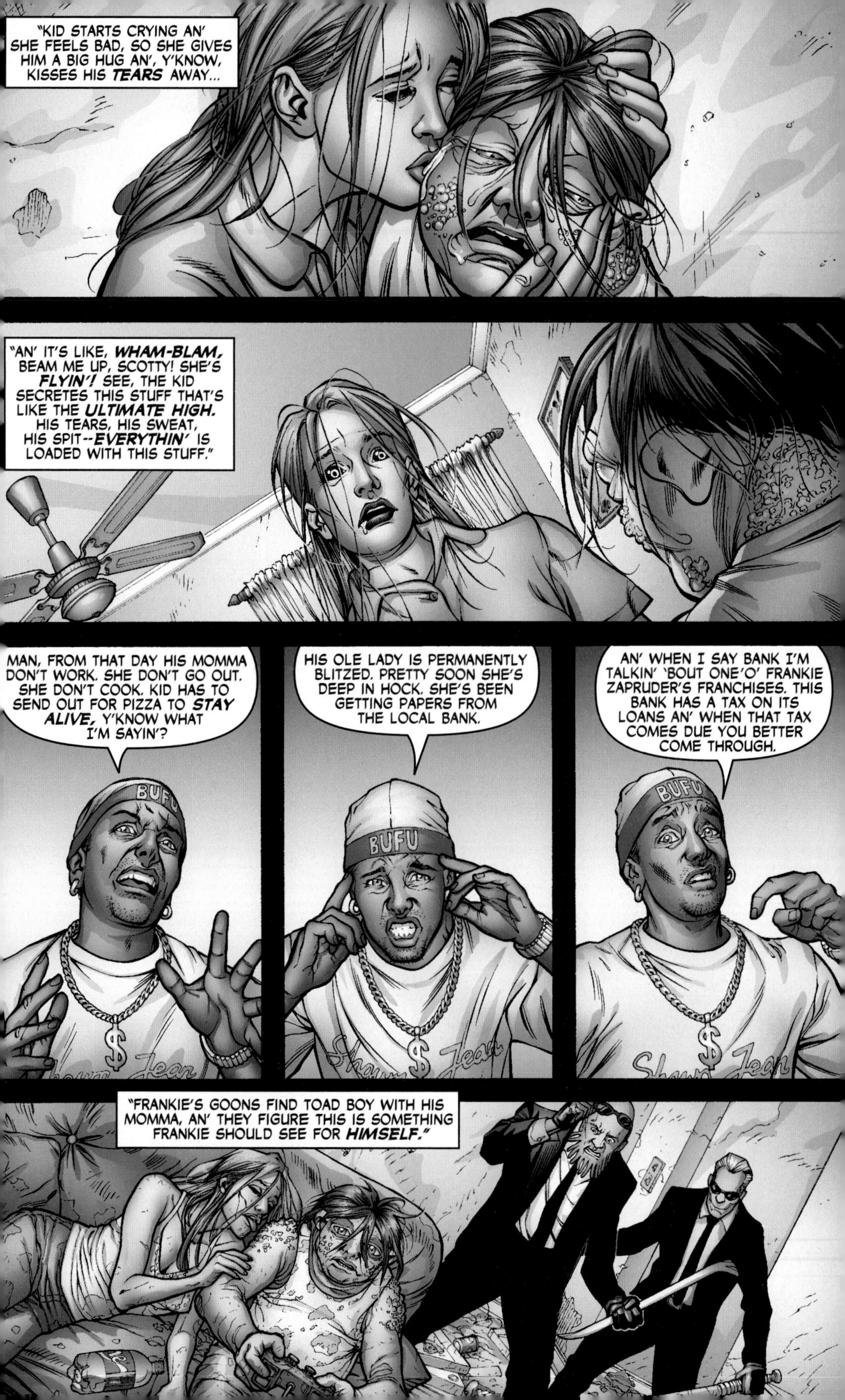
"KID STARTS CRYING AN' SHE FEELS BAD, SO SHE GIVES HIM A BIG HUG AN', Y'KNOW, KISSES HIS TEARS AWAY...
"AN' IT'S LIKE, WHAM-BLAM, BEAM ME UP, SCOTTY! SHE'S FLYIN'! SEE, THE KID SECRETES THIS STUFF THAT'S LIKE THE ULTIMATE HIGH. HIS TEARS, HIS SWEAT, HIS SPIT--EVERYTHIN' IS LOADED WITH THIS STUFF."
MAN, FROM THAT DAY HIS MOMMA DON'T WORK. SHE DON'T GO OUT. SHE DON'T COOK. KID HAS TO SEND OUT FOR PIZZA TO STAY ALIVE, Y'KNOW WHAT I'M SAYIN'?
BUFU
HIS OLE LADY IS PERMANENTLY BLITZED. PRETTY SOON SHE'S DEEP IN HOCK. SHE'S BEEN GETTING PAPERS FROM THE LOCAL BANK.
BUFU
AN' WHEN I SAY BANK I'M TALKIN' 'BOUT ONE 'O' FRANKIE ZAPRUDER'S FRANCHISES. THIS BANK HAS A TAX ON ITS LOANS AN' WHEN THAT TAX COMES DUE YOU BETTER COME THROUGH.
BUFU
"FRANKIE'S GOONS FIND TOAD BOY WITH HIS MOMMA, AN' THEY FIGURE THIS IS SOMETHING FRANKIE SHOULD SEE FOR HIMSELF."

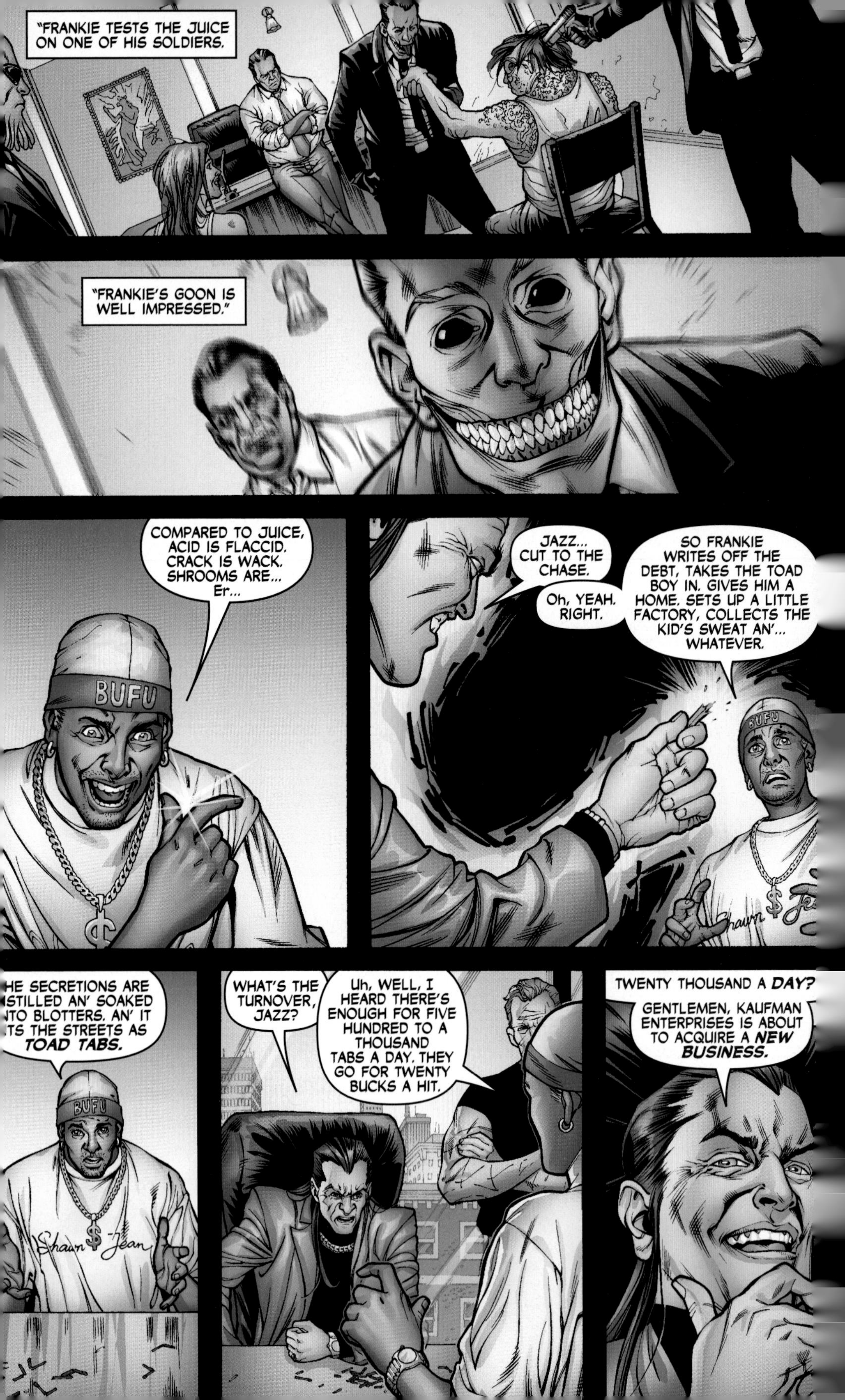
"FRANKIE TESTS THE JUICE ON ONE OF HIS SOLDIERS.
"FRANKIE'S GOON IS WELL IMPRESSED."
COMPARED TO JUICE, ACID IS FLACCID. CRACK IS WACK. SHROOMS ARE... Er...
BUFU
JAZZ... CUT TO THE CHASE.
Oh, YEAH. RIGHT.
SO FRANKIE WRITES OFF THE DEBT, TAKES THE TOAD BOY IN, GIVES HIM A HOME, SETS UP A LITTLE FACTORY, COLLECTS THE KID'S SWEAT AN'... WHATEVER.
BUFU
HE SECRETIONS ARE STILLED AN' SOAKED NTO BLOTTERS, AN' IT TS THE STREETS AS TOAD TABS.
BUFU
Shawn $ Jean
WHAT'S THE TURNOVER, JAZZ?
Uh, WELL, I HEARD THERE'S ENOUGH FOR FIVE HUNDRED TO A THOUSAND TABS A DAY. THEY GO FOR TWENTY BUCKS A HIT.
TWENTY THOUSAND A DAY?
GENTLEMEN, KAUFMAN ENTERPRISES IS ABOUT TO ACQUIRE A NEW BUSINESS.

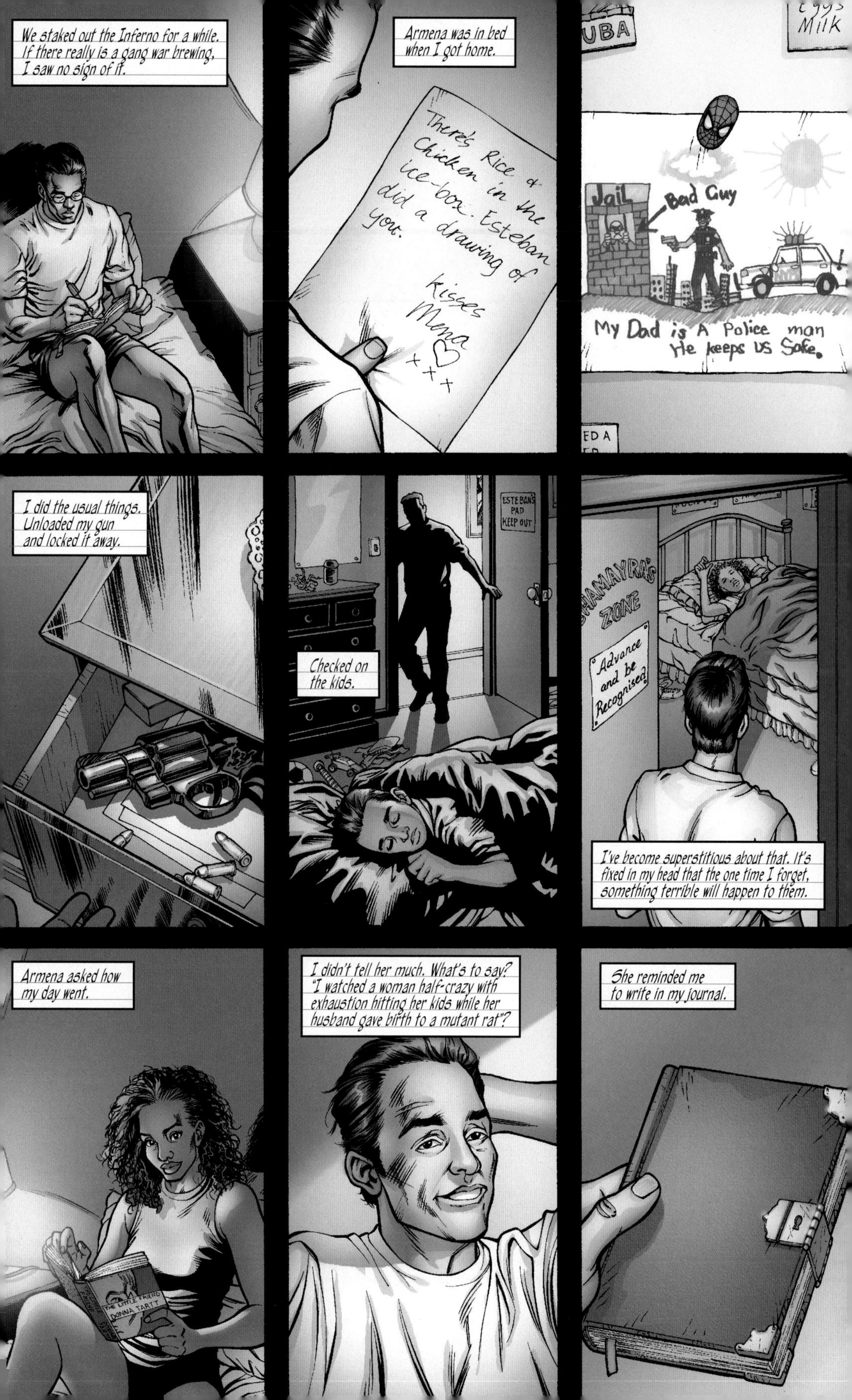
We staked out the Inferno for a while. If there really is a gang war brewing, I saw no sign of it.
Armena was in bed when I got home.
There's Rice & Chicken in the ice-box. Esteban did a drawing of you.
kisses Mena
xxx
Milk
Jail
Bad Guy
My Dad is A Police man He keeps US Safe.
I did the usual things. Unloaded my gun and locked it away.
ESTEBAN'S PAD KEEP OUT
Checked on the kids.
SHAMAYRA'S ZONE
Advance and be Recognised
I've become superstitious about that. It's fixed in my head that the one time I forget, something terrible will happen to them.
Armena asked how my day went.
THE LITTLE FRIEND DONNA TARTT
I didn't tell her much. What's to say? "I watched a woman half-crazy with exhaustion hitting her kids while her husband gave birth to a mutant rat"?
She reminded me to write in my journal.

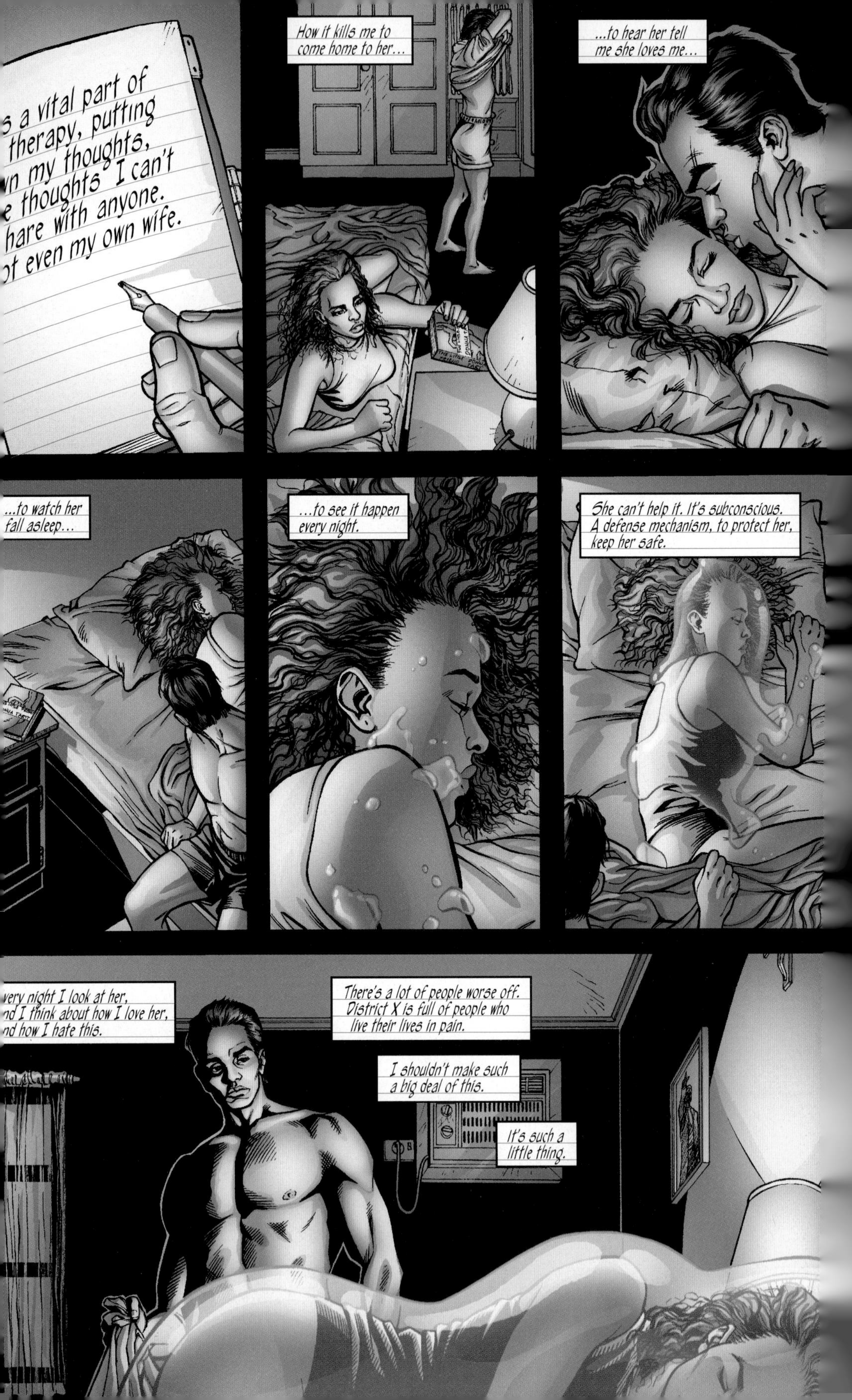
s a vital part of
therapy, putting
n my thoughts,
e thoughts I can't
hare with anyone.
ot even my own wife.
How it kills me to come home to her...
...to hear her tell me she loves me...
...to watch her fall asleep...
...to see it happen every night.
She can't help it. It's subconscious. A defense mechanism, to protect her, keep her safe.
very night I look at her.
nd I think about how I love her.
nd how I hate this.
There's a lot of people worse off. District X is full of people who live their lives in pain.
I shouldn't make such a big deal of this.
It's such a little thing.

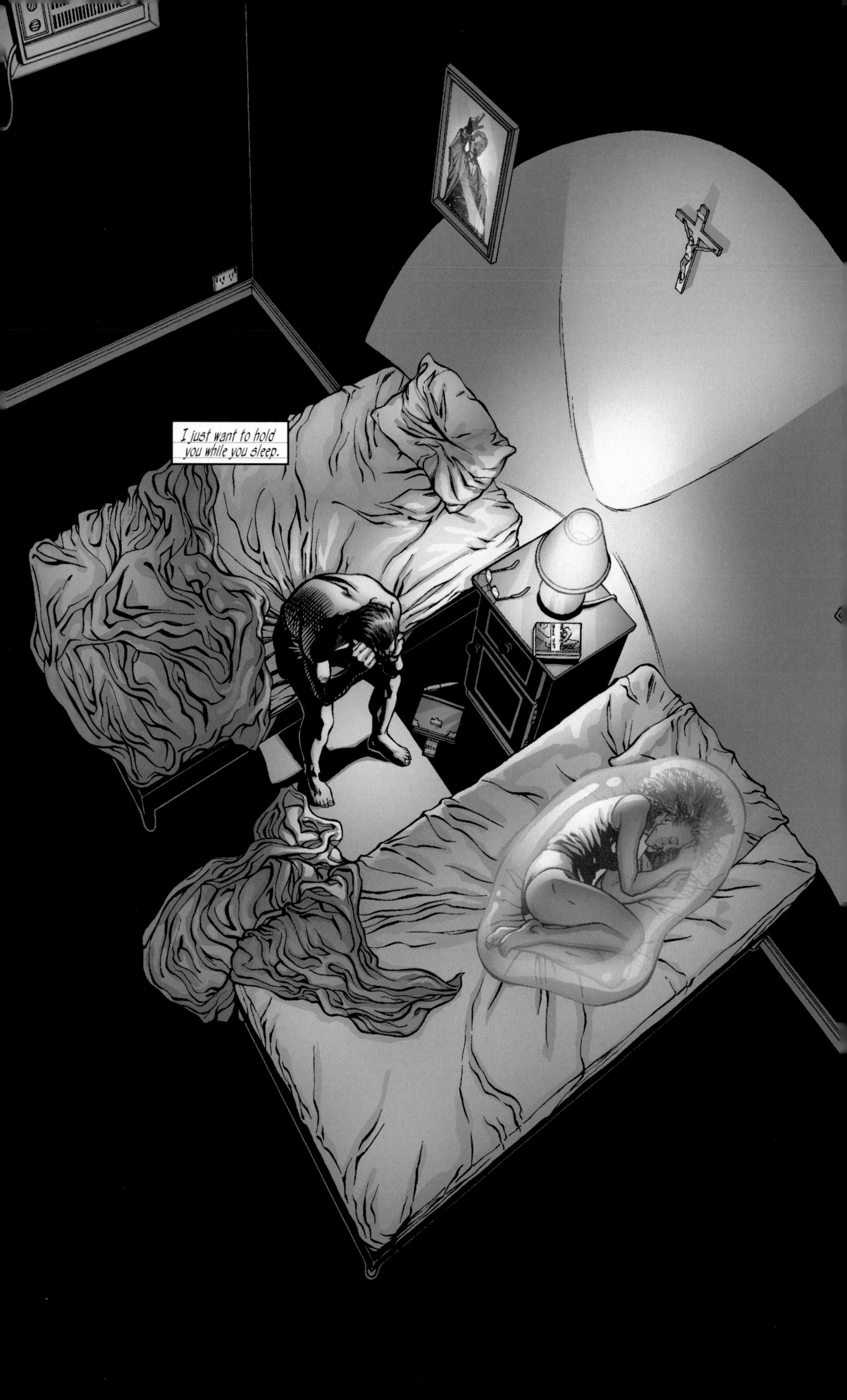
I just want to hold you while you sleep.

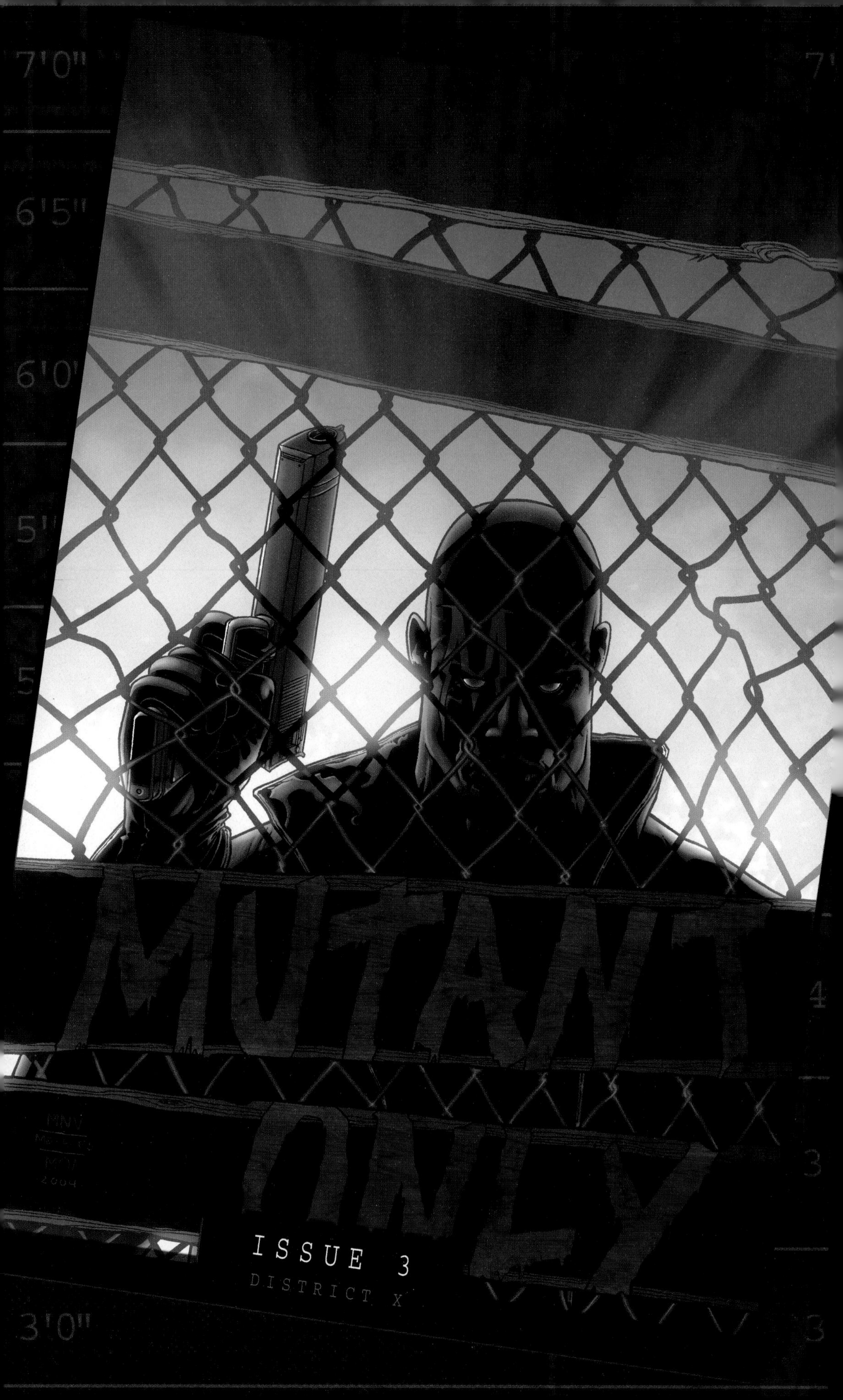
7'0"
6'5"
6'0"
3'0"
ISSUE 3
DISTRICT X

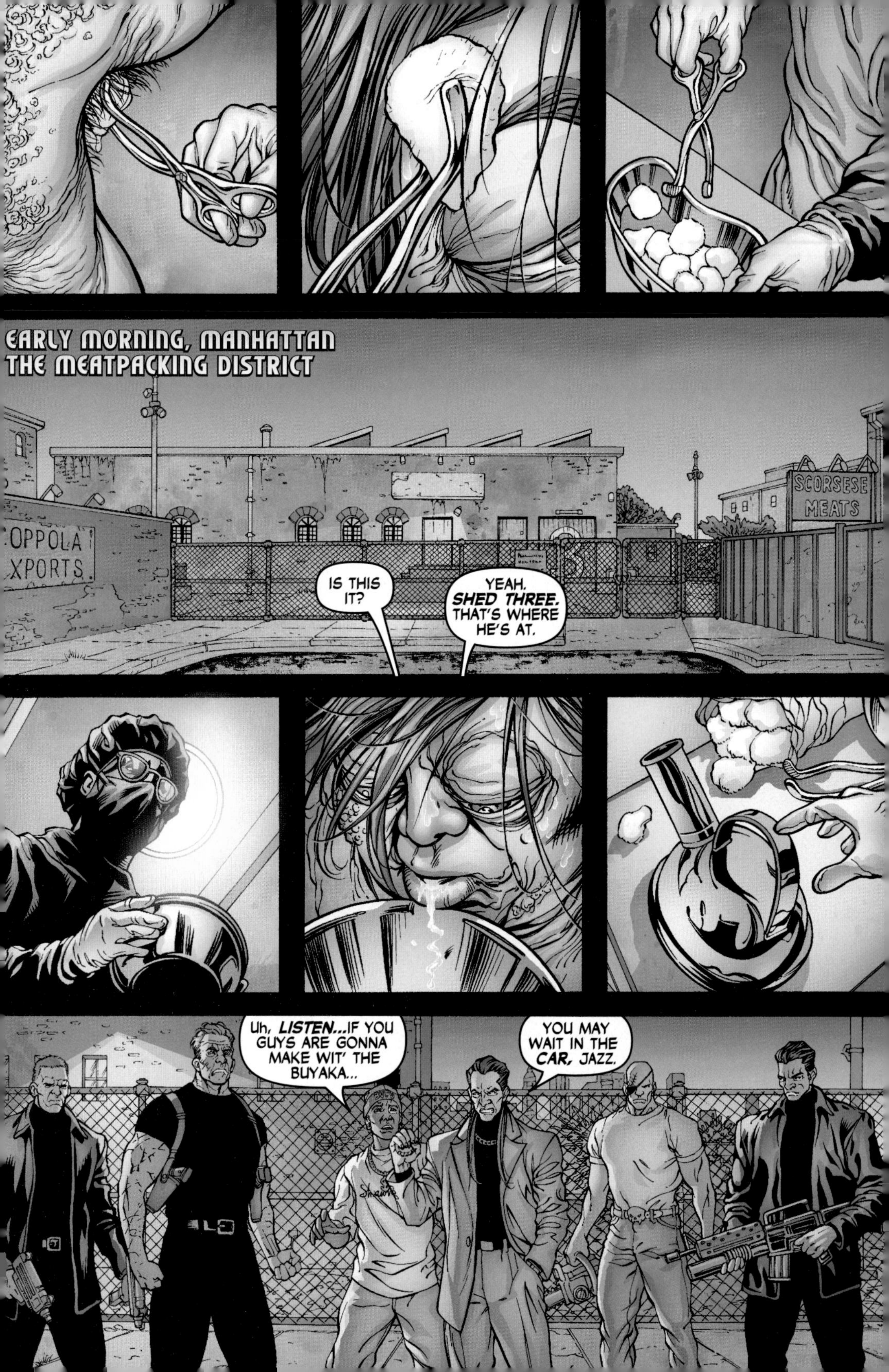
EARLY MORNING, MANHATTAN
THE MEATPACKING DISTRICT
OPPOLA
XPORTS
SCORSESE
MEATS
IS THIS IT?
YEAH. SHED THREE. THAT'S WHERE HE'S AT.
Uh, LISTEN...IF YOU GUYS ARE GONNA MAKE WIT' THE BUYAKA...
YOU MAY WAIT IN THE CAR, JAZZ.

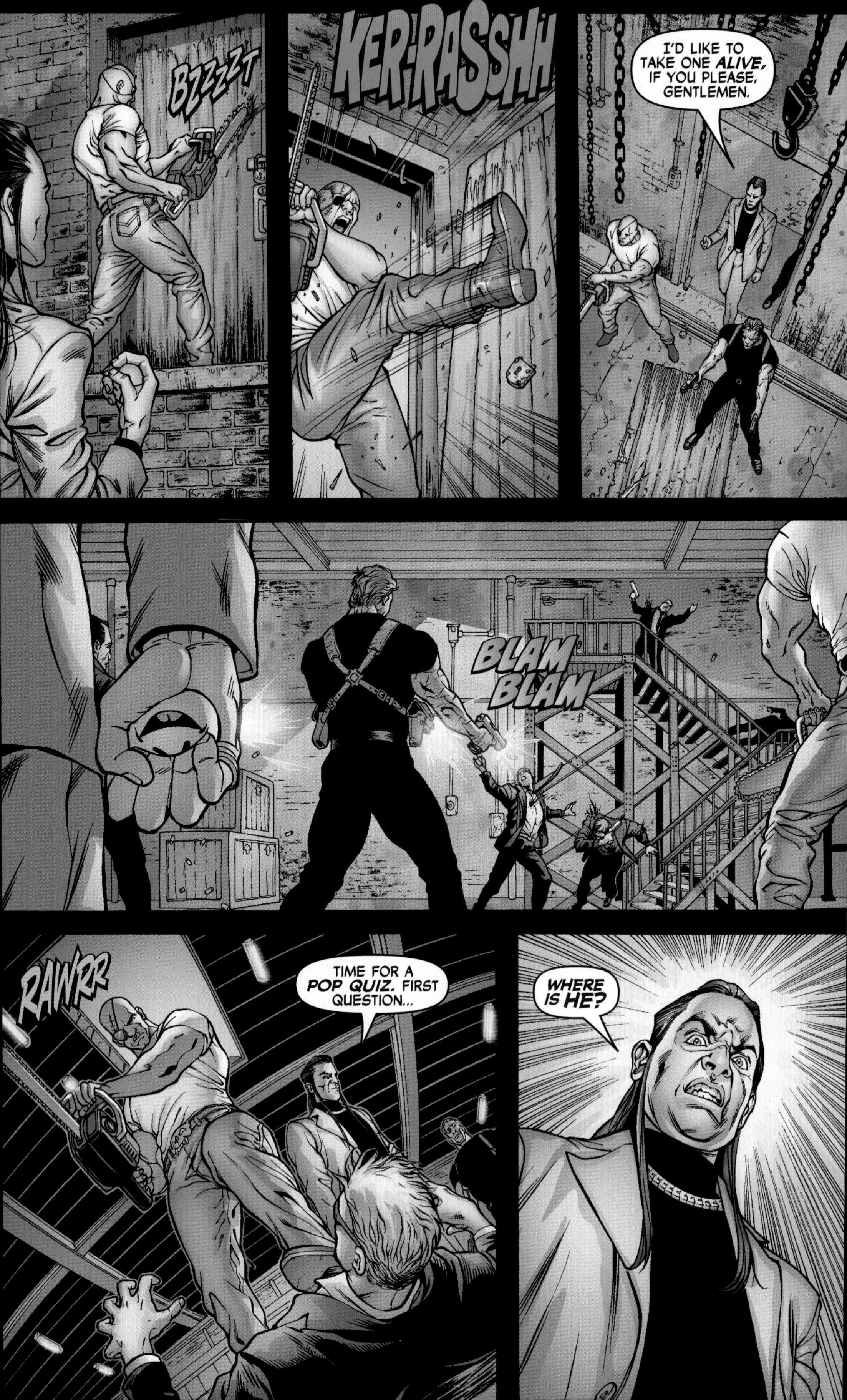
BZZZZT
KER-RASSHH
I'D LIKE TO TAKE ONE ALIVE, IF YOU PLEASE, GENTLEMEN.
BLAM BLAM
RAWRR
TIME FOR A POP QUIZ. FIRST QUESTION...
WHERE IS HE?

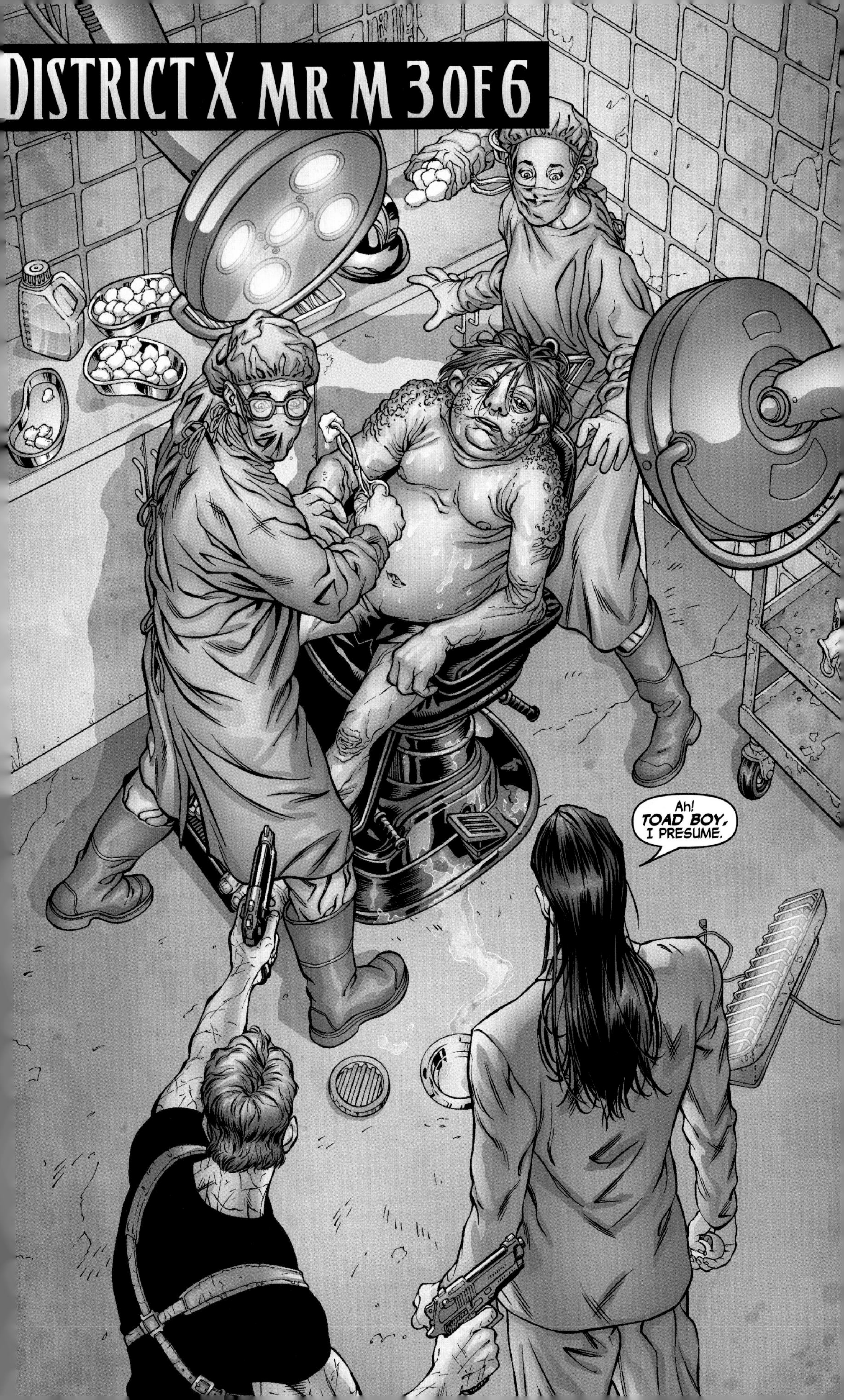
DISTRICT X MR M 3 OF 6
Ah! TOAD BOY, I PRESUME.

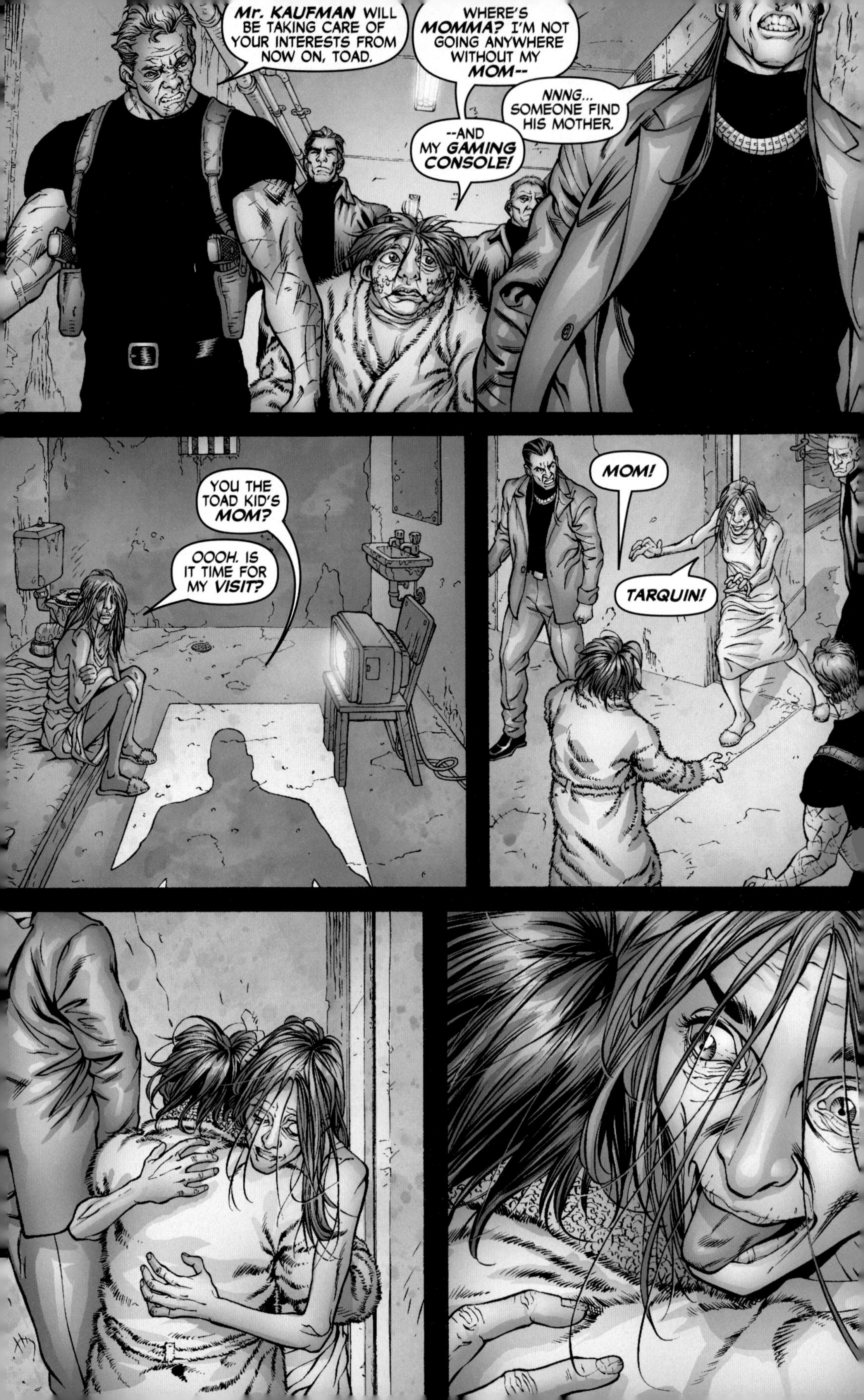

Mr. KAUFMAN WILL BE TAKING CARE OF YOUR INTERESTS FROM NOW ON, TOAD.
WHERE'S MOMMA? I'M NOT GOING ANYWHERE WITHOUT MY MOM--
--AND MY GAMING CONSOLE!
NNNG... SOMEONE FIND HIS MOTHER.
YOU THE TOAD KID'S MOM?
OOOH. IS IT TIME FOR MY VISIT?
MOM!
TARQUIN!

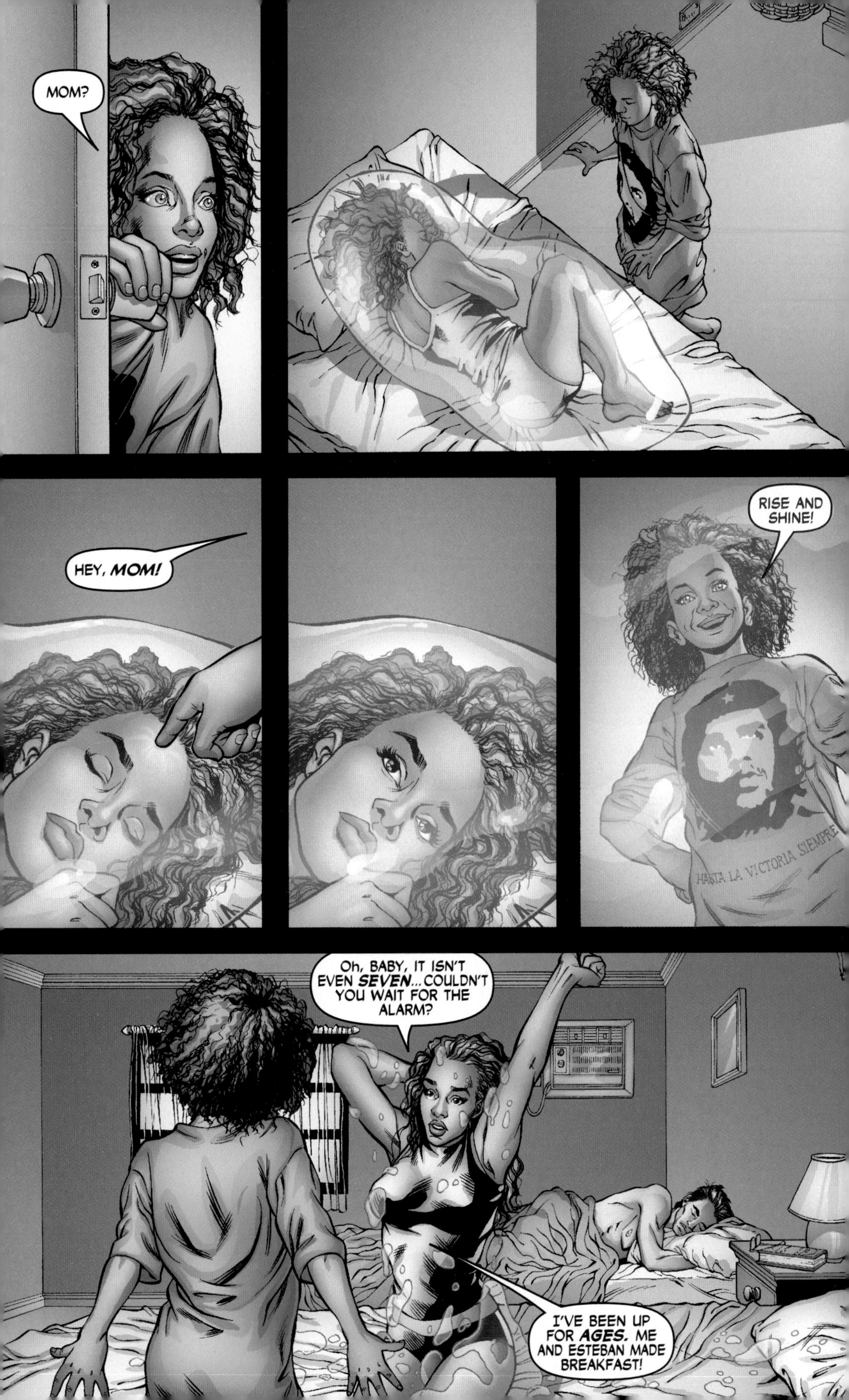
MOM?
HEY, **MOM!**
RISE AND SHINE!
HASTA LA VICTORIA SIEMPRE
Oh, BABY, IT ISN'T EVEN ***SEVEN***... COULDN'T YOU WAIT FOR THE ALARM?
I'VE BEEN UP FOR ***AGES.*** ME AND ESTEBAN MADE BREAKFAST!

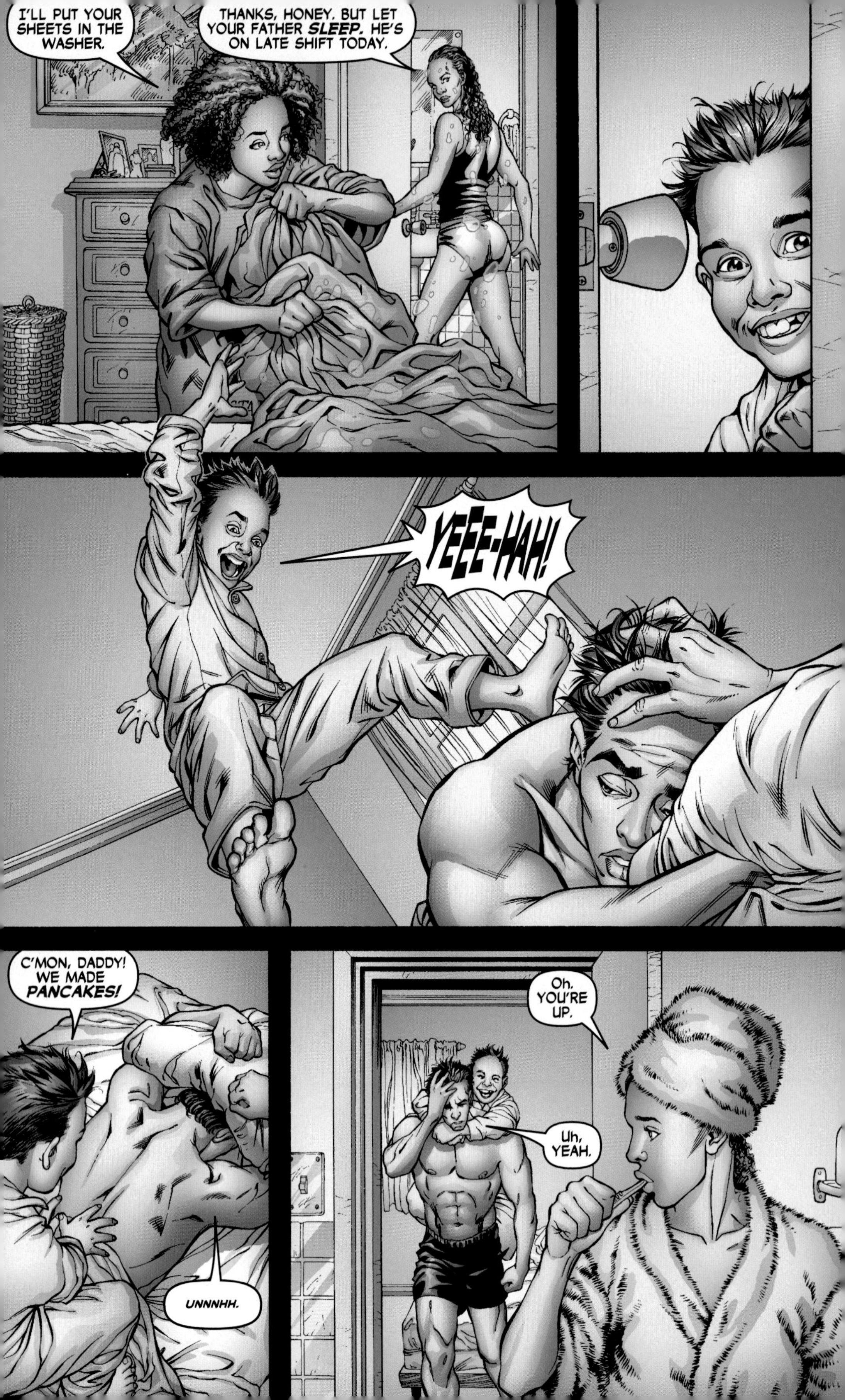
I'LL PUT YOUR SHEETS IN THE WASHER.
THANKS, HONEY. BUT LET YOUR FATHER SLEEP. HE'S ON LATE SHIFT TODAY.
YEEE-HAH!
C'MON, DADDY! WE MADE PANCAKES!
UNNNHH.
Oh, YOU'RE UP.
Uh, YEAH.

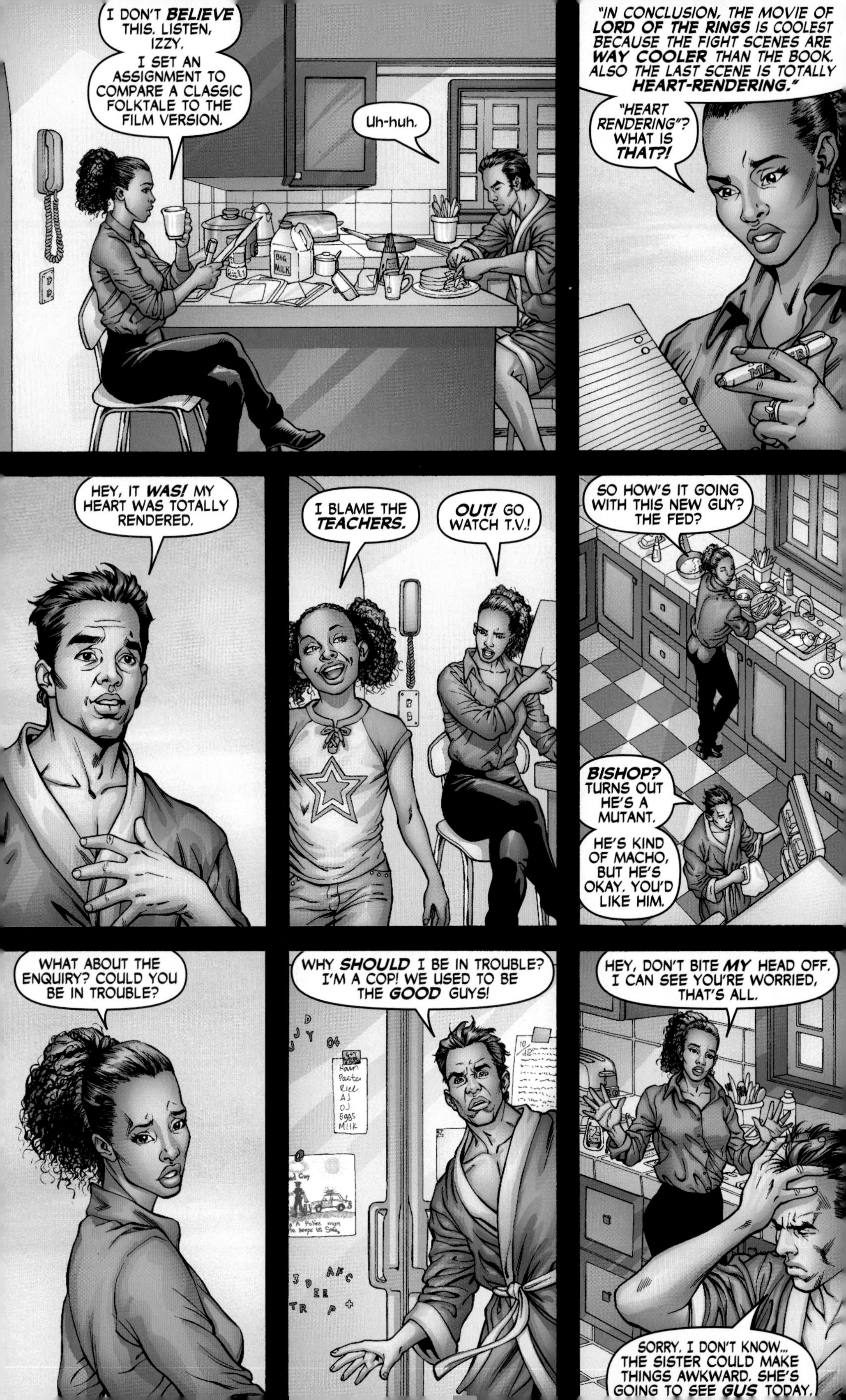
I DON'T **BELIEVE** THIS. LISTEN, IZZY.
I SET AN ASSIGNMENT TO COMPARE A CLASSIC FOLKTALE TO THE FILM VERSION.
Uh-huh.
BIG MILK
"IN CONCLUSION, THE MOVIE OF **LORD OF THE RINGS** IS COOLEST BECAUSE THE FIGHT SCENES ARE **WAY COOLER** THAN THE BOOK. ALSO THE LAST SCENE IS TOTALLY **HEART-RENDERING.**"
"HEART RENDERING"? WHAT IS **THAT?!**
HEY, IT **WAS!** MY HEART WAS TOTALLY RENDERED.
I BLAME THE **TEACHERS.**
OUT! GO WATCH T.V.!
SO HOW'S IT GOING WITH THIS NEW GUY? THE FED?
BISHOP? TURNS OUT HE'S A MUTANT.
HE'S KIND OF MACHO, BUT HE'S OKAY. YOU'D LIKE HIM.
WHAT ABOUT THE ENQUIRY? COULD YOU BE IN TROUBLE?
WHY **SHOULD** I BE IN TROUBLE? I'M A COP! WE USED TO BE THE **GOOD** GUYS!
Ham
Pasta
Rice
AJ
OJ
Eggs
Milk
HEY, DON'T BITE **MY** HEAD OFF. I CAN SEE YOU'RE WORRIED, THAT'S ALL.
SORRY. I DON'T KNOW... THE SISTER COULD MAKE THINGS AWKWARD. SHE'S GOING TO SEE **GUS** TODAY.

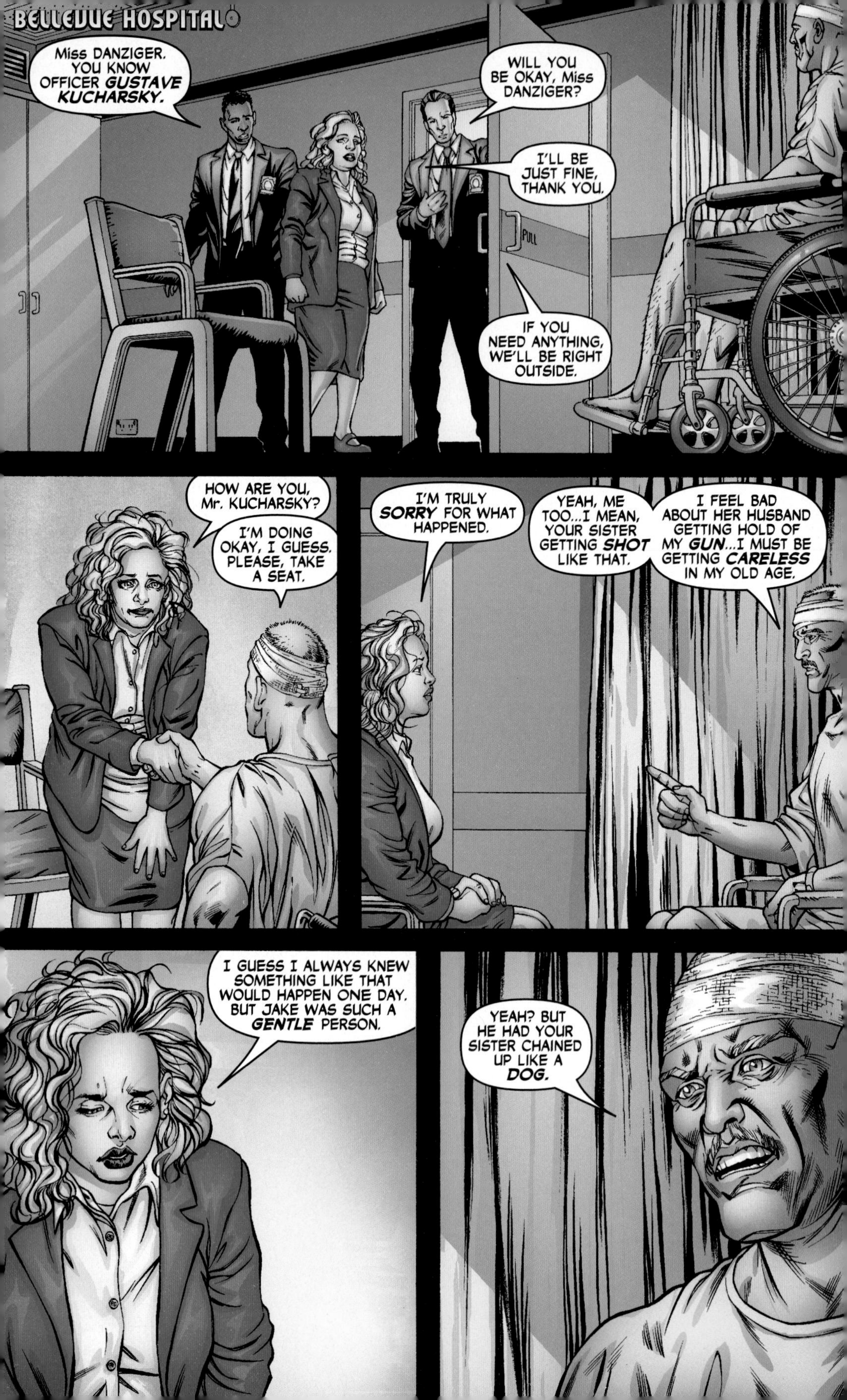
BELLEVUE HOSPITAL
Miss DANZIGER. YOU KNOW OFFICER GUSTAVE KUCHARSKY.
WILL YOU BE OKAY, Miss DANZIGER?
I'LL BE JUST FINE, THANK YOU.
IF YOU NEED ANYTHING, WE'LL BE RIGHT OUTSIDE.
PULL
HOW ARE YOU, Mr. KUCHARSKY?
I'M DOING OKAY, I GUESS. PLEASE, TAKE A SEAT.
I'M TRULY SORRY FOR WHAT HAPPENED.
YEAH, ME TOO...I MEAN, YOUR SISTER GETTING SHOT LIKE THAT.
I FEEL BAD ABOUT HER HUSBAND GETTING HOLD OF MY GUN...I MUST BE GETTING CARELESS IN MY OLD AGE.
I GUESS I ALWAYS KNEW SOMETHING LIKE THAT WOULD HAPPEN ONE DAY. BUT JAKE WAS SUCH A GENTLE PERSON.
YEAH? BUT HE HAD YOUR SISTER CHAINED UP LIKE A DOG.

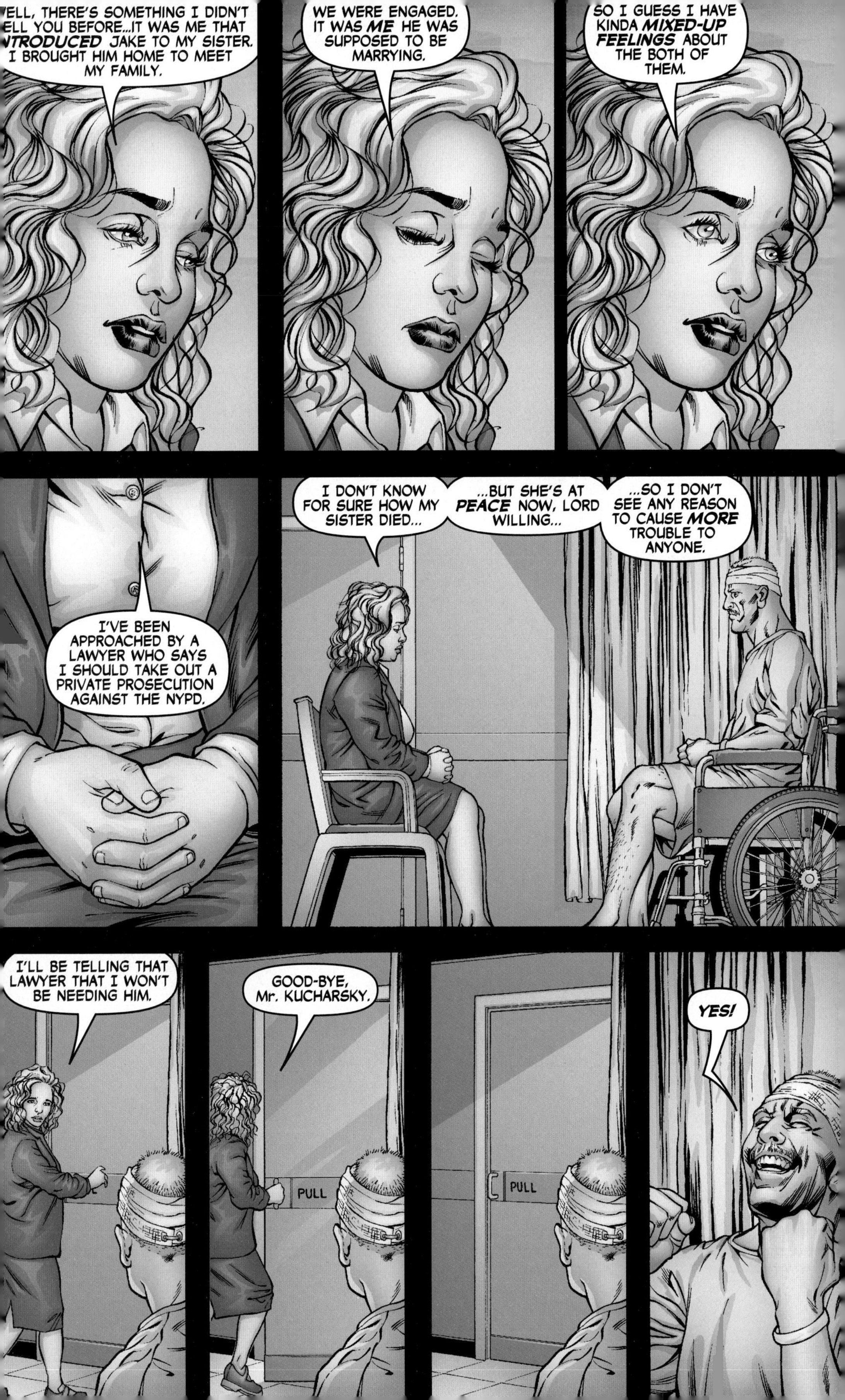

'ELL, THERE'S SOMETHING I DIDN'T
ELL YOU BEFORE...IT WAS ME THAT
ITRODUCED JAKE TO MY SISTER.
I BROUGHT HIM HOME TO MEET MY FAMILY.
WE WERE ENGAGED. IT WAS ME HE WAS SUPPOSED TO BE MARRYING.
SO I GUESS I HAVE KINDA MIXED-UP FEELINGS ABOUT THE BOTH OF THEM.
I'VE BEEN APPROACHED BY A LAWYER WHO SAYS I SHOULD TAKE OUT A PRIVATE PROSECUTION AGAINST THE NYPD.
I DON'T KNOW FOR SURE HOW MY SISTER DIED...
...BUT SHE'S AT PEACE NOW, LORD WILLING...
...SO I DON'T SEE ANY REASON TO CAUSE MORE TROUBLE TO ANYONE.
I'LL BE TELLING THAT LAWYER THAT I WON'T BE NEEDING HIM.
GOOD-BYE, Mr. KUCHARSKY.
PULL
PULL
YES!

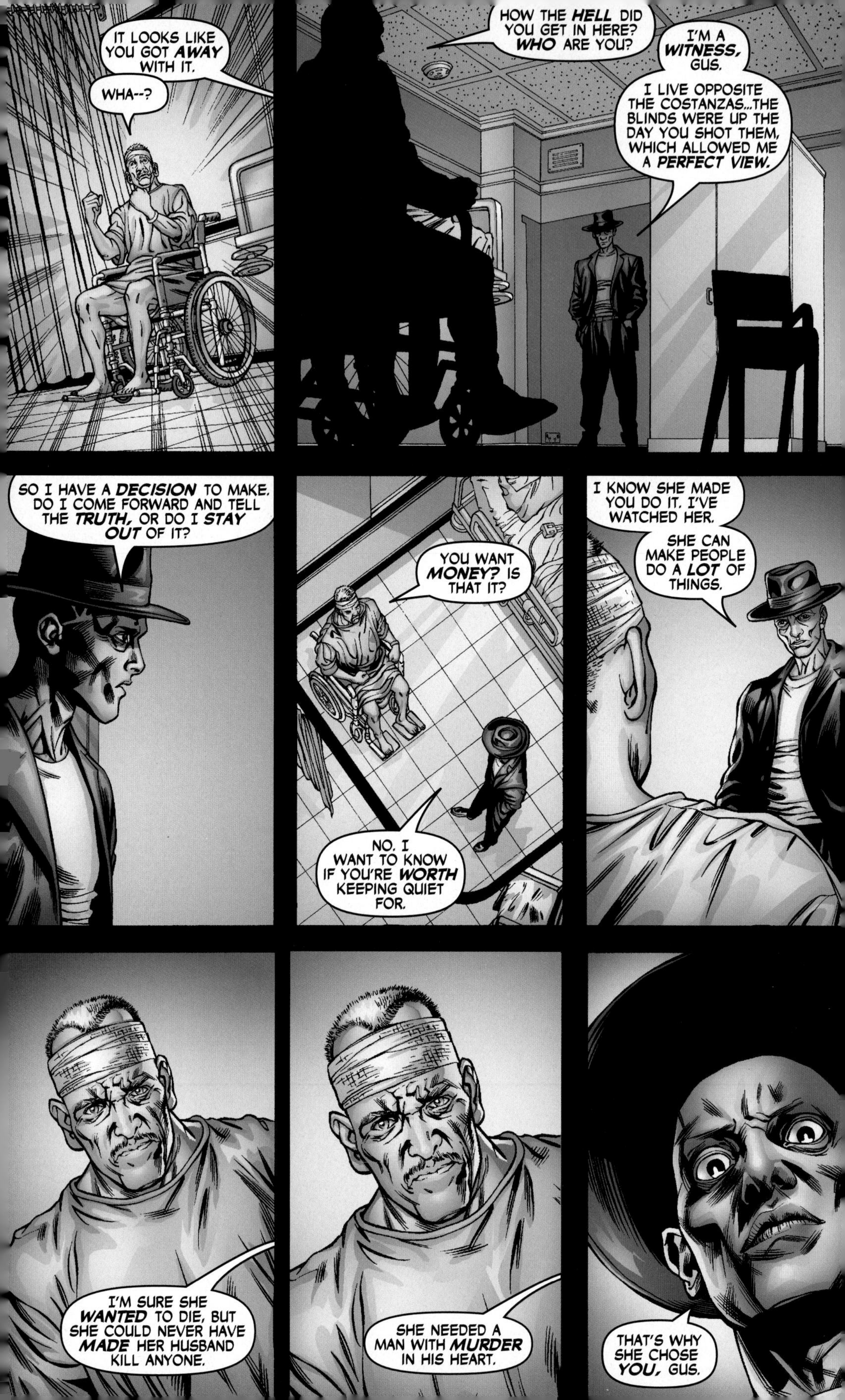
IT LOOKS LIKE YOU GOT AWAY WITH IT.
WHA--?
HOW THE HELL DID YOU GET IN HERE? WHO ARE YOU?
I'M A WITNESS, GUS.
I LIVE OPPOSITE THE COSTANZAS...THE BLINDS WERE UP THE DAY YOU SHOT THEM, WHICH ALLOWED ME A PERFECT VIEW.
SO I HAVE A DECISION TO MAKE. DO I COME FORWARD AND TELL THE TRUTH, OR DO I STAY OUT OF IT?
YOU WANT MONEY? IS THAT IT?
NO. I WANT TO KNOW IF YOU'RE WORTH KEEPING QUIET FOR.
I KNOW SHE MADE YOU DO IT. I'VE WATCHED HER.
SHE CAN MAKE PEOPLE DO A LOT OF THINGS.
I'M SURE SHE WANTED TO DIE, BUT SHE COULD NEVER HAVE MADE HER HUSBAND KILL ANYONE.
SHE NEEDED A MAN WITH MURDER IN HIS HEART.
THAT'S WHY SHE CHOSE YOU, GUS.

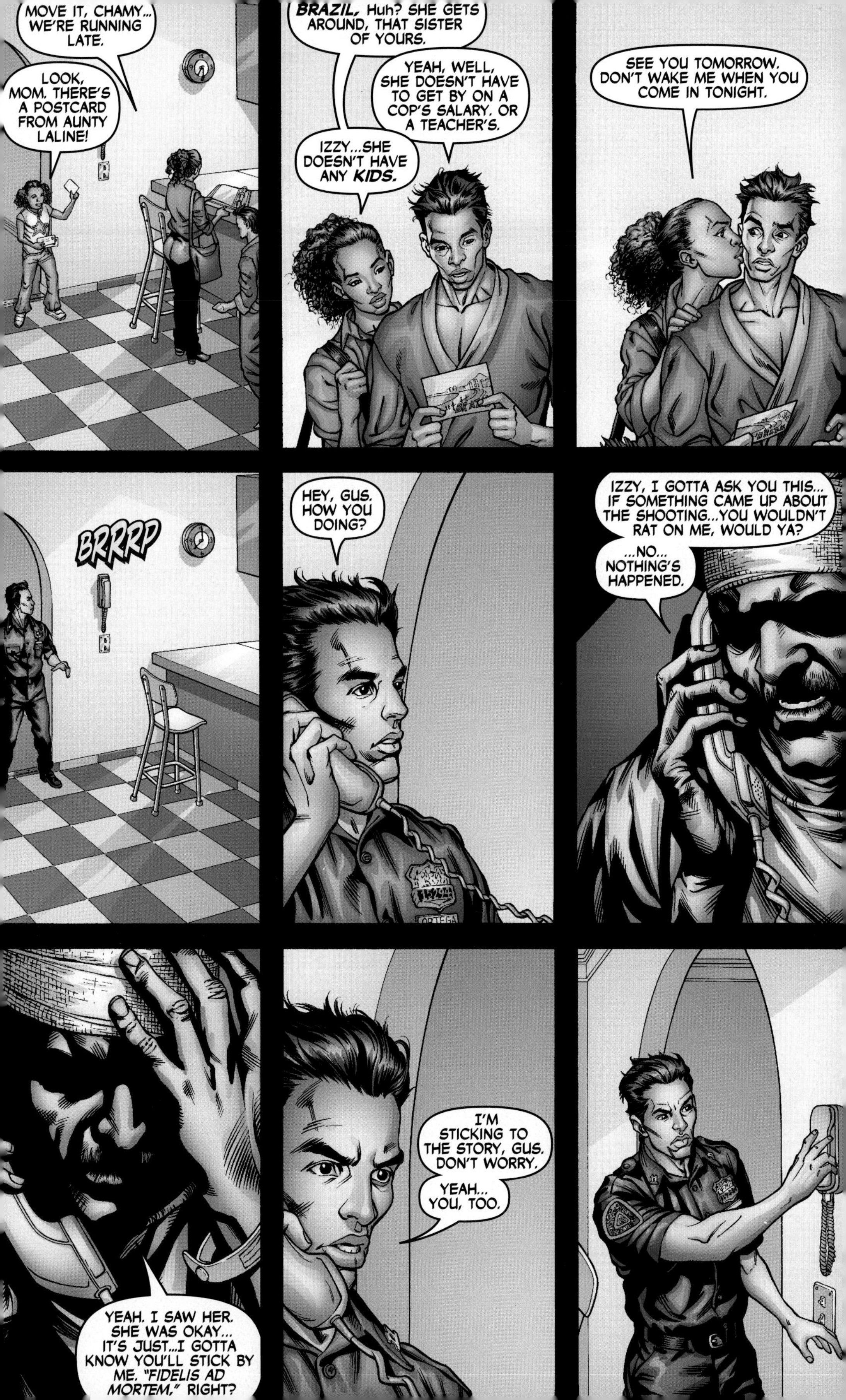
MOVE IT, CHAMY... WE'RE RUNNING LATE.
LOOK, MOM. THERE'S A POSTCARD FROM AUNTY LALINE!
BRAZIL, Huh? SHE GETS AROUND, THAT SISTER OF YOURS.
YEAH, WELL, SHE DOESN'T HAVE TO GET BY ON A COP'S SALARY. OR A TEACHER'S.
IZZY...SHE DOESN'T HAVE ANY KIDS.
SEE YOU TOMORROW. DON'T WAKE ME WHEN YOU COME IN TONIGHT.
BRRRP
HEY, GUS. HOW YOU DOING?
IZZY, I GOTTA ASK YOU THIS... IF SOMETHING CAME UP ABOUT THE SHOOTING...YOU WOULDN'T RAT ON ME, WOULD YA?
...NO... NOTHING'S HAPPENED.
YEAH. I SAW HER. SHE WAS OKAY... IT'S JUST...I GOTTA KNOW YOU'LL STICK BY ME. "FIDELIS AD MORTEM," RIGHT?
I'M STICKING TO THE STORY, GUS. DON'T WORRY.
YEAH... YOU, TOO.

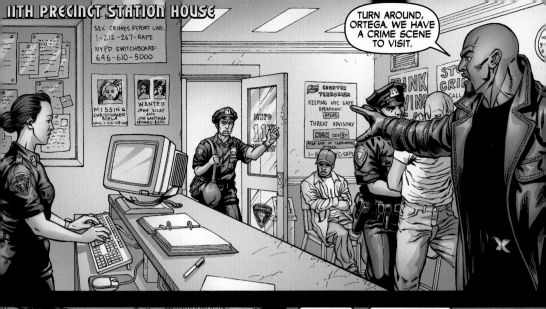

SEX CRIMES REPORT LINE:
1-212-267-RAPE

NYPD SWITCHBOARD:
646-610-5000

MISSING
CHRISTOPHER
BUELL
CALL: 1-212-478-2143

WANTED
JOHN SICAT
AND
JON SANTANA
REWARD: $500

COUNTER
TERRORISM
KEEPING NYC SAFE
OPERATION:
ATLAS
THREAT ADVISORY
HIGH

TURN AROUND, ORTEGA. WE HAVE A CRIME SCENE TO VISIT.

SHED THREE

LOOKS LIKE *SOMEONE* FORGOT HIS KEYS.

YOU *BISHOP*?

ME SCENE - DO NOT ENTER - CRIMES

DETECTIVE KLEIN.

WHAT HAPPENED HERE, DETECTIVE?

7

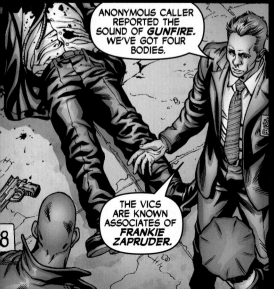

ANONYMOUS CALLER REPORTED THE SOUND OF *GUNFIRE*. WE'VE GOT FOUR BODIES.

THE VICS ARE KNOWN ASSOCIATES OF *FRANKIE ZAPRUDER*.

8

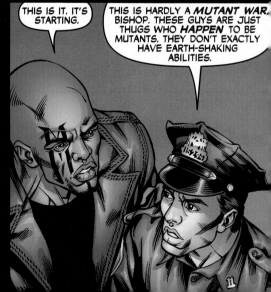

THIS IS IT. IT'S STARTING.

THIS IS HARDLY A *MUTANT WAR*, BISHOP. THESE GUYS ARE JUST THUGS WHO *HAPPEN* TO BE MUTANTS. THEY DON'T EXACTLY HAVE EARTH-SHAKING ABILITIES.

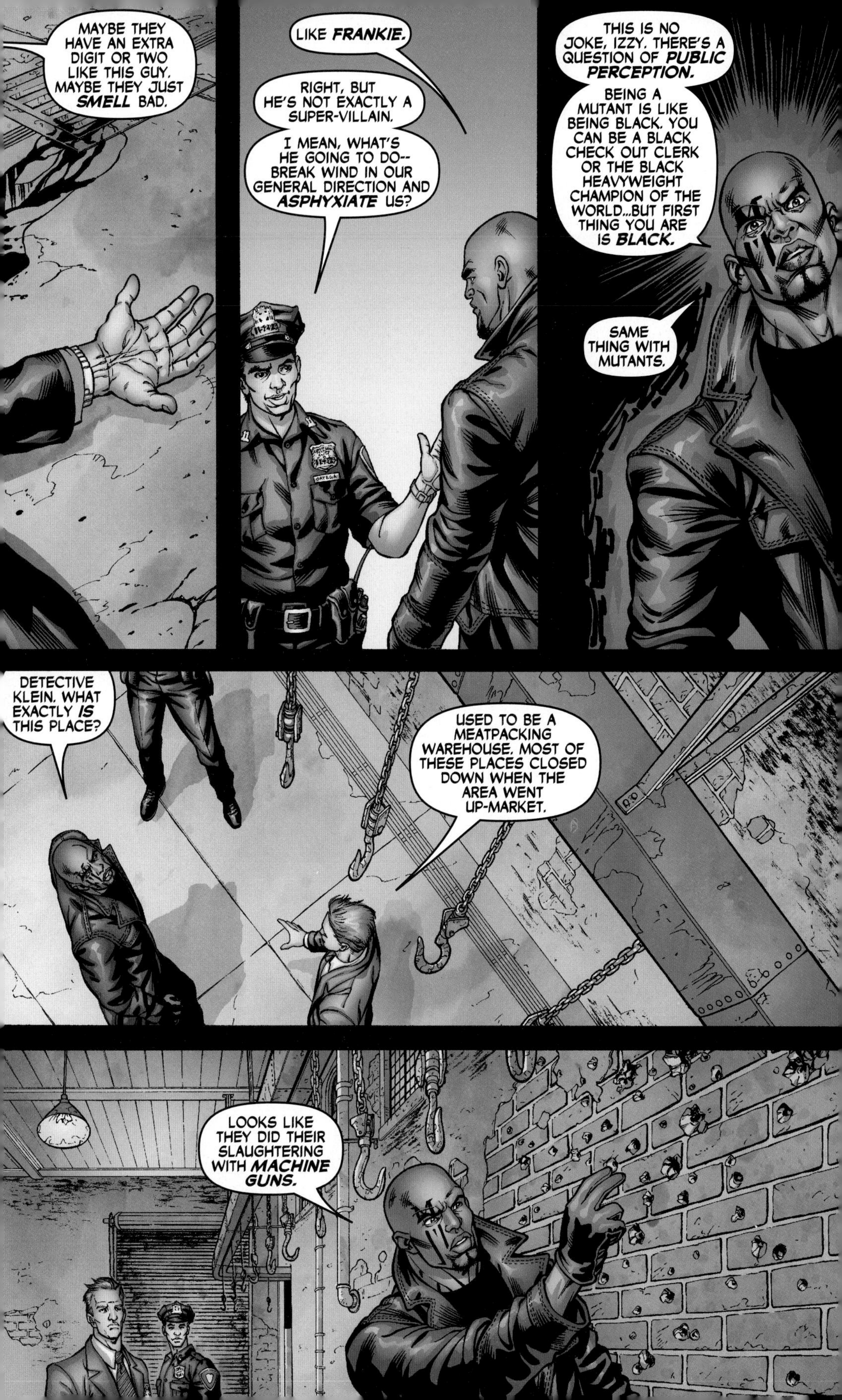
MAYBE THEY HAVE AN EXTRA DIGIT OR TWO LIKE THIS GUY. MAYBE THEY JUST SMELL BAD.
LIKE FRANKIE.
RIGHT, BUT HE'S NOT EXACTLY A SUPER-VILLAIN.
I MEAN, WHAT'S HE GOING TO DO-- BREAK WIND IN OUR GENERAL DIRECTION AND ASPHYXIATE US?
THIS IS NO JOKE, IZZY. THERE'S A QUESTION OF PUBLIC PERCEPTION.
BEING A MUTANT IS LIKE BEING BLACK. YOU CAN BE A BLACK CHECK OUT CLERK OR THE BLACK HEAVYWEIGHT CHAMPION OF THE WORLD...BUT FIRST THING YOU ARE IS BLACK.
SAME THING WITH MUTANTS.
DETECTIVE KLEIN. WHAT EXACTLY IS THIS PLACE?
USED TO BE A MEATPACKING WAREHOUSE. MOST OF THESE PLACES CLOSED DOWN WHEN THE AREA WENT UP-MARKET.
LOOKS LIKE THEY DID THEIR SLAUGHTERING WITH MACHINE GUNS.

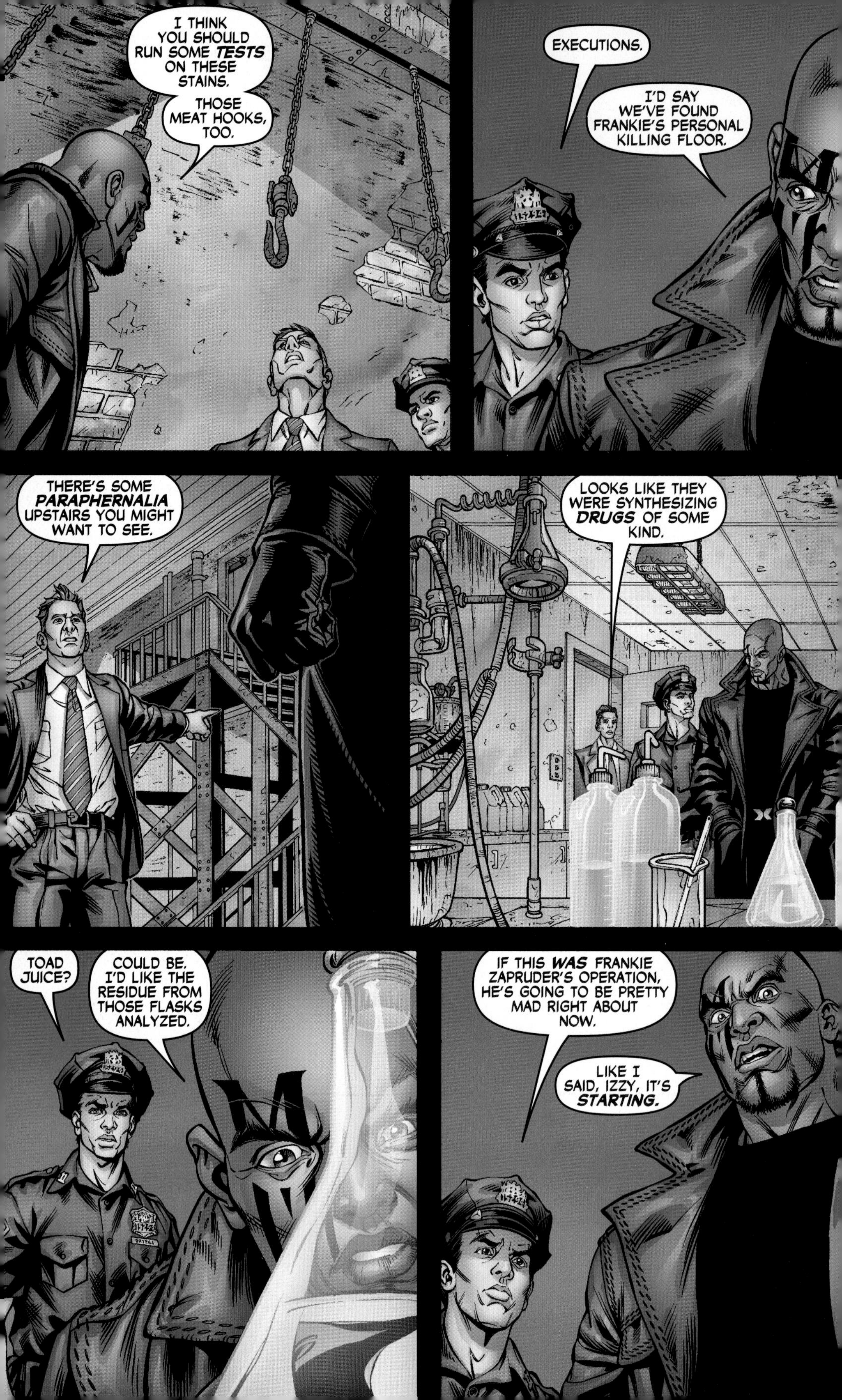

I THINK YOU SHOULD RUN SOME *TESTS* ON THESE STAINS.
THOSE MEAT HOOKS, TOO.
EXECUTIONS.
I'D SAY WE'VE FOUND FRANKIE'S PERSONAL KILLING FLOOR.
THERE'S SOME *PARAPHERNALIA* UPSTAIRS YOU MIGHT WANT TO SEE.
LOOKS LIKE THEY WERE SYNTHESIZING *DRUGS* OF SOME KIND.
TOAD JUICE?
COULD BE. I'D LIKE THE RESIDUE FROM THOSE FLASKS ANALYZED.
IF THIS *WAS* FRANKIE ZAPRUDER'S OPERATION, HE'S GOING TO BE PRETTY MAD RIGHT ABOUT NOW.
LIKE I SAID, IZZY, IT'S *STARTING.*

I'LL **KILL** HIM!

WE GONNA HIT **KAUFMAN**, Mr. ZAPRUDER?

Oh YEAH, WE'RE GONNA **HIT** HIM, WE'RE GONNA **SHUT HIM DOWN!** THEN I AM PERSONALLY GOING TO TAKE THAT NANCE APART!

THEN I'M GONNA **EAT** HIM!

FRANKIEEE...

WHAT? WHAT IS IT?!

IT'S JUST... YOU KNOW HOW IT IS WHEN YOU GET **UPSET**.

YOU DON'T LIKE THE WAY I **SMELL**, YOU GET OUT OF MY FACE! **GO!** TAKE A HIKE!

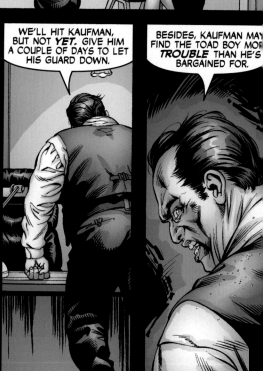

WE'LL HIT KAUFMAN, BUT NOT **YET**. GIVE HIM A COUPLE OF DAYS TO LET HIS GUARD DOWN.

BESIDES, KAUFMAN MAY FIND THE TOAD BOY MOR **TROUBLE** THAN HE'S BARGAINED FOR.

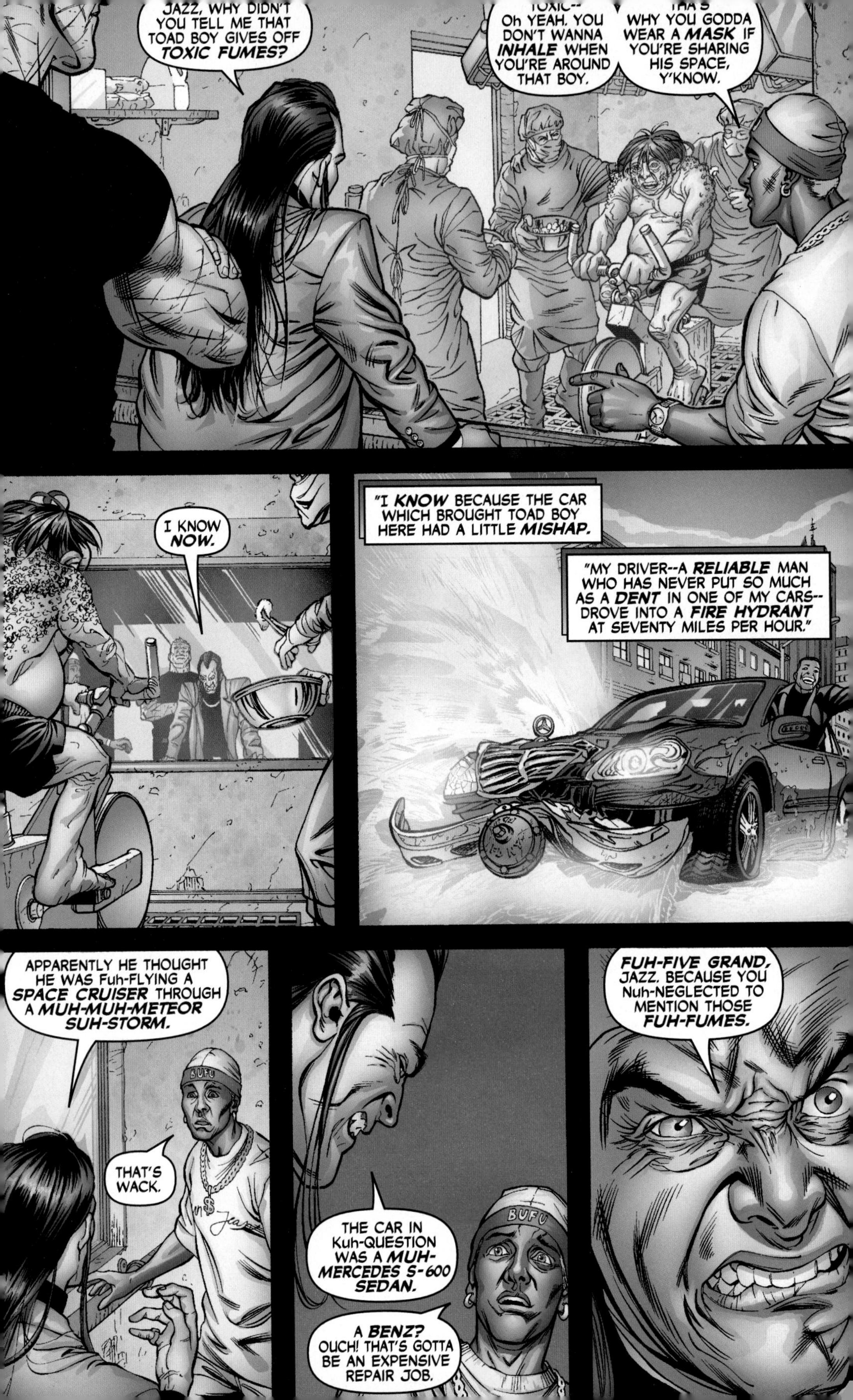
JAZZ, WHY DIDN'T YOU TELL ME THAT TOAD BOY GIVES OFF TOXIC FUMES?
TOXIC--
Oh YEAH, YOU DON'T WANNA INHALE WHEN YOU'RE AROUND THAT BOY.
WHY YOU GODDA WEAR A MASK IF YOU'RE SHARING HIS SPACE, Y'KNOW.
I KNOW NOW.
"I KNOW BECAUSE THE CAR WHICH BROUGHT TOAD BOY HERE HAD A LITTLE MISHAP.
"MY DRIVER--A RELIABLE MAN WHO HAS NEVER PUT SO MUCH AS A DENT IN ONE OF MY CARS--DROVE INTO A FIRE HYDRANT AT SEVENTY MILES PER HOUR."
APPARENTLY HE THOUGHT HE WAS Fuh-FLYING A SPACE CRUISER THROUGH A MUH-MUH-METEOR SUH-STORM.
BUFU
THAT'S WACK.
THE CAR IN Kuh-QUESTION WAS A MUH-MERCEDES S-600 SEDAN.
BUFU
A BENZ? OUCH! THAT'S GOTTA BE AN EXPENSIVE REPAIR JOB.
FUH-FIVE GRAND, JAZZ. BECAUSE YOU Nuh-NEGLECTED TO MENTION THOSE FUH-FUMES.

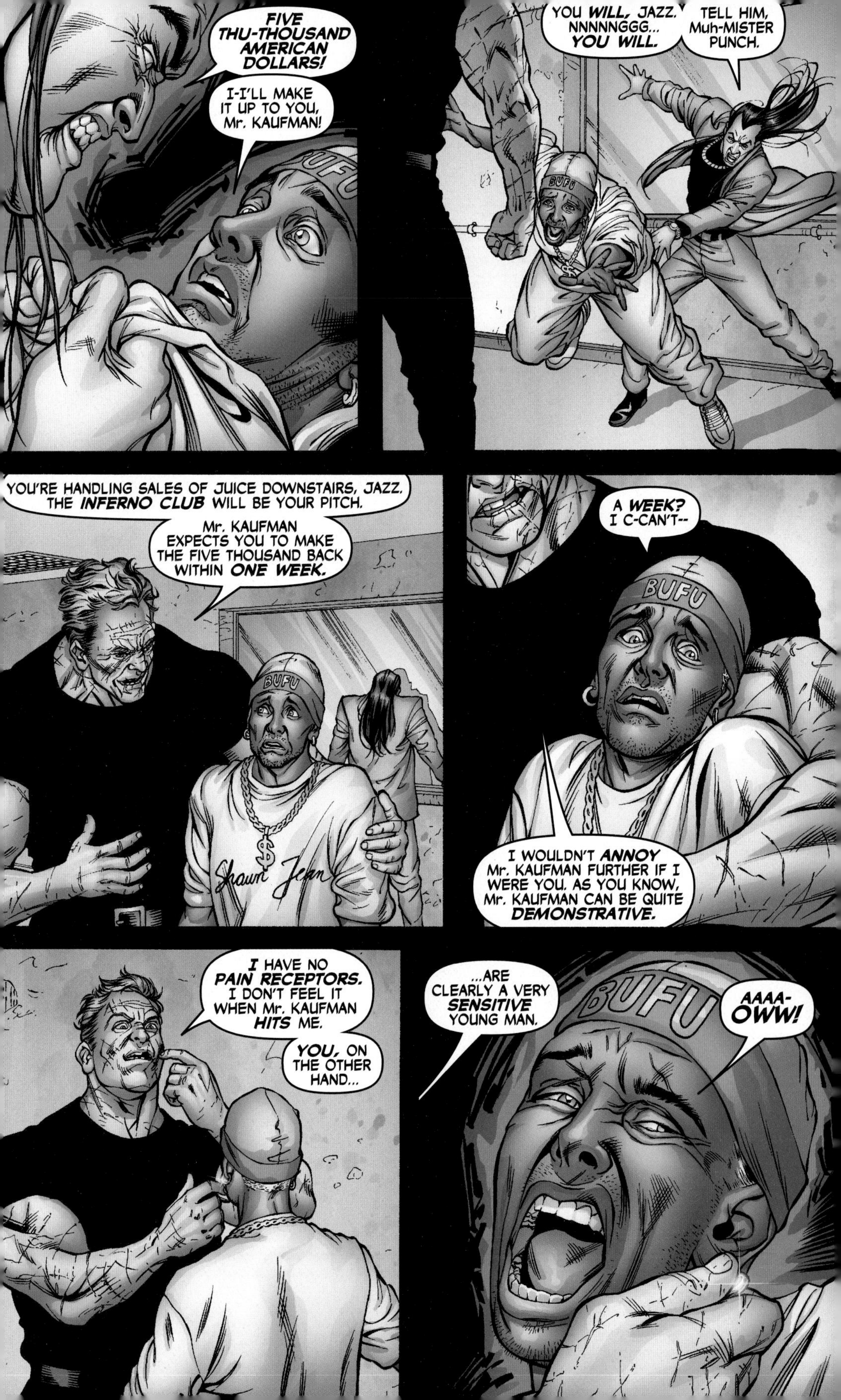
FIVE THU-THOUSAND AMERICAN DOLLARS!
I-I'LL MAKE IT UP TO YOU, Mr. KAUFMAN!
BUFU
YOU WILL, JAZZ. NNNNNGGG... YOU WILL.
TELL HIM, Muh-MISTER PUNCH.
BUFU
YOU'RE HANDLING SALES OF JUICE DOWNSTAIRS, JAZZ. THE INFERNO CLUB WILL BE YOUR PITCH.
Mr. KAUFMAN EXPECTS YOU TO MAKE THE FIVE THOUSAND BACK WITHIN ONE WEEK.
BUFU
A WEEK? I C-CAN'T--
BUFU
I WOULDN'T ANNOY Mr. KAUFMAN FURTHER IF I WERE YOU. AS YOU KNOW, Mr. KAUFMAN CAN BE QUITE DEMONSTRATIVE.
I HAVE NO PAIN RECEPTORS. I DON'T FEEL IT WHEN Mr. KAUFMAN HITS ME.
YOU, ON THE OTHER HAND...
...ARE CLEARLY A VERY SENSITIVE YOUNG MAN.
AAAA-OWW!
BUFU

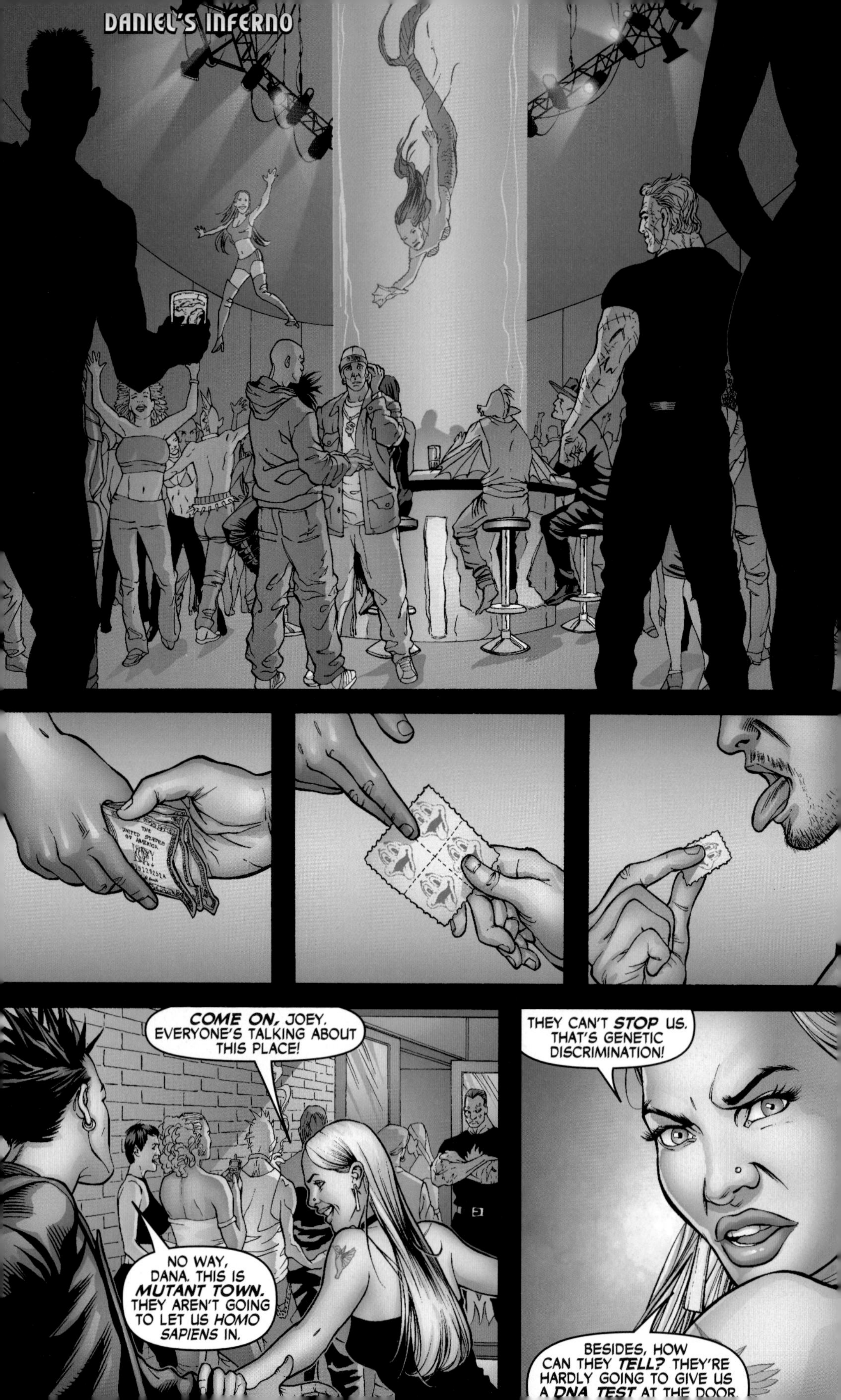

DANIEL'S INFERNO
COME ON, JOEY. EVERYONE'S TALKING ABOUT THIS PLACE!
NO WAY, DANA. THIS IS MUTANT TOWN. THEY AREN'T GOING TO LET US HOMO SAPIENS IN.
THEY CAN'T STOP US. THAT'S GENETIC DISCRIMINATION!
BESIDES, HOW CAN THEY TELL? THEY'RE HARDLY GOING TO GIVE US A DNA TEST AT THE DOOR

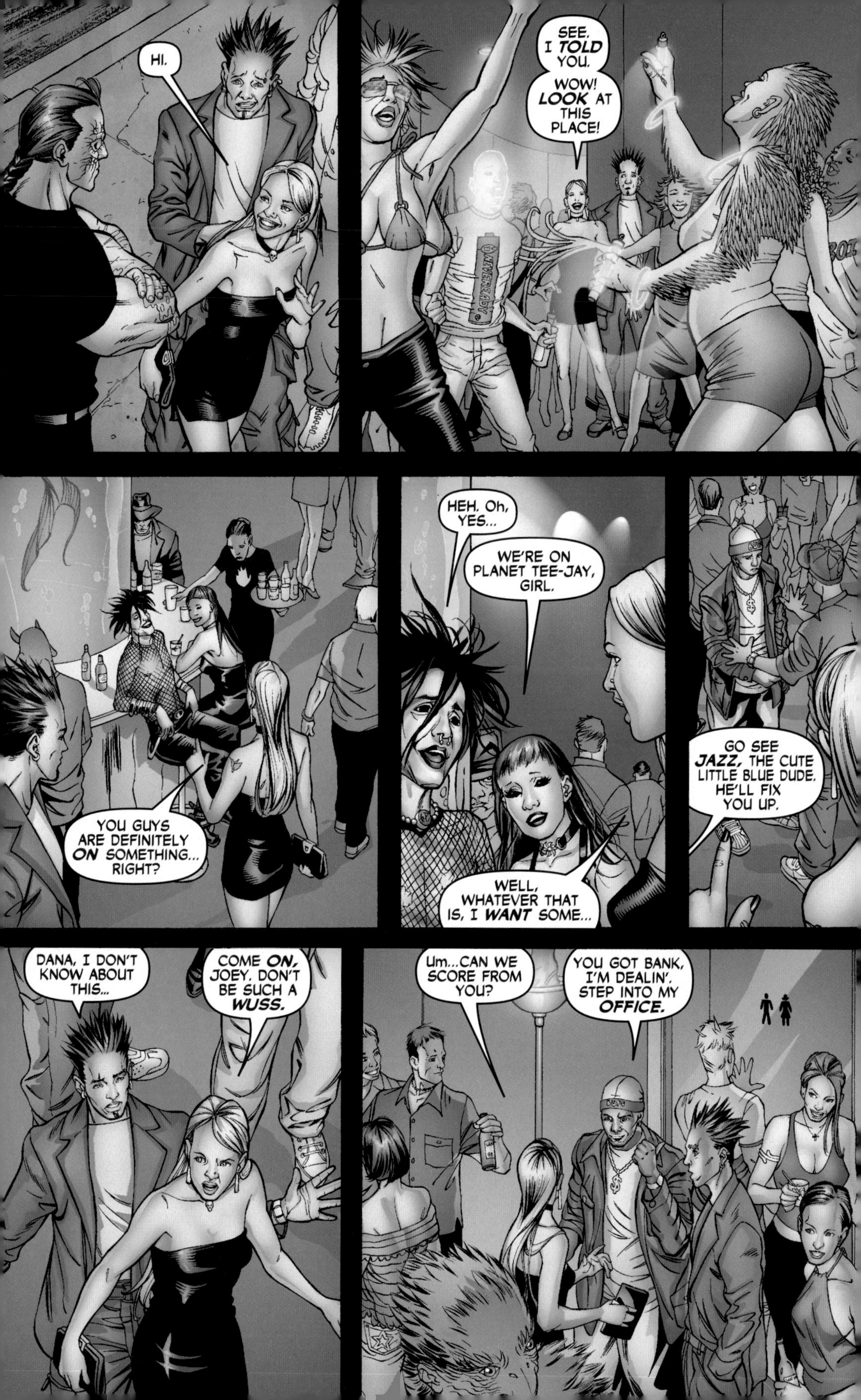
HI.
SEE. I TOLD YOU.
WOW! LOOK AT THIS PLACE!
EVEREADY
YOU GUYS ARE DEFINITELY ON SOMETHING... RIGHT?
HEH. Oh, YES...
WE'RE ON PLANET TEE-JAY, GIRL.
WELL, WHATEVER THAT IS, I WANT SOME...
GO SEE JAZZ, THE CUTE LITTLE BLUE DUDE. HE'LL FIX YOU UP.
DANA, I DON'T KNOW ABOUT THIS...
COME ON, JOEY. DON'T BE SUCH A WUSS.
Um...CAN WE SCORE FROM YOU?
YOU GOT BANK, I'M DEALIN'. STEP INTO MY OFFICE.

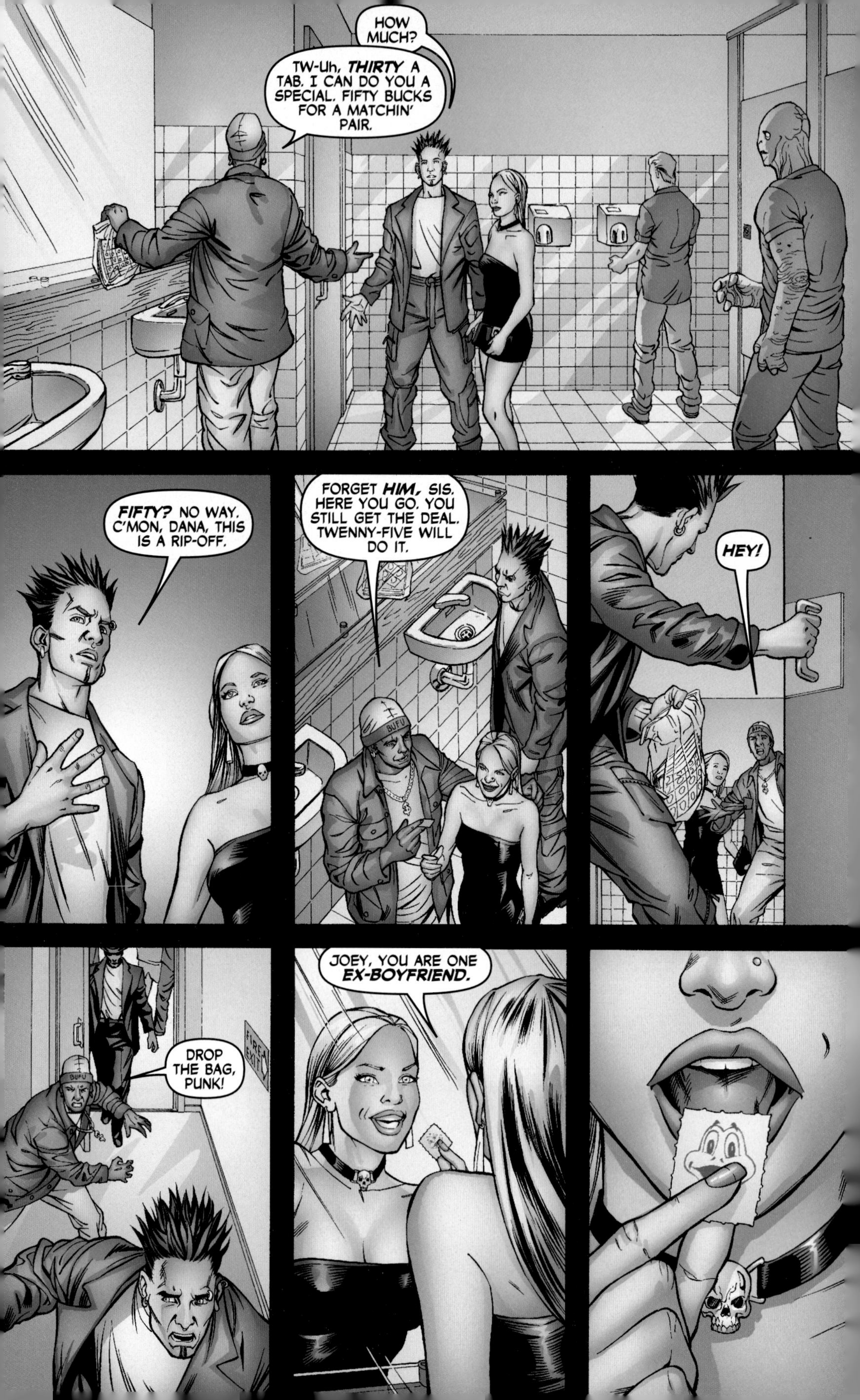
HOW MUCH?
TW-Uh, *THIRTY* A TAB. I CAN DO YOU A SPECIAL. FIFTY BUCKS FOR A MATCHIN' PAIR.
FIFTY? NO WAY. C'MON, DANA, THIS IS A RIP-OFF.
FORGET *HIM,* SIS. HERE YOU GO. YOU STILL GET THE DEAL. TWENNY-FIVE WILL DO IT.
BUFU
HEY!
DROP THE BAG, PUNK!
FIRE EXIT
JOEY, YOU ARE ONE *EX-BOYFRIEND.*

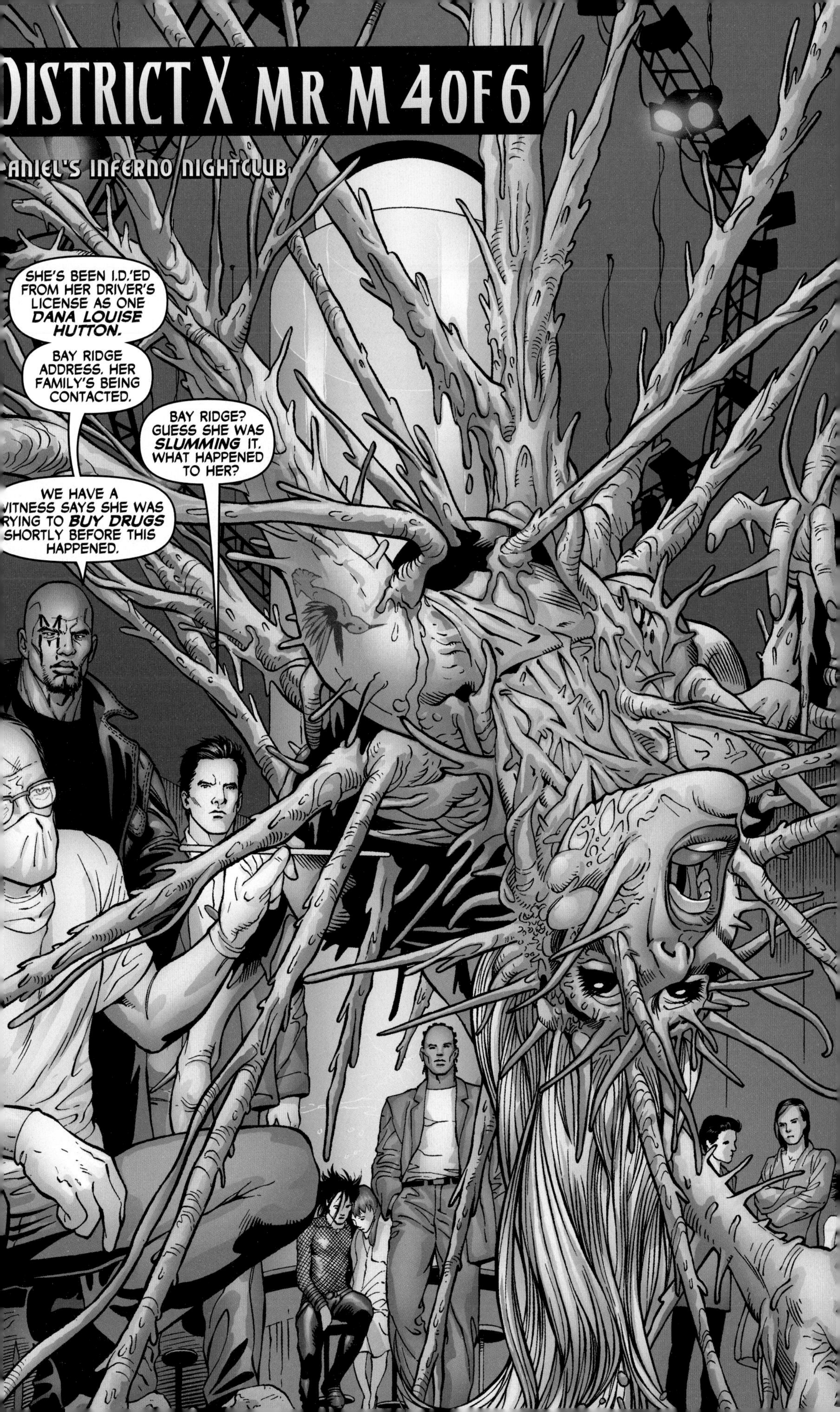
DISTRICT X MR M 4 OF 6
ANIEL'S INFERNO NIGHTCLUB
SHE'S BEEN I.D.'ED FROM HER DRIVER'S LICENSE AS ONE DANA LOUISE HUTTON.
BAY RIDGE ADDRESS. HER FAMILY'S BEING CONTACTED.
BAY RIDGE? GUESS SHE WAS SLUMMING IT. WHAT HAPPENED TO HER?
WE HAVE A WITNESS SAYS SHE WAS RYING TO BUY DRUGS SHORTLY BEFORE THIS HAPPENED.

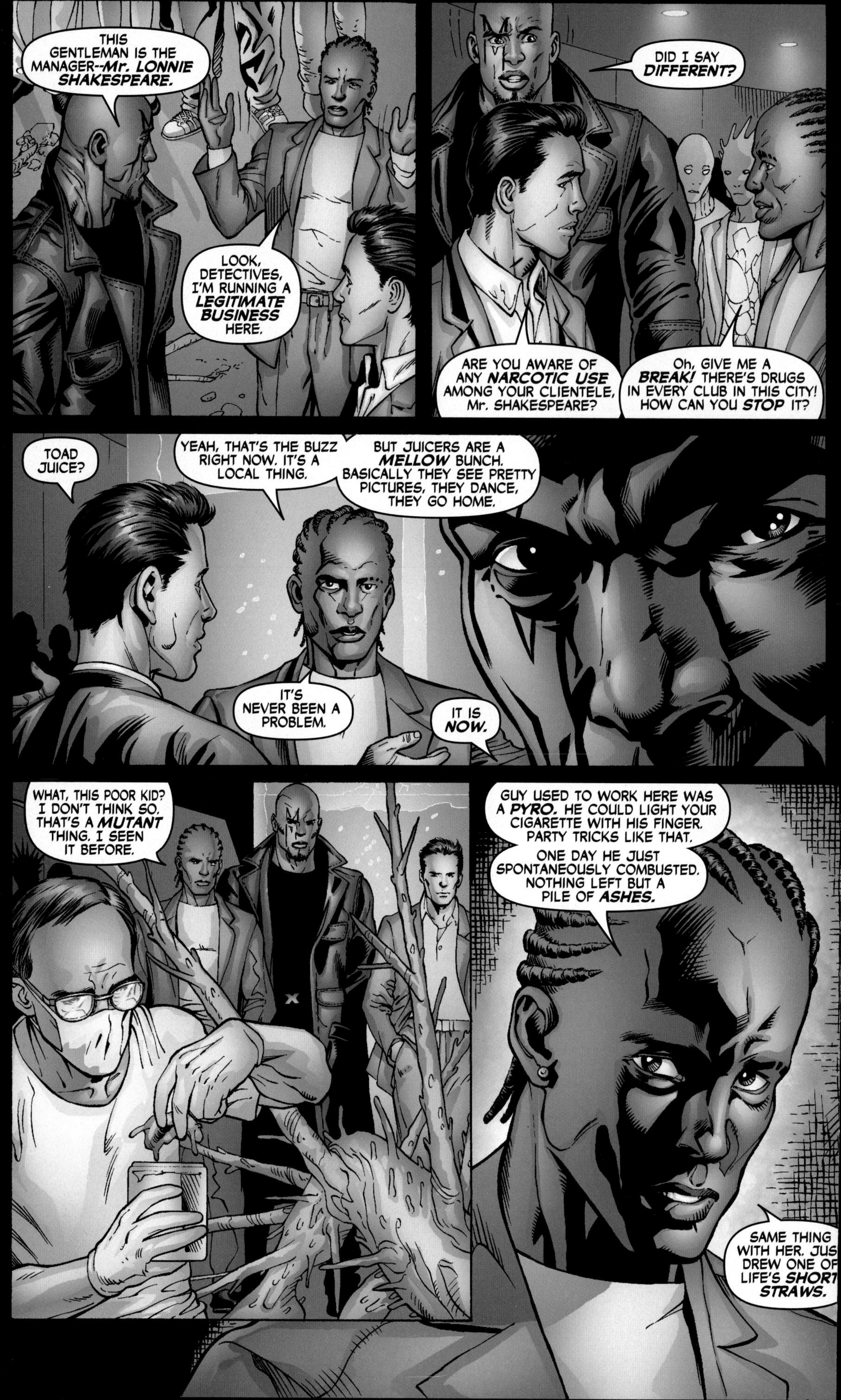

THIS GENTLEMAN IS THE MANAGER--Mr. LONNIE SHAKESPEARE.
LOOK, DETECTIVES, I'M RUNNING A LEGITIMATE BUSINESS HERE.
DID I SAY DIFFERENT?
ARE YOU AWARE OF ANY NARCOTIC USE AMONG YOUR CLIENTELE, Mr. SHAKESPEARE?
Oh, GIVE ME A BREAK! THERE'S DRUGS IN EVERY CLUB IN THIS CITY! HOW CAN YOU STOP IT?
TOAD JUICE?
YEAH, THAT'S THE BUZZ RIGHT NOW. IT'S A LOCAL THING.
BUT JUICERS ARE A MELLOW BUNCH. BASICALLY THEY SEE PRETTY PICTURES, THEY DANCE, THEY GO HOME.
IT'S NEVER BEEN A PROBLEM.
IT IS NOW.
WHAT, THIS POOR KID? I DON'T THINK SO. THAT'S A MUTANT THING. I SEEN IT BEFORE.
GUY USED TO WORK HERE WAS A PYRO. HE COULD LIGHT YOUR CIGARETTE WITH HIS FINGER. PARTY TRICKS LIKE THAT.
ONE DAY HE JUST SPONTANEOUSLY COMBUSTED. NOTHING LEFT BUT A PILE OF ASHES.
SAME THING WITH HER. JUS DREW ONE OF LIFE'S SHORT STRAWS.

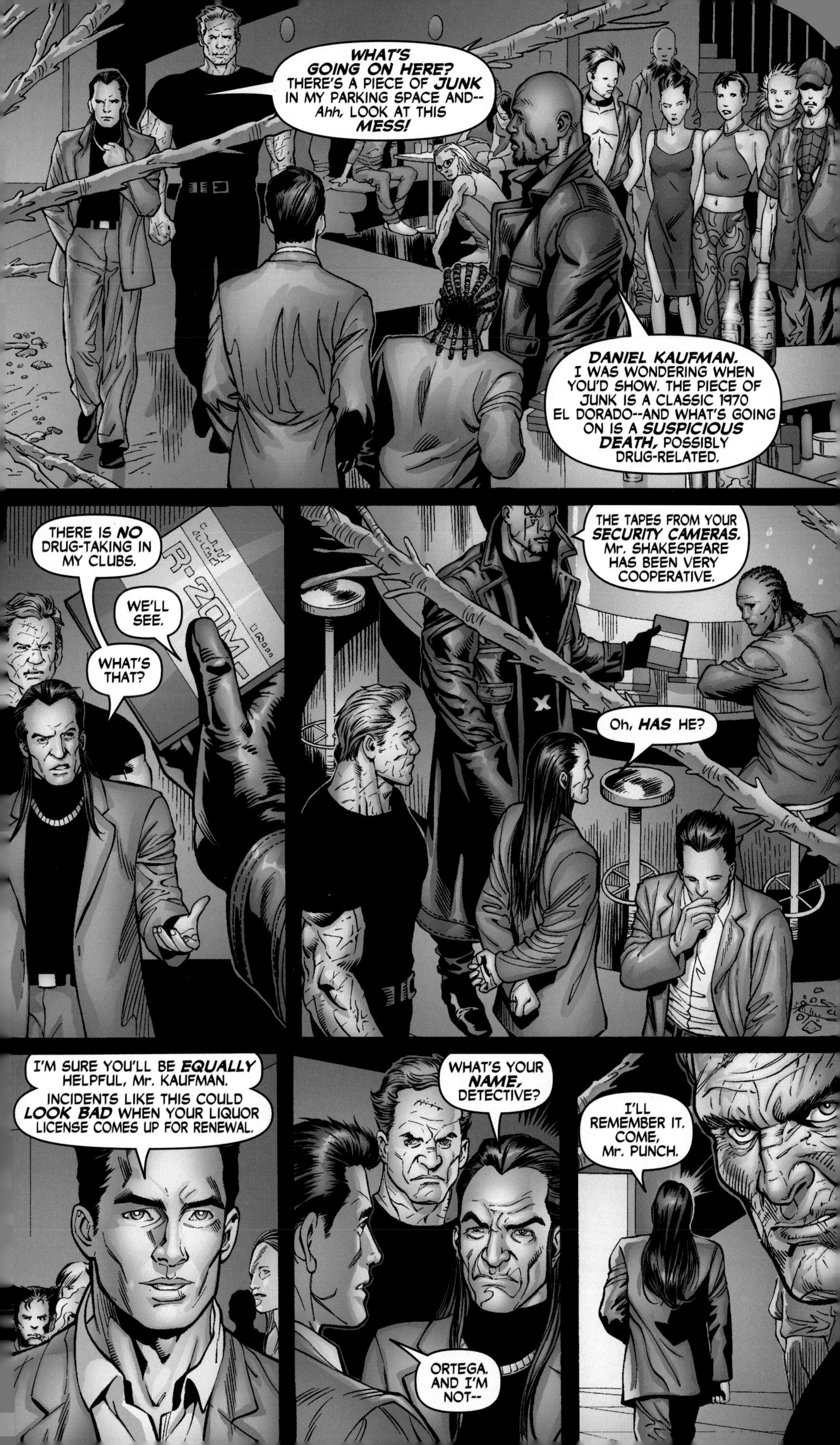
WHAT'S GOING ON HERE? THERE'S A PIECE OF JUNK IN MY PARKING SPACE AND-- Ahh, LOOK AT THIS MESS!
DANIEL KAUFMAN. I WAS WONDERING WHEN YOU'D SHOW. THE PIECE OF JUNK IS A CLASSIC 1970 EL DORADO--AND WHAT'S GOING ON IS A SUSPICIOUS DEATH, POSSIBLY DRUG-RELATED.
THERE IS NO DRUG-TAKING IN MY CLUBS.
WE'LL SEE.
WHAT'S THAT?
THE TAPES FROM YOUR SECURITY CAMERAS. Mr. SHAKESPEARE HAS BEEN VERY COOPERATIVE.
Oh, HAS HE?
I'M SURE YOU'LL BE EQUALLY HELPFUL, Mr. KAUFMAN. INCIDENTS LIKE THIS COULD LOOK BAD WHEN YOUR LIQUOR LICENSE COMES UP FOR RENEWAL.
WHAT'S YOUR NAME, DETECTIVE?
ORTEGA. AND I'M NOT--
I'LL REMEMBER IT. COME, Mr. PUNCH.

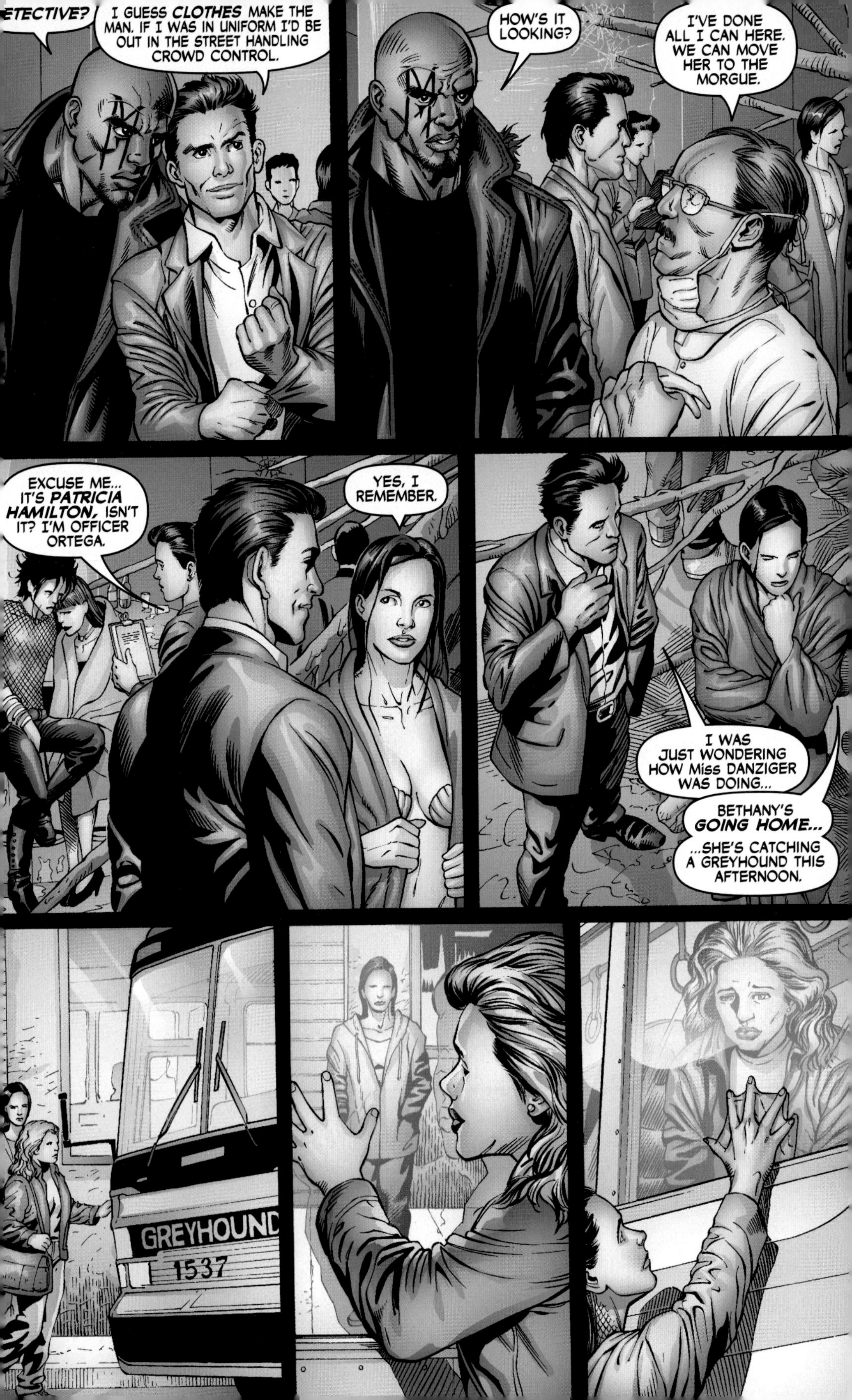
ETECTIVE?
I GUESS CLOTHES MAKE THE MAN. IF I WAS IN UNIFORM I'D BE OUT IN THE STREET HANDLING CROWD CONTROL.
HOW'S IT LOOKING?
I'VE DONE ALL I CAN HERE. WE CAN MOVE HER TO THE MORGUE.
EXCUSE ME... IT'S PATRICIA HAMILTON, ISN'T IT? I'M OFFICER ORTEGA.
YES, I REMEMBER.
I WAS JUST WONDERING HOW Miss DANZIGER WAS DOING...
BETHANY'S GOING HOME...
...SHE'S CATCHING A GREYHOUND THIS AFTERNOON.
GREYHOUND
1537

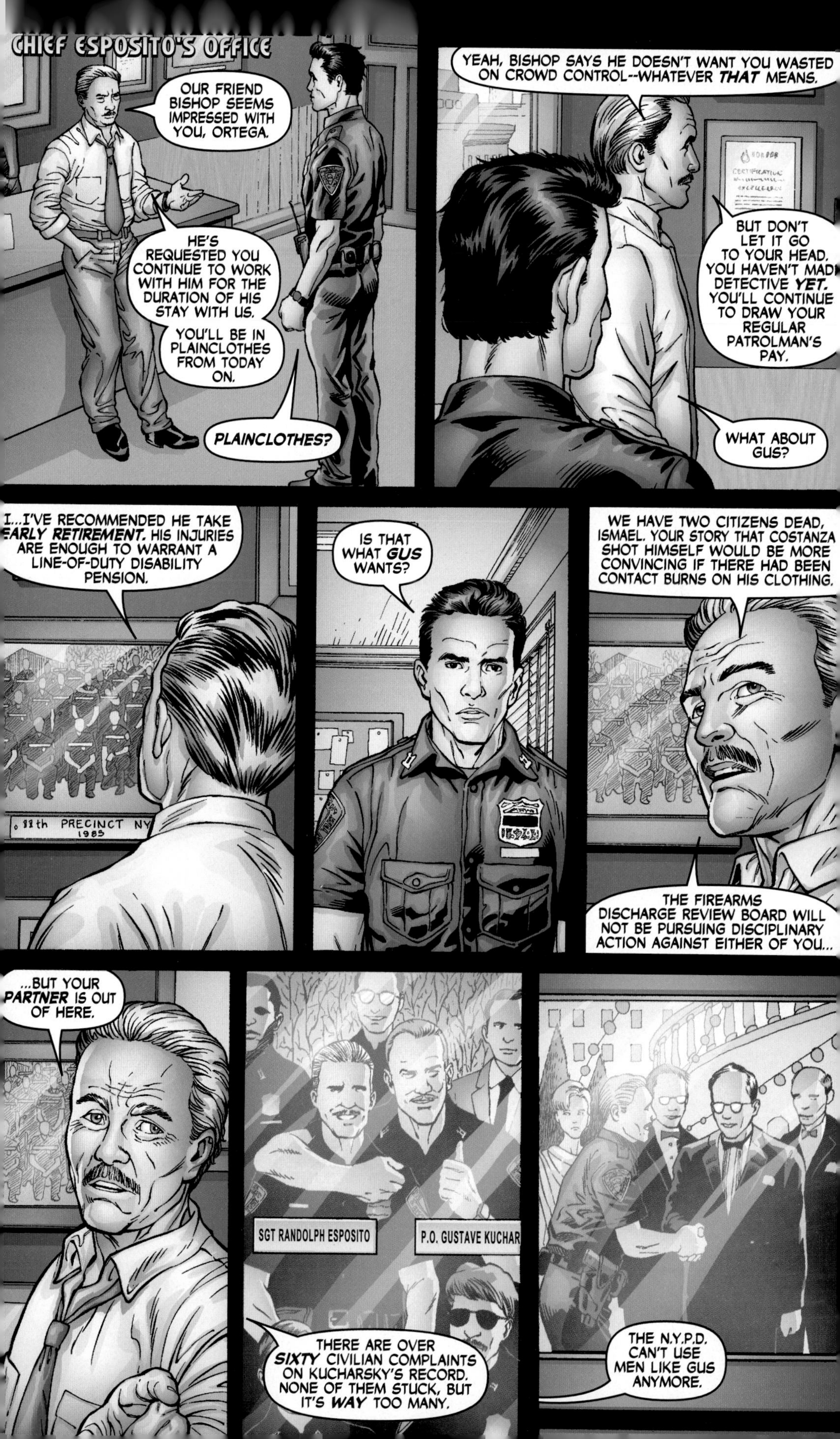
CHIEF ESPOSITO'S OFFICE
OUR FRIEND BISHOP SEEMS IMPRESSED WITH YOU, ORTEGA.
HE'S REQUESTED YOU CONTINUE TO WORK WITH HIM FOR THE DURATION OF HIS STAY WITH US.
YOU'LL BE IN PLAINCLOTHES FROM TODAY ON.
PLAINCLOTHES?
YEAH, BISHOP SAYS HE DOESN'T WANT YOU WASTED ON CROWD CONTROL--WHATEVER THAT MEANS.
BUT DON'T LET IT GO TO YOUR HEAD. YOU HAVEN'T MADE DETECTIVE YET. YOU'LL CONTINUE TO DRAW YOUR REGULAR PATROLMAN'S PAY.
WHAT ABOUT GUS?
I...I'VE RECOMMENDED HE TAKE EARLY RETIREMENT. HIS INJURIES ARE ENOUGH TO WARRANT A LINE-OF-DUTY DISABILITY PENSION.
11th PRECINCT NY 1985
IS THAT WHAT GUS WANTS?
WE HAVE TWO CITIZENS DEAD, ISMAEL. YOUR STORY THAT COSTANZA SHOT HIMSELF WOULD BE MORE CONVINCING IF THERE HAD BEEN CONTACT BURNS ON HIS CLOTHING.
THE FIREARMS DISCHARGE REVIEW BOARD WILL NOT BE PURSUING DISCIPLINARY ACTION AGAINST EITHER OF YOU...
...BUT YOUR PARTNER IS OUT OF HERE.
SGT RANDOLPH ESPOSITO
P.O. GUSTAVE KUCHAR
THERE ARE OVER SIXTY CIVILIAN COMPLAINTS ON KUCHARSKY'S RECORD. NONE OF THEM STUCK, BUT IT'S WAY TOO MANY.
THE N.Y.P.D. CAN'T USE MEN LIKE GUS ANYMORE.

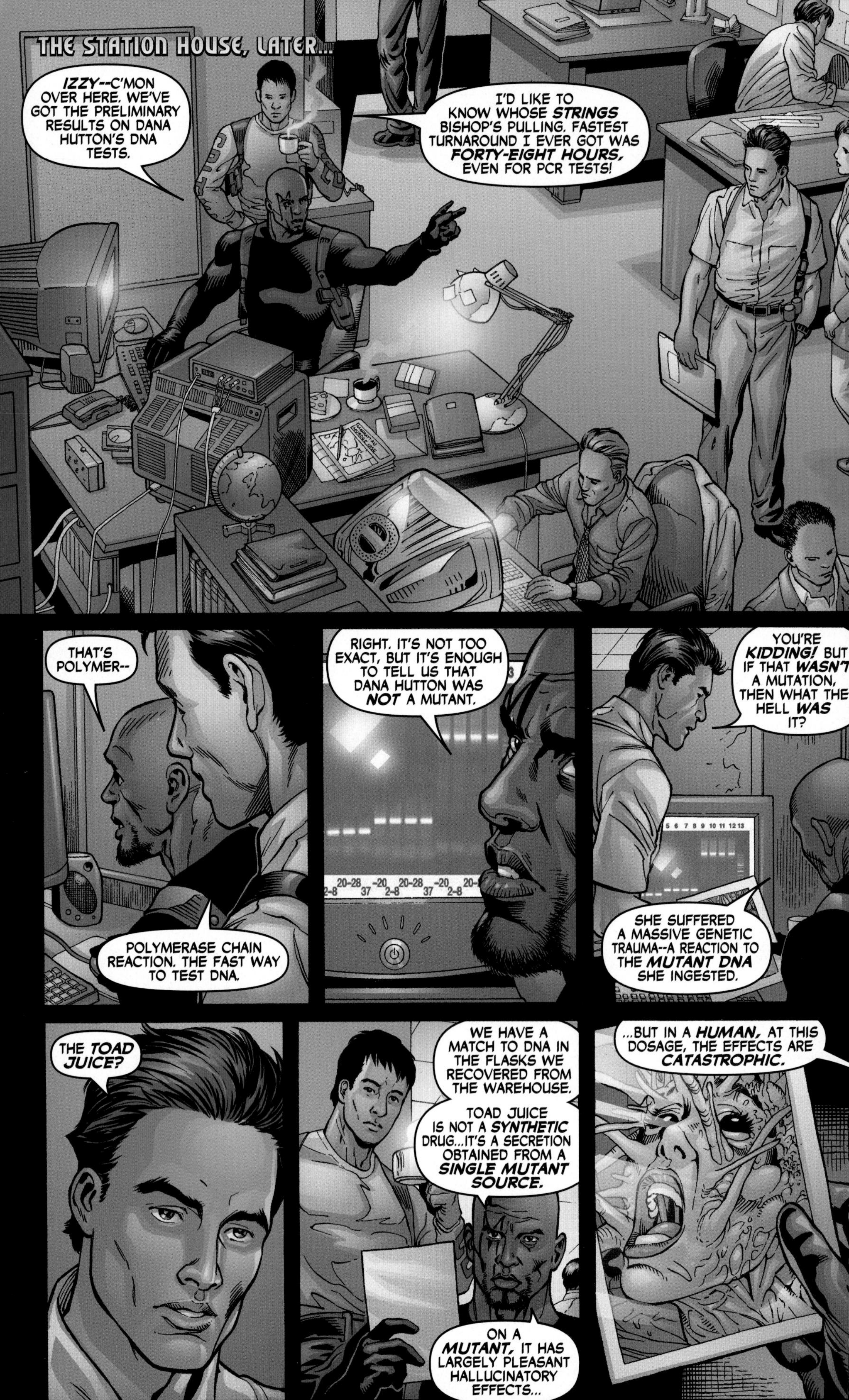
THE STATION HOUSE, LATER...
IZZY--C'MON OVER HERE. WE'VE GOT THE PRELIMINARY RESULTS ON DANA HUTTON'S DNA TESTS.
I'D LIKE TO KNOW WHOSE STRINGS BISHOP'S PULLING. FASTEST TURNAROUND I EVER GOT WAS FORTY-EIGHT HOURS, EVEN FOR PCR TESTS!
THAT'S POLYMER--
POLYMERASE CHAIN REACTION. THE FAST WAY TO TEST DNA.
RIGHT. IT'S NOT TOO EXACT, BUT IT'S ENOUGH TO TELL US THAT DANA HUTTON WAS NOT A MUTANT.
YOU'RE KIDDING! BUT IF THAT WASN'T A MUTATION, THEN WHAT THE HELL WAS IT?
SHE SUFFERED A MASSIVE GENETIC TRAUMA--A REACTION TO THE MUTANT DNA SHE INGESTED.
THE TOAD JUICE?
WE HAVE A MATCH TO DNA IN THE FLASKS WE RECOVERED FROM THE WAREHOUSE.
TOAD JUICE IS NOT A SYNTHETIC DRUG...IT'S A SECRETION OBTAINED FROM A SINGLE MUTANT SOURCE.
ON A MUTANT, IT HAS LARGELY PLEASANT HALLUCINATORY EFFECTS...
...BUT IN A HUMAN, AT THIS DOSAGE, THE EFFECTS ARE CATASTROPHIC.

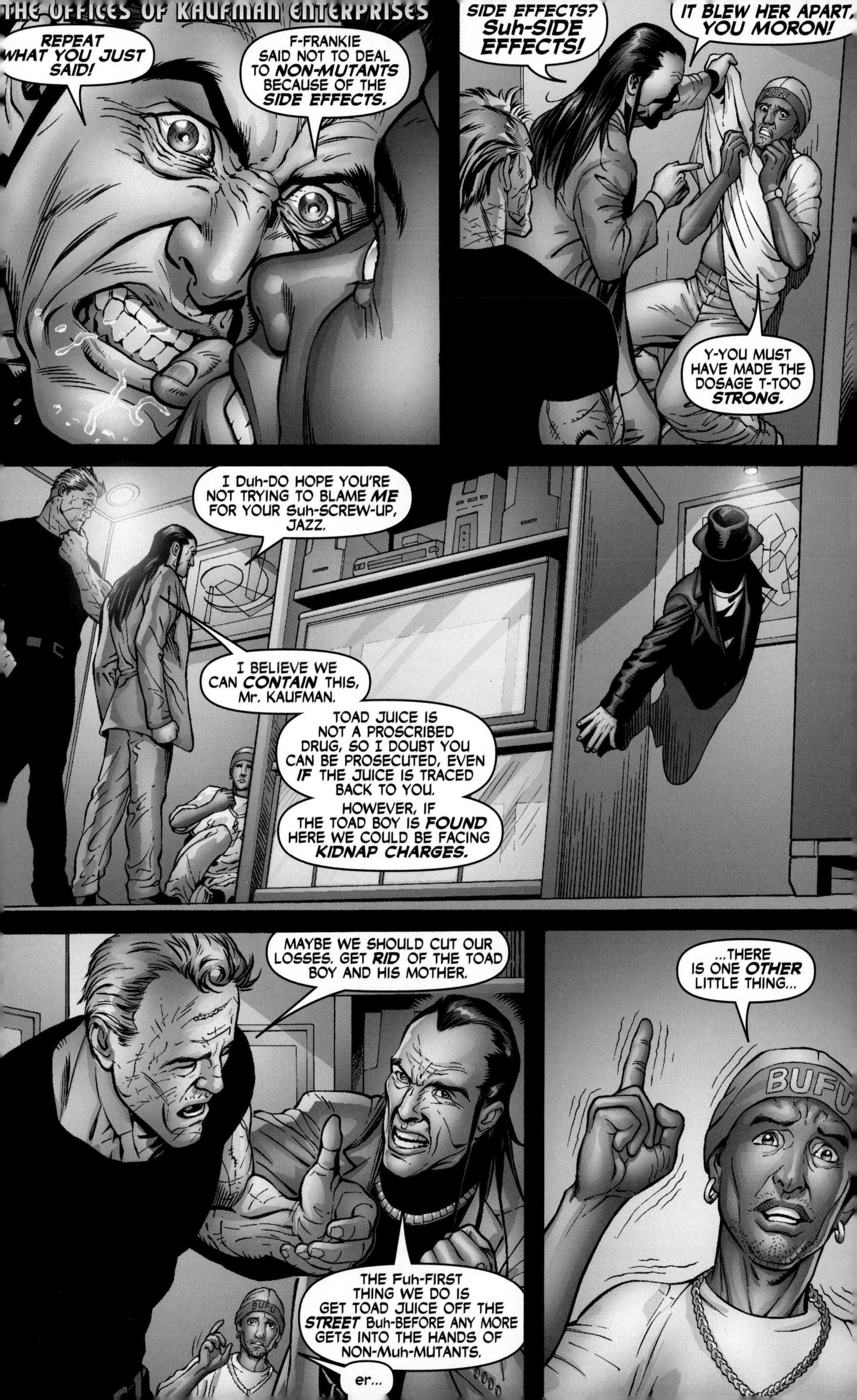
THE OFFICES OF KAUFMAN ENTERPRISES
REPEAT WHAT YOU JUST SAID!
F-FRANKIE SAID NOT TO DEAL TO NON-MUTANTS BECAUSE OF THE SIDE EFFECTS.
SIDE EFFECTS? Suh-SIDE EFFECTS!
IT BLEW HER APART, YOU MORON!
Y-YOU MUST HAVE MADE THE DOSAGE T-TOO STRONG.
I Duh-DO HOPE YOU'RE NOT TRYING TO BLAME ME FOR YOUR Suh-SCREW-UP, JAZZ.
I BELIEVE WE CAN CONTAIN THIS, Mr. KAUFMAN.
TOAD JUICE IS NOT A PROSCRIBED DRUG, SO I DOUBT YOU CAN BE PROSECUTED, EVEN IF THE JUICE IS TRACED BACK TO YOU.
HOWEVER, IF THE TOAD BOY IS FOUND HERE WE COULD BE FACING KIDNAP CHARGES.
MAYBE WE SHOULD CUT OUR LOSSES. GET RID OF THE TOAD BOY AND HIS MOTHER.
THE Fuh-FIRST THING WE DO IS GET TOAD JUICE OFF THE STREET Buh-BEFORE ANY MORE GETS INTO THE HANDS OF NON-Muh-MUTANTS.
er...
...THERE IS ONE OTHER LITTLE THING...
BUFU

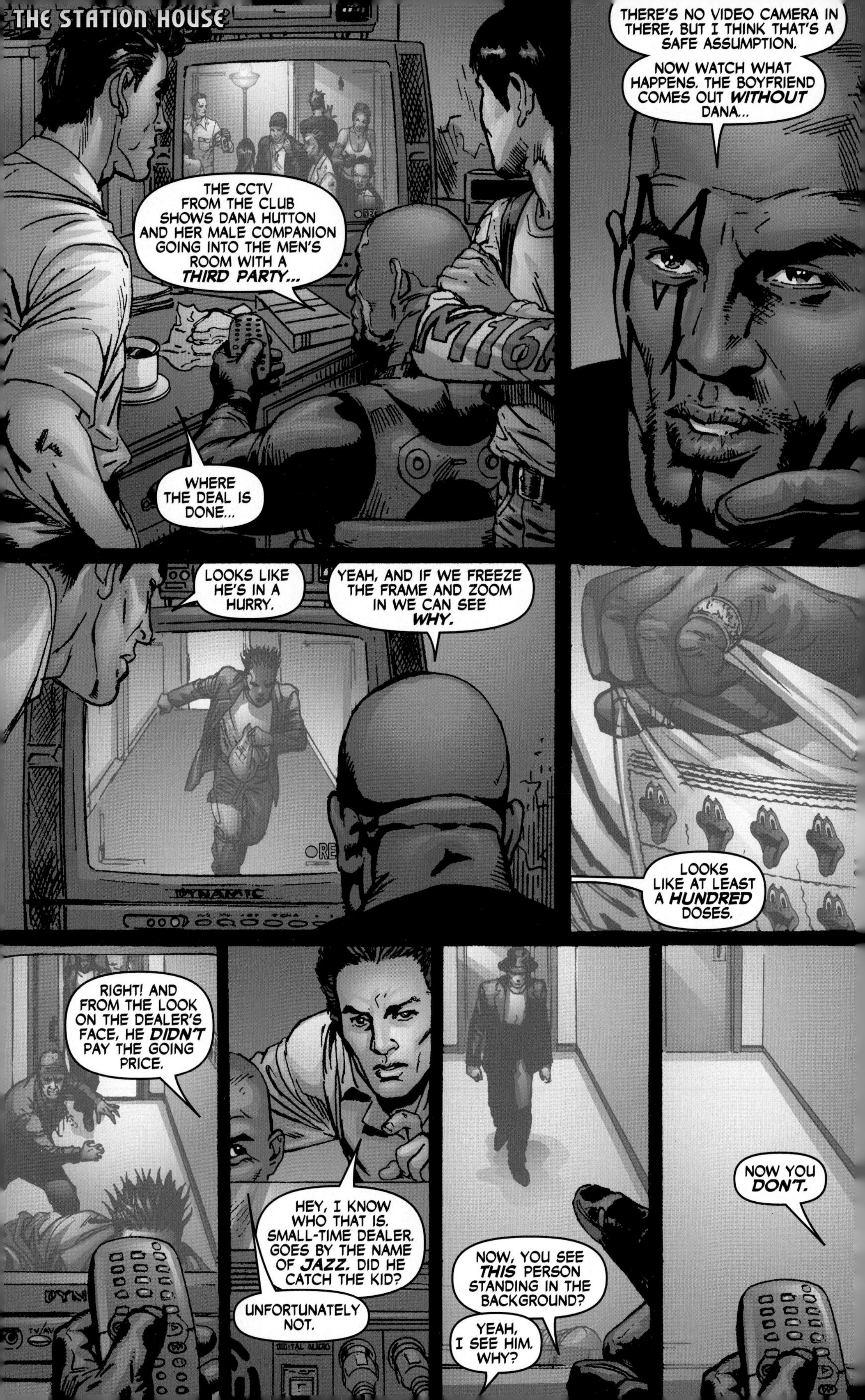
THE STATION HOUSE
THE CCTV FROM THE CLUB SHOWS DANA HUTTON AND HER MALE COMPANION GOING INTO THE MEN'S ROOM WITH A THIRD PARTY...
WHERE THE DEAL IS DONE...
THERE'S NO VIDEO CAMERA IN THERE, BUT I THINK THAT'S A SAFE ASSUMPTION.
NOW WATCH WHAT HAPPENS. THE BOYFRIEND COMES OUT WITHOUT DANA...
LOOKS LIKE HE'S IN A HURRY.
YEAH, AND IF WE FREEZE THE FRAME AND ZOOM IN WE CAN SEE WHY.
LOOKS LIKE AT LEAST A HUNDRED DOSES.
RIGHT! AND FROM THE LOOK ON THE DEALER'S FACE, HE DIDN'T PAY THE GOING PRICE.
HEY, I KNOW WHO THAT IS. SMALL-TIME DEALER. GOES BY THE NAME OF JAZZ. DID HE CATCH THE KID?
UNFORTUNATELY NOT.
NOW, YOU SEE THIS PERSON STANDING IN THE BACKGROUND?
YEAH, I SEE HIM. WHY?
NOW YOU DON'T.

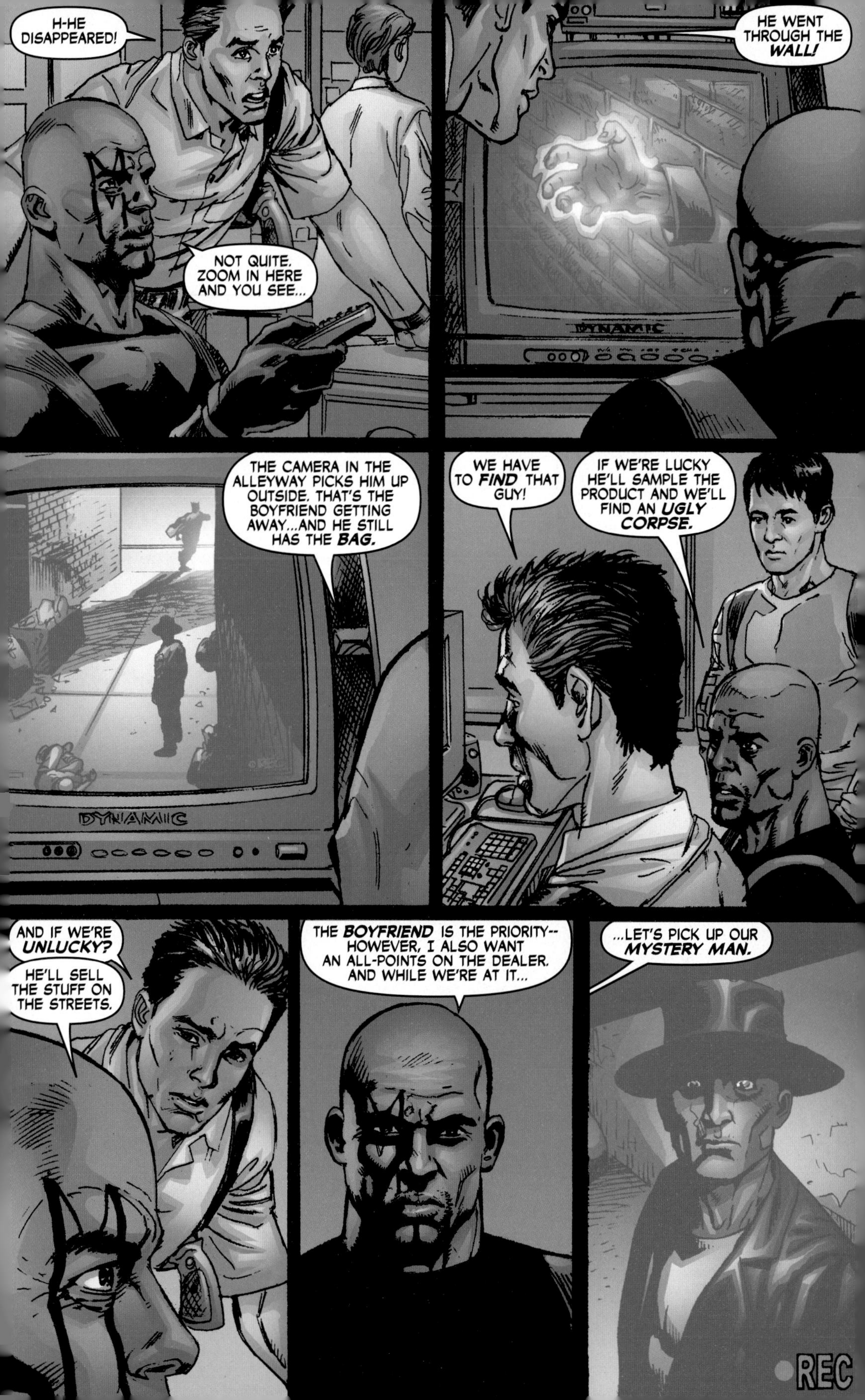
H-HE DISAPPEARED!
NOT QUITE. ZOOM IN HERE AND YOU SEE...
HE WENT THROUGH THE *WALL!*
DYNAMIC
THE CAMERA IN THE ALLEYWAY PICKS HIM UP OUTSIDE. THAT'S THE BOYFRIEND GETTING AWAY...AND HE STILL HAS THE *BAG.*
DYNAMIC
WE HAVE TO *FIND* THAT GUY!
IF WE'RE LUCKY HE'LL SAMPLE THE PRODUCT AND WE'LL FIND AN *UGLY CORPSE.*
AND IF WE'RE *UNLUCKY?*
HE'LL SELL THE STUFF ON THE STREETS.
THE *BOYFRIEND* IS THE PRIORITY-- HOWEVER, I ALSO WANT AN ALL-POINTS ON THE DEALER. AND WHILE WE'RE AT IT...
...LET'S PICK UP OUR *MYSTERY MAN.*
REC

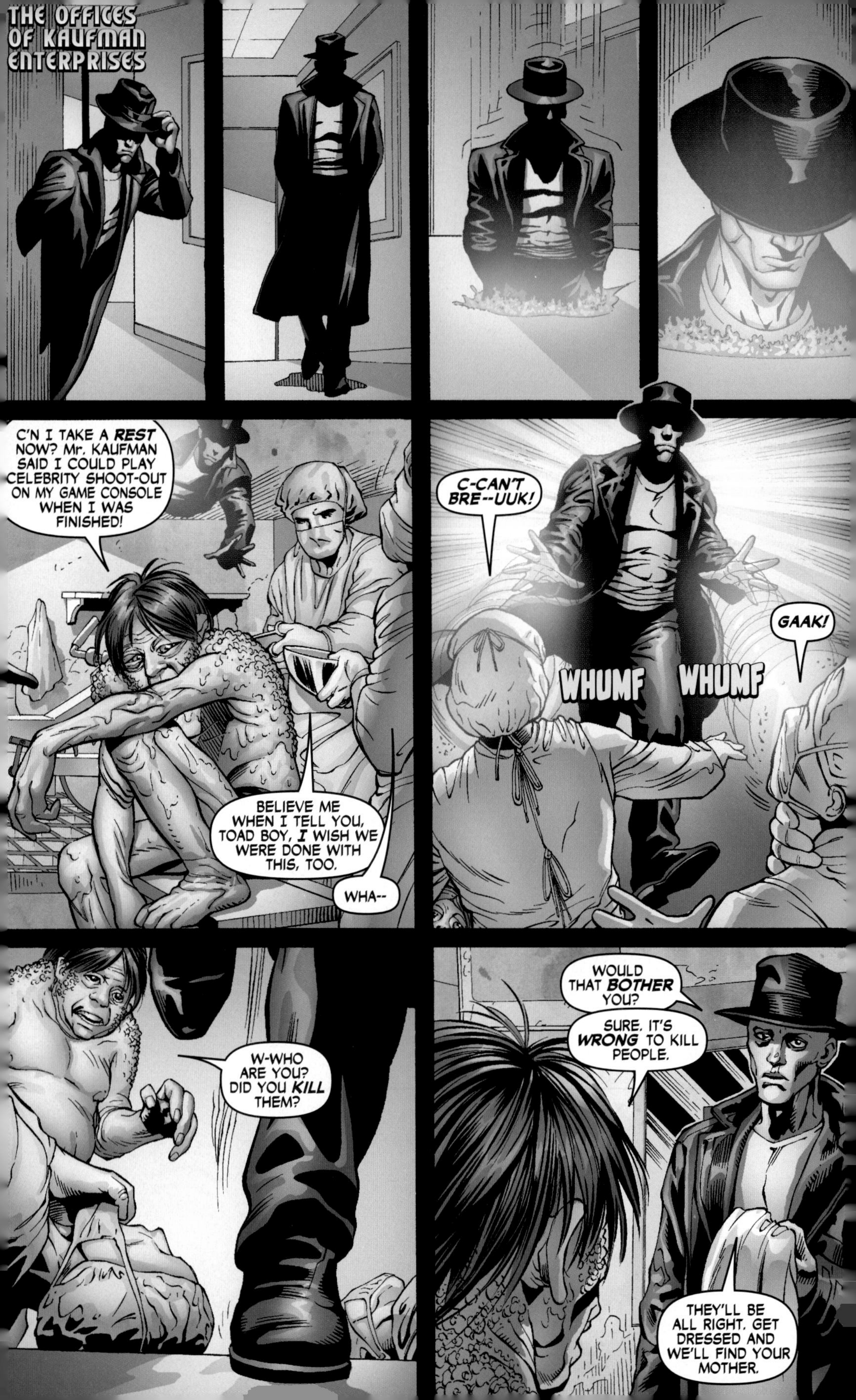
THE OFFICES OF KAUFMAN ENTERPRISES
C'N I TAKE A REST NOW? Mr. KAUFMAN SAID I COULD PLAY CELEBRITY SHOOT-OUT ON MY GAME CONSOLE WHEN I WAS FINISHED!
BELIEVE ME WHEN I TELL YOU, TOAD BOY, I WISH WE WERE DONE WITH THIS, TOO.
WHA--
C-CAN'T BRE--UUK!
GAAK!
WHUMF
WHUMF
W-WHO ARE YOU? DID YOU KILL THEM?
WOULD THAT BOTHER YOU?
SURE. IT'S WRONG TO KILL PEOPLE.
THEY'LL BE ALL RIGHT. GET DRESSED AND WE'LL FIND YOUR MOTHER.

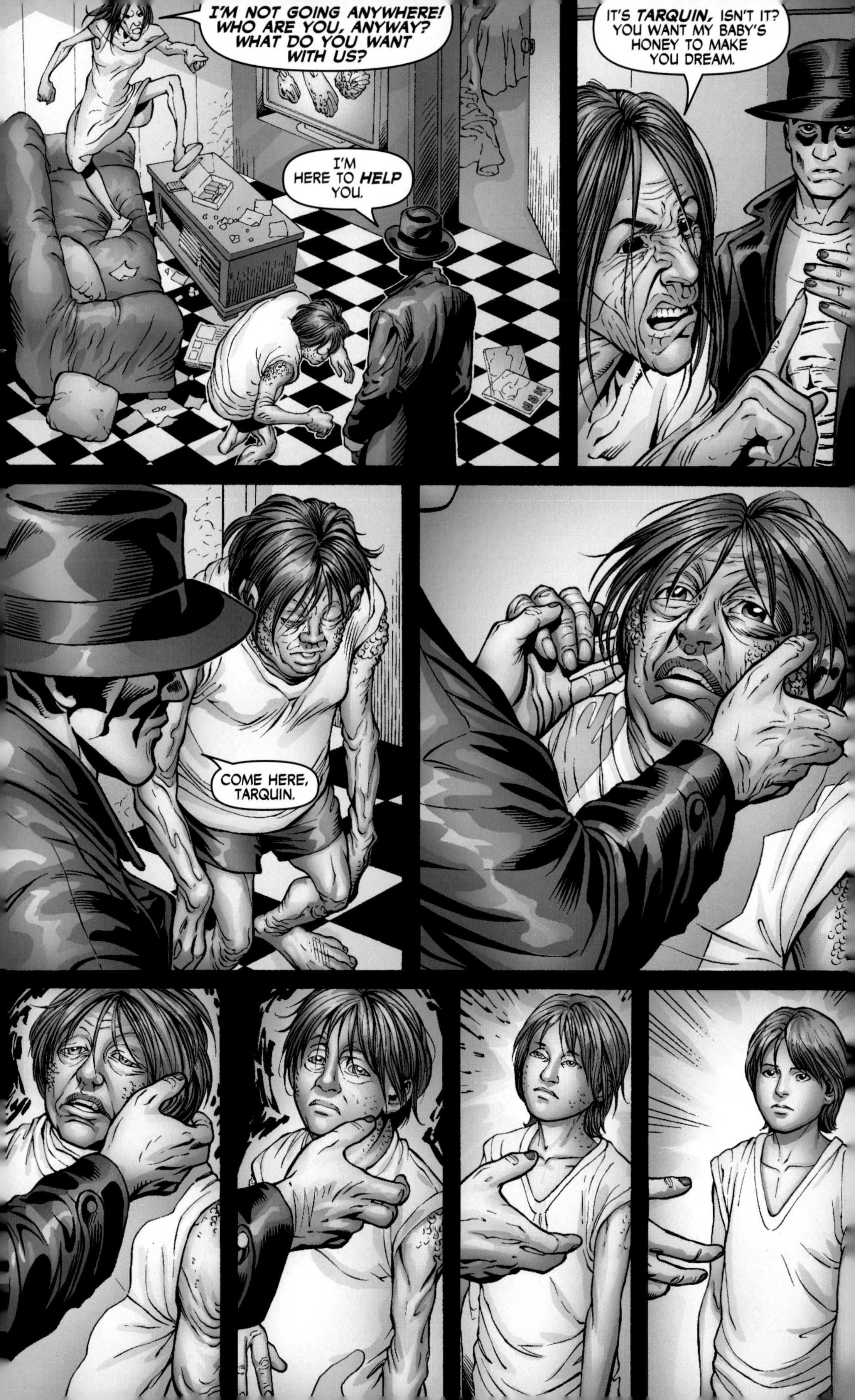
I'M NOT GOING ANYWHERE! WHO ARE YOU, ANYWAY? WHAT DO YOU WANT WITH US?
I'M HERE TO HELP YOU.
IT'S TARQUIN, ISN'T IT? YOU WANT MY BABY'S HONEY TO MAKE YOU DREAM.
COME HERE, TARQUIN.

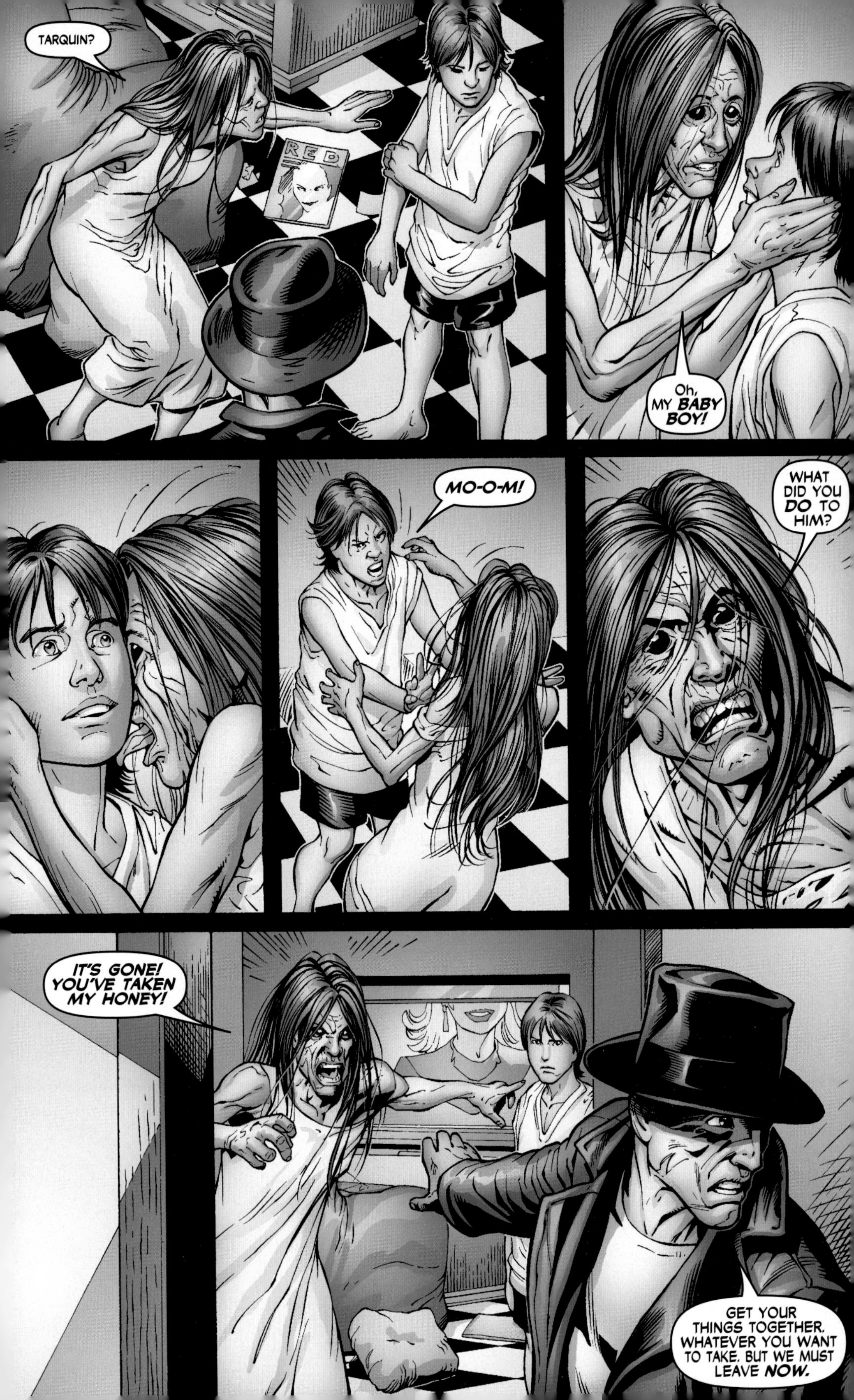
TARQUIN?
Oh, MY BABY BOY!
MO-O-M!
WHAT DID YOU DO TO HIM?
IT'S GONE! YOU'VE TAKEN MY HONEY!
GET YOUR THINGS TOGETHER. WHATEVER YOU WANT TO TAKE. BUT WE MUST LEAVE NOW.

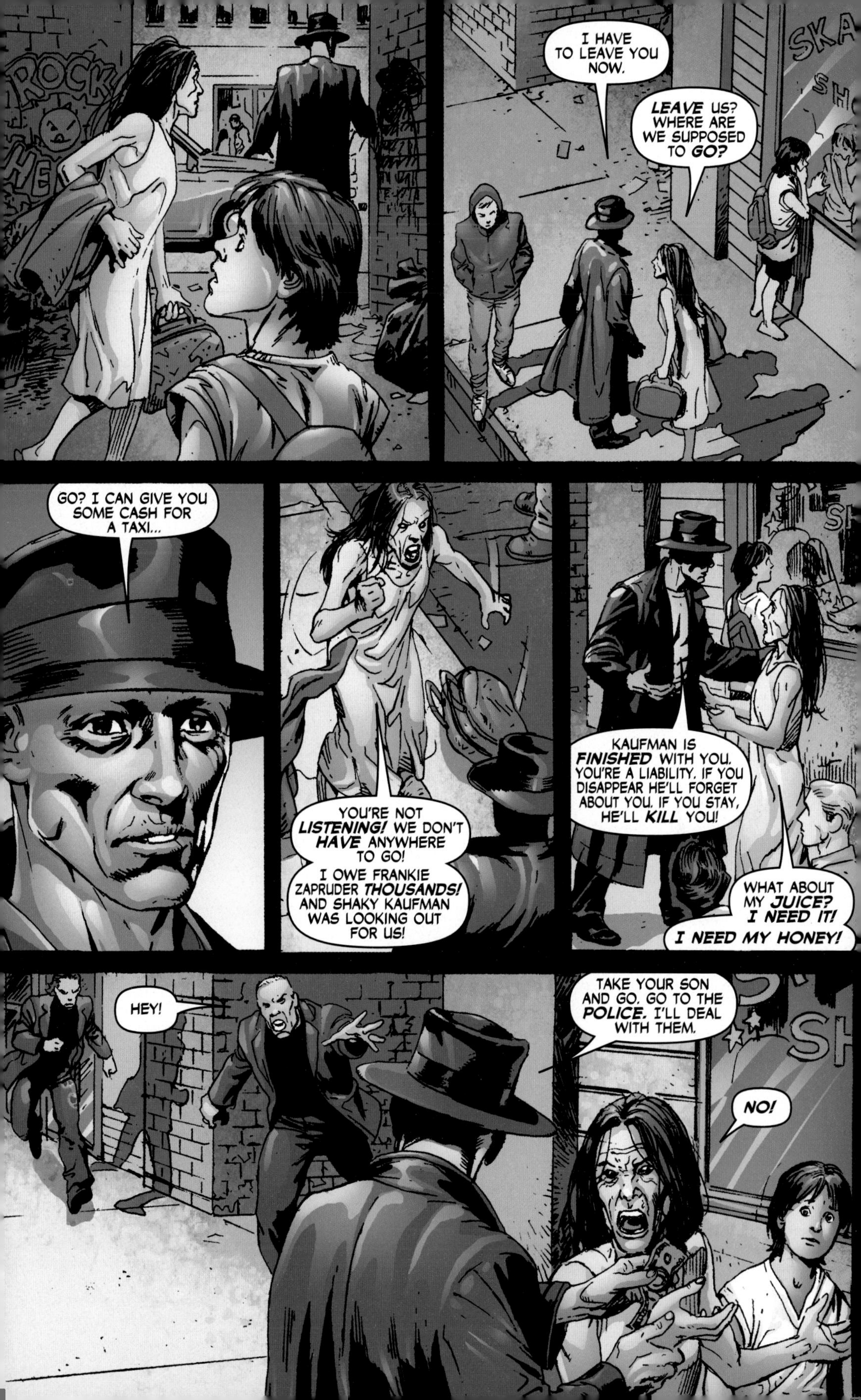
ROCK
I HAVE TO LEAVE YOU NOW.
LEAVE US? WHERE ARE WE SUPPOSED TO GO?
GO? I CAN GIVE YOU SOME CASH FOR A TAXI...
YOU'RE NOT LISTENING! WE DON'T HAVE ANYWHERE TO GO!
I OWE FRANKIE ZAPRUDER THOUSANDS! AND SHAKY KAUFMAN WAS LOOKING OUT FOR US!
KAUFMAN IS FINISHED WITH YOU. YOU'RE A LIABILITY. IF YOU DISAPPEAR HE'LL FORGET ABOUT YOU. IF YOU STAY, HE'LL KILL YOU!
WHAT ABOUT MY JUICE? I NEED IT!
I NEED MY HONEY!
HEY!
TAKE YOUR SON AND GO. GO TO THE POLICE. I'LL DEAL WITH THEM.
NO!

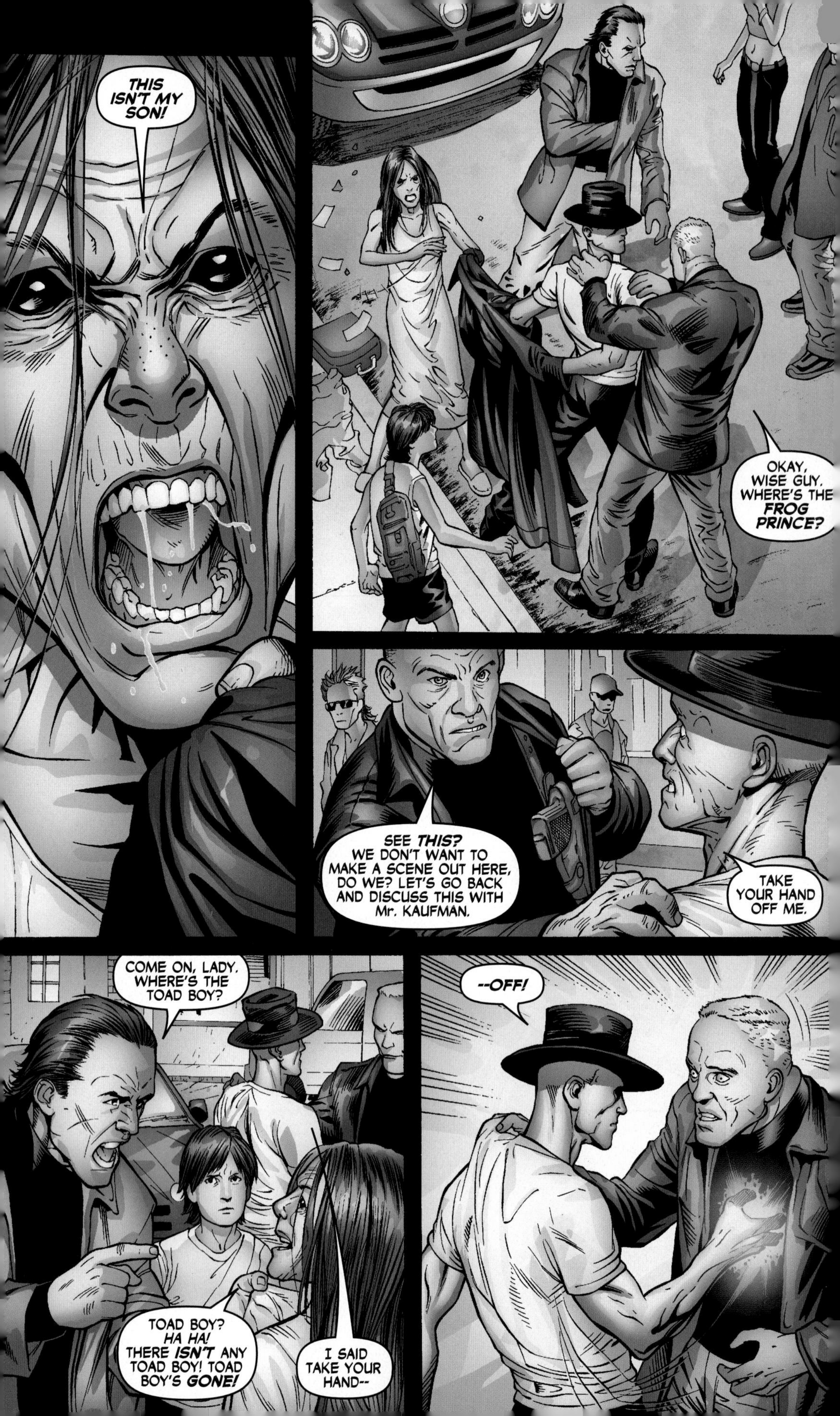
THIS ISN'T MY SON!
OKAY, WISE GUY. WHERE'S THE FROG PRINCE?
SEE THIS? WE DON'T WANT TO MAKE A SCENE OUT HERE, DO WE? LET'S GO BACK AND DISCUSS THIS WITH Mr. KAUFMAN.
TAKE YOUR HAND OFF ME.
COME ON, LADY. WHERE'S THE TOAD BOY?
TOAD BOY? HA HA! THERE ISN'T ANY TOAD BOY! TOAD BOY'S GONE!
I SAID TAKE YOUR HAND--
--OFF!

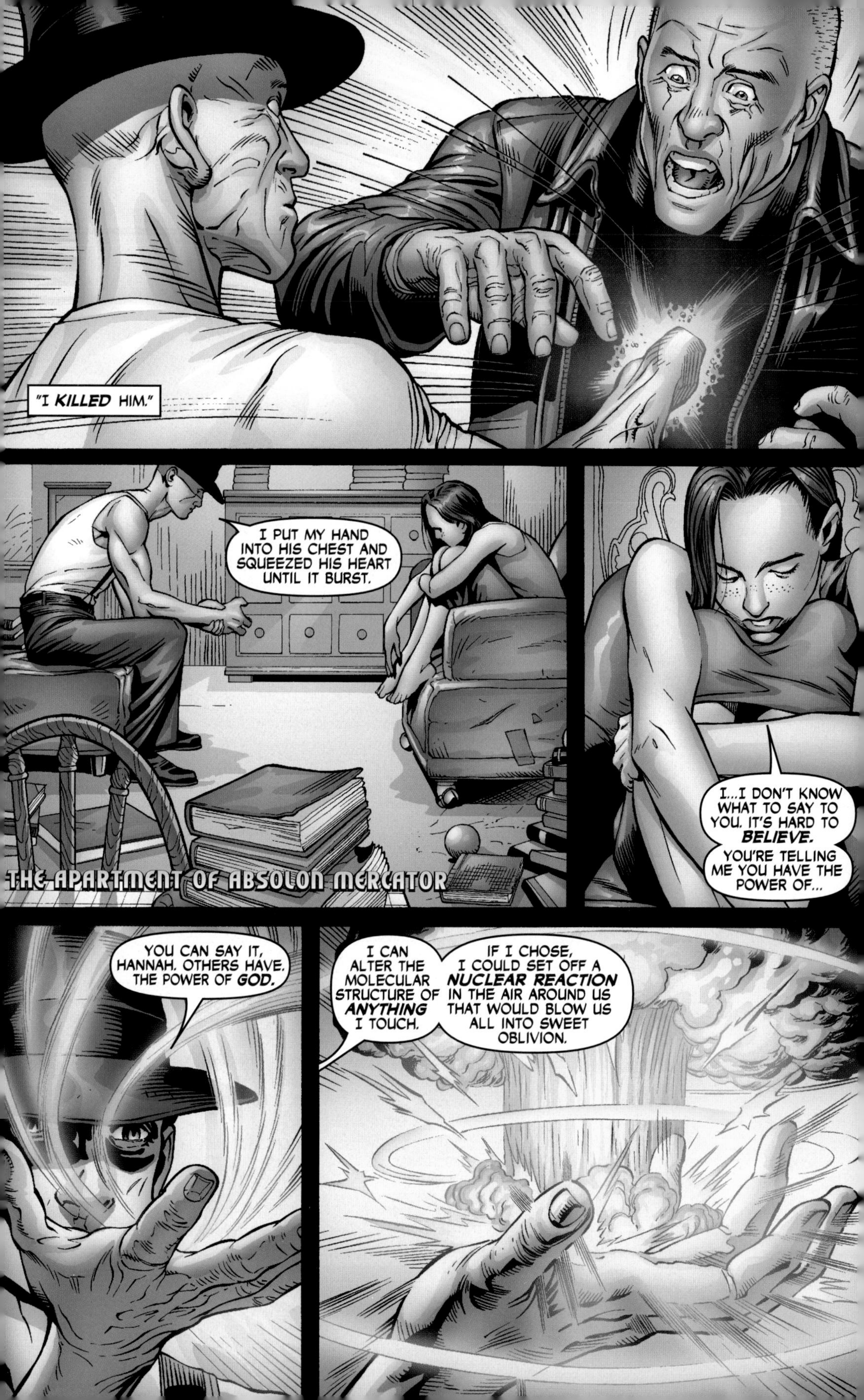
"I KILLED HIM."
I PUT MY HAND INTO HIS CHEST AND SQUEEZED HIS HEART UNTIL IT BURST.
THE APARTMENT OF ABSOLON MERCATOR
I...I DON'T KNOW WHAT TO SAY TO YOU. IT'S HARD TO BELIEVE.
YOU'RE TELLING ME YOU HAVE THE POWER OF...
YOU CAN SAY IT, HANNAH. OTHERS HAVE. THE POWER OF GOD.
I CAN ALTER THE MOLECULAR STRUCTURE OF ANYTHING I TOUCH.
IF I CHOSE, I COULD SET OFF A NUCLEAR REACTION IN THE AIR AROUND US THAT WOULD BLOW US ALL INTO SWEET OBLIVION.

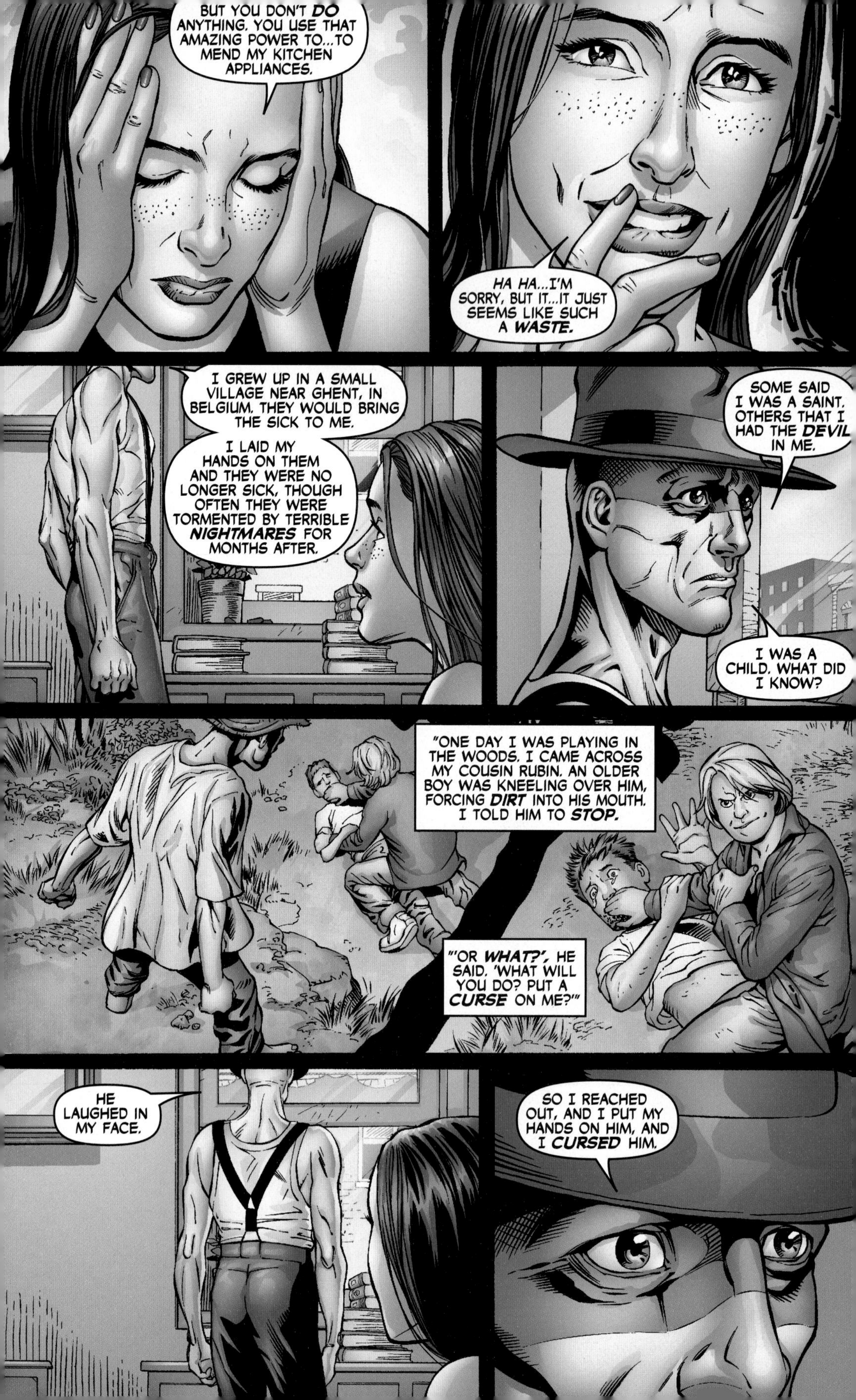
BUT YOU DON'T DO ANYTHING. YOU USE THAT AMAZING POWER TO...TO MEND MY KITCHEN APPLIANCES.
HA HA...I'M SORRY, BUT IT...IT JUST SEEMS LIKE SUCH A WASTE.
I GREW UP IN A SMALL VILLAGE NEAR GHENT, IN BELGIUM. THEY WOULD BRING THE SICK TO ME.
I LAID MY HANDS ON THEM AND THEY WERE NO LONGER SICK, THOUGH OFTEN THEY WERE TORMENTED BY TERRIBLE NIGHTMARES FOR MONTHS AFTER.
SOME SAID I WAS A SAINT. OTHERS THAT I HAD THE DEVIL IN ME.
I WAS A CHILD. WHAT DID I KNOW?
"ONE DAY I WAS PLAYING IN THE WOODS. I CAME ACROSS MY COUSIN RUBIN. AN OLDER BOY WAS KNEELING OVER HIM, FORCING DIRT INTO HIS MOUTH. I TOLD HIM TO STOP.
"'OR WHAT?', HE SAID. 'WHAT WILL YOU DO? PUT A CURSE ON ME?'"
HE LAUGHED IN MY FACE.
SO I REACHED OUT, AND I PUT MY HANDS ON HIM, AND I CURSED HIM.

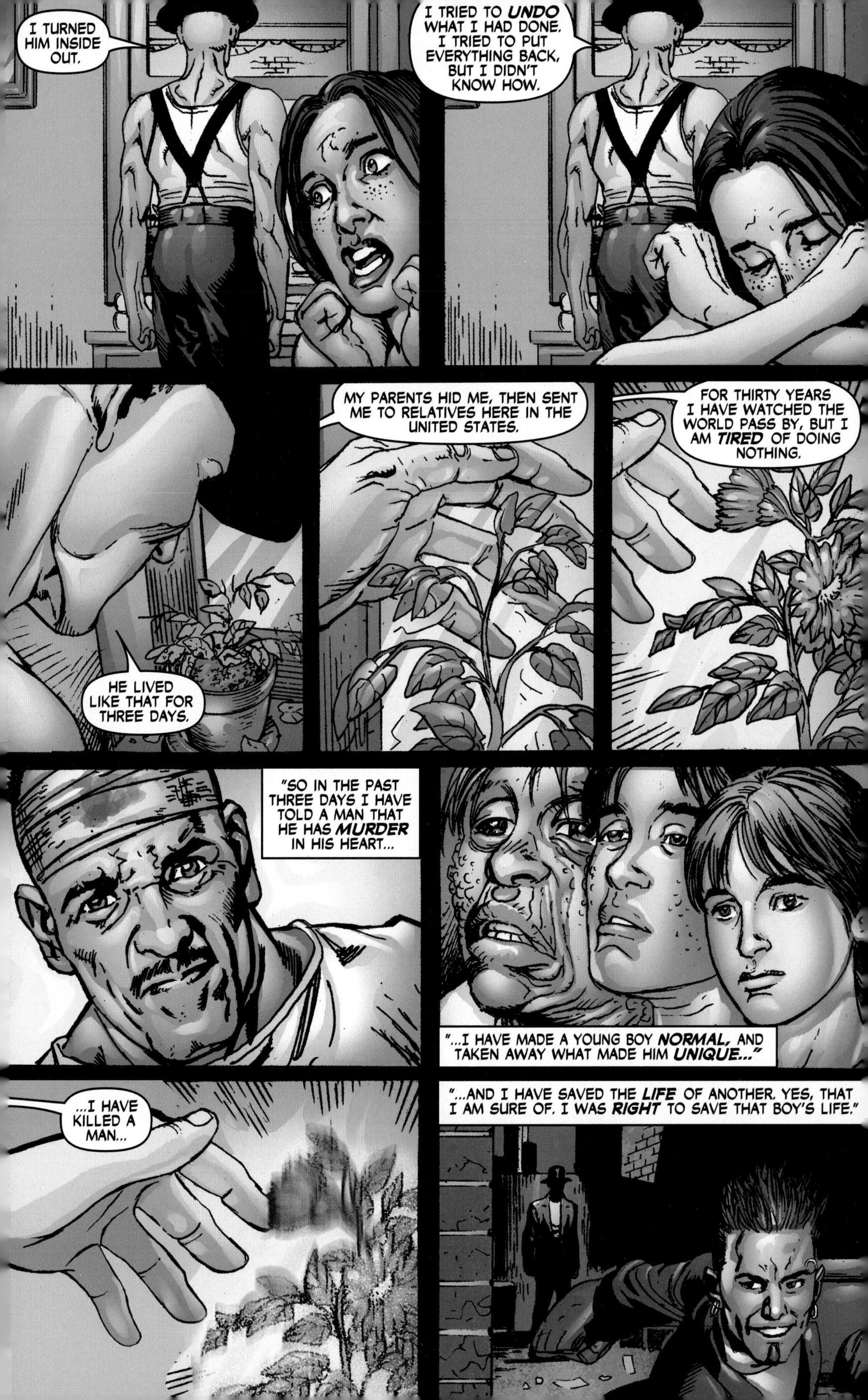
I TURNED HIM INSIDE OUT.
I TRIED TO UNDO WHAT I HAD DONE. I TRIED TO PUT EVERYTHING BACK, BUT I DIDN'T KNOW HOW.
HE LIVED LIKE THAT FOR THREE DAYS.
MY PARENTS HID ME, THEN SENT ME TO RELATIVES HERE IN THE UNITED STATES.
FOR THIRTY YEARS I HAVE WATCHED THE WORLD PASS BY, BUT I AM TIRED OF DOING NOTHING.
"SO IN THE PAST THREE DAYS I HAVE TOLD A MAN THAT HE HAS MURDER IN HIS HEART...
"...I HAVE MADE A YOUNG BOY NORMAL, AND TAKEN AWAY WHAT MADE HIM UNIQUE..."
...I HAVE KILLED A MAN...
"...AND I HAVE SAVED THE LIFE OF ANOTHER. YES, THAT I AM SURE OF. I WAS RIGHT TO SAVE THAT BOY'S LIFE."

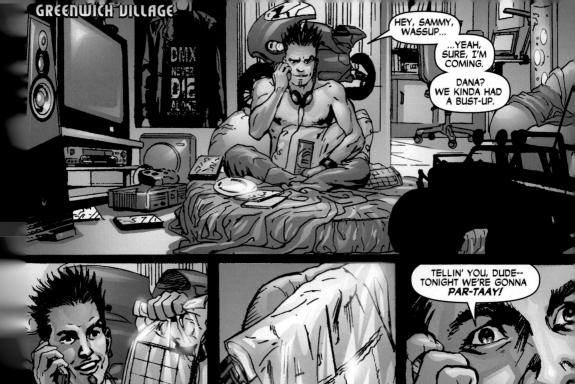

GREENWICH VILLAGE
HEY, SAMMY, WASSUP...
...YEAH, SURE, I'M COMING.
DANA? WE KINDA HAD A BUST-UP.
DMX
NEVER
DIE
ALONE
HEY, IT'S NO BIG DEAL. LISTEN UP, WILLYA? I'M TRYING TO TELL YOU I GOT THE GOODIES SORTED FOR TONIGHT.
NOPE, THIS IS TOTALLY NEW. PICKED IT UP IN MUTANT TOWN. TOAD JUICE. IT'S DA BOMB!
TELLIN' YOU, DUDE-- TONIGHT WE'RE GONNA PAR-TAAY!
11TH PRECINCT, CHIEF ESPOSITO'S OFFICE
CHIEF, WE HAVE TO GO PUBLIC WITH THIS. NOW!
I DON'T KNOW, BISHOP. THIS IS GOING TO DRAW DOWN A LOT OF ATTENTION.
YOU SAY WE HAVE THE SOURCE OF TOAD JUICE?
WE'RE WAITING ON DNA TESTS. THE MOTHER'S CONFUSED.
"ONE MINUTE HER SON'S THE TOAD BOY, THE NEXT HE'S NOT EVEN HER SON. THE KID'S NOT TALKING."
WHETHER HE'S THE SOURCE OR NOT, THERE'S STILL A LOT OF JUICE OUT THERE. WE NEED TO BROADCAST A WARNING. ALL MAJOR TV AND RADIO NETWORKS.

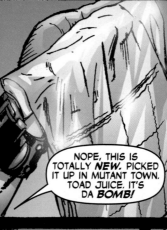

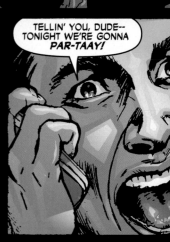

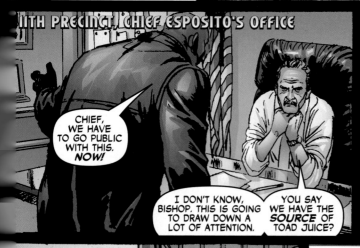

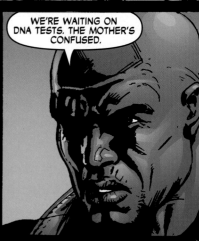

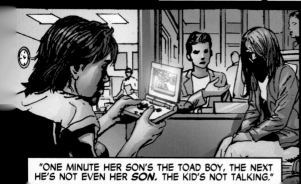

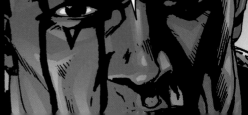

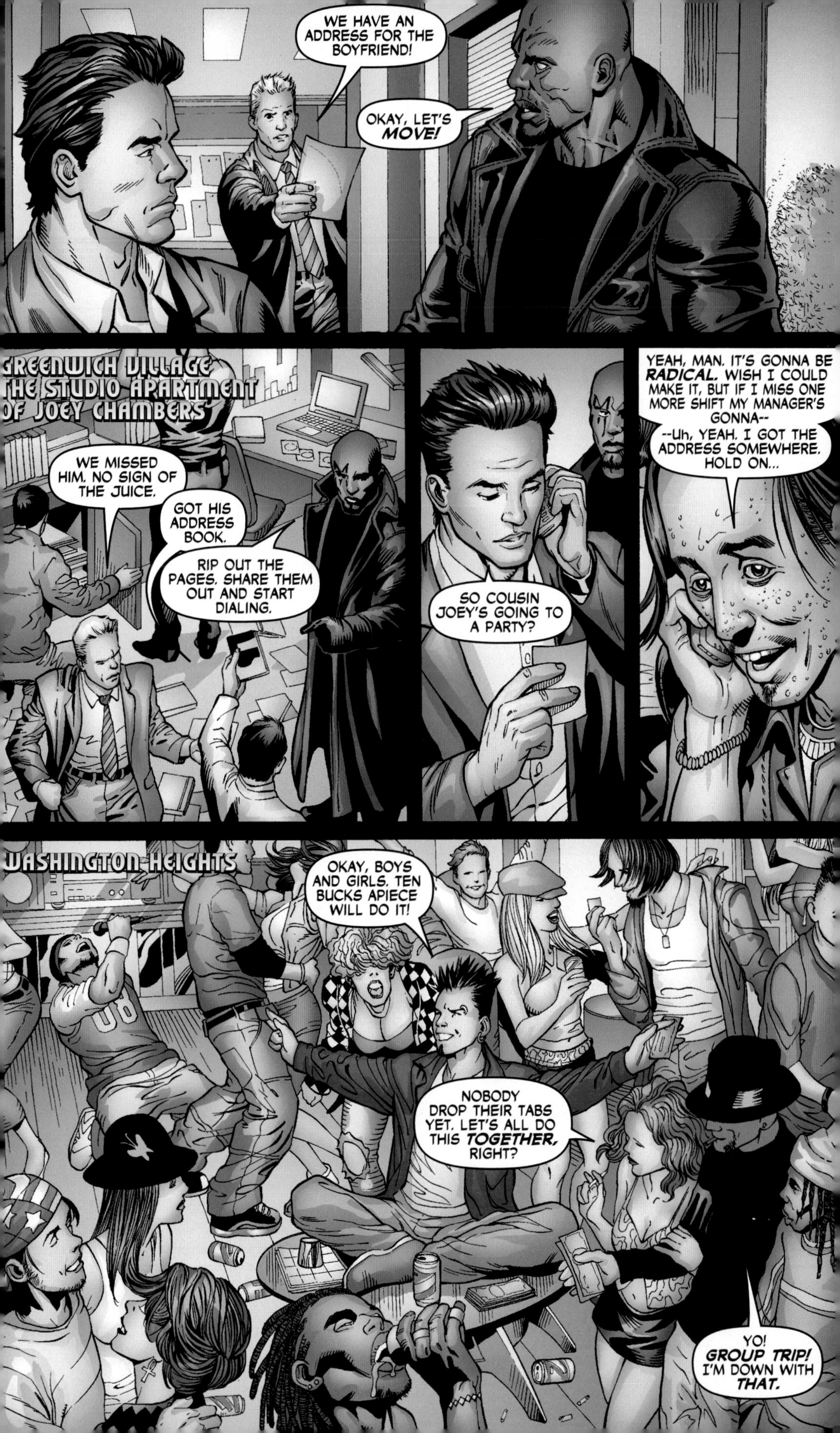
WE HAVE AN ADDRESS FOR THE BOYFRIEND!
OKAY, LET'S *MOVE!*
GREENWICH VILLAGE THE STUDIO APARTMENT OF JOEY CHAMBERS
WE MISSED HIM. NO SIGN OF THE JUICE.
GOT HIS ADDRESS BOOK.
RIP OUT THE PAGES. SHARE THEM OUT AND START DIALING.
SO COUSIN JOEY'S GOING TO A PARTY?
YEAH, MAN. IT'S GONNA BE *RADICAL.* WISH I COULD MAKE IT, BUT IF I MISS ONE MORE SHIFT MY MANAGER'S GONNA--
--Uh, YEAH. I GOT THE ADDRESS SOMEWHERE. HOLD ON...
WASHINGTON HEIGHTS
OKAY, BOYS AND GIRLS. TEN BUCKS APIECE WILL DO IT!
NOBODY DROP THEIR TABS YET. LET'S ALL DO THIS *TOGETHER,* RIGHT?
YO! *GROUP TRIP!* I'M DOWN WITH *THAT.*

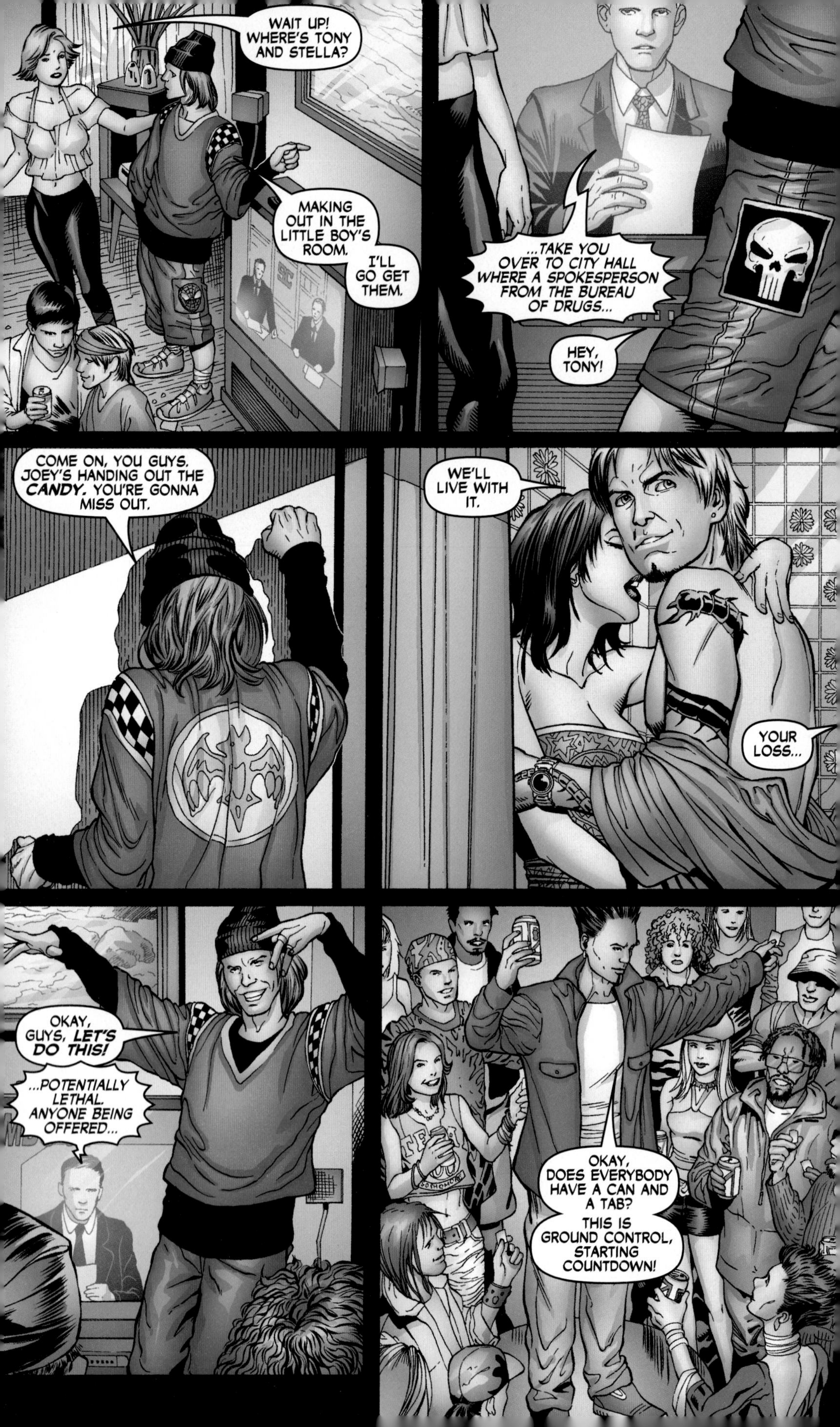
WAIT UP! WHERE'S TONY AND STELLA?
MAKING OUT IN THE LITTLE BOY'S ROOM.
I'LL GO GET THEM.
...TAKE YOU OVER TO CITY HALL WHERE A SPOKESPERSON FROM THE BUREAU OF DRUGS...
HEY, TONY!
COME ON, YOU GUYS. JOEY'S HANDING OUT THE *CANDY.* YOU'RE GONNA MISS OUT.
WE'LL LIVE WITH IT.
YOUR LOSS...
OKAY, GUYS, ***LET'S DO THIS!***
...POTENTIALLY LETHAL. ANYONE BEING OFFERED...
OKAY, DOES EVERYBODY HAVE A CAN AND A TAB?
THIS IS GROUND CONTROL, STARTING COUNTDOWN!

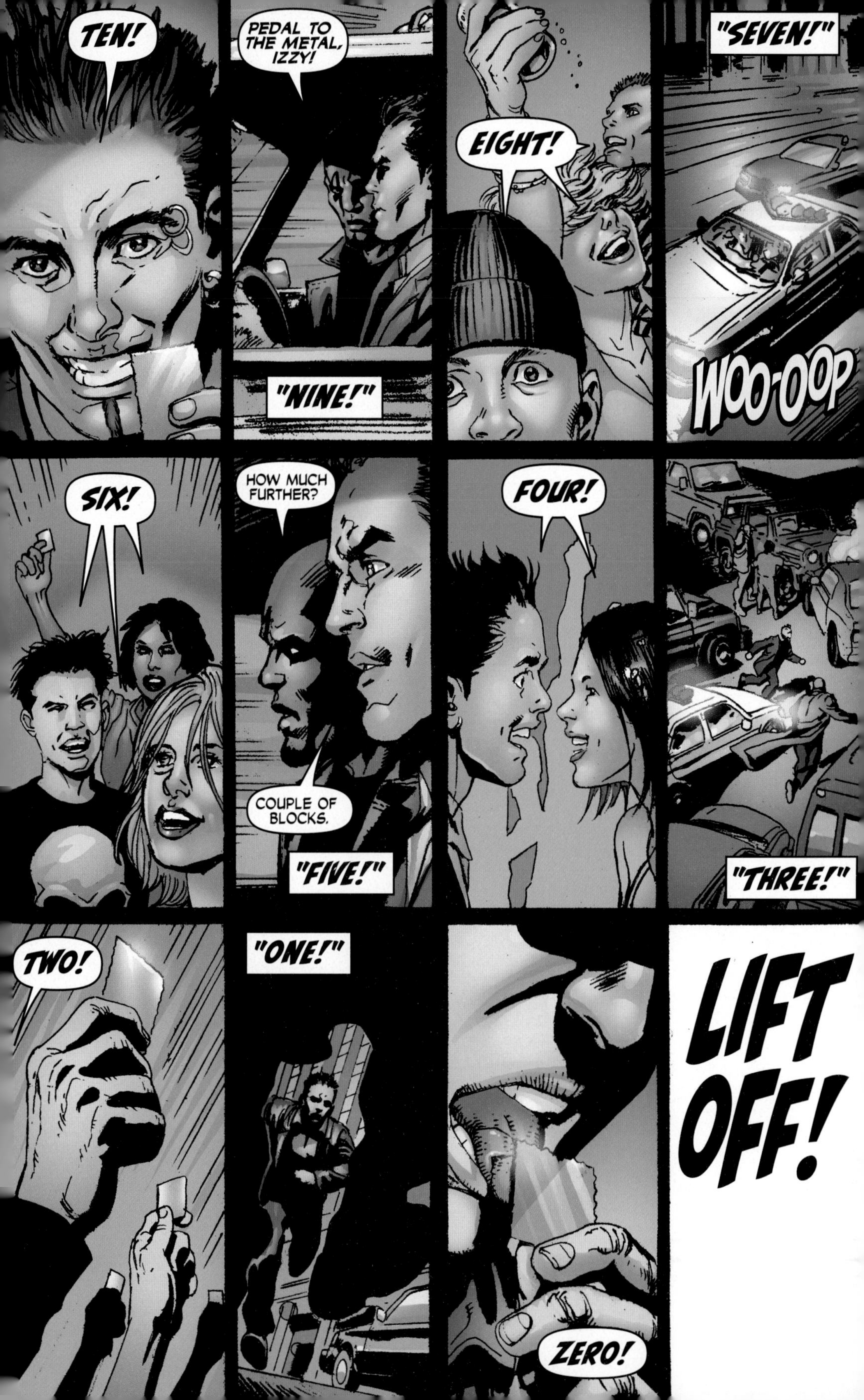
TEN!
PEDAL TO THE METAL, IZZY!
"NINE!"
EIGHT!
"SEVEN!"
WOO-OOP
SIX!
HOW MUCH FURTHER?
COUPLE OF BLOCKS.
"FIVE!"
FOUR!
"THREE!"
TWO!
"ONE!"
ZERO!
LIFT OFF!

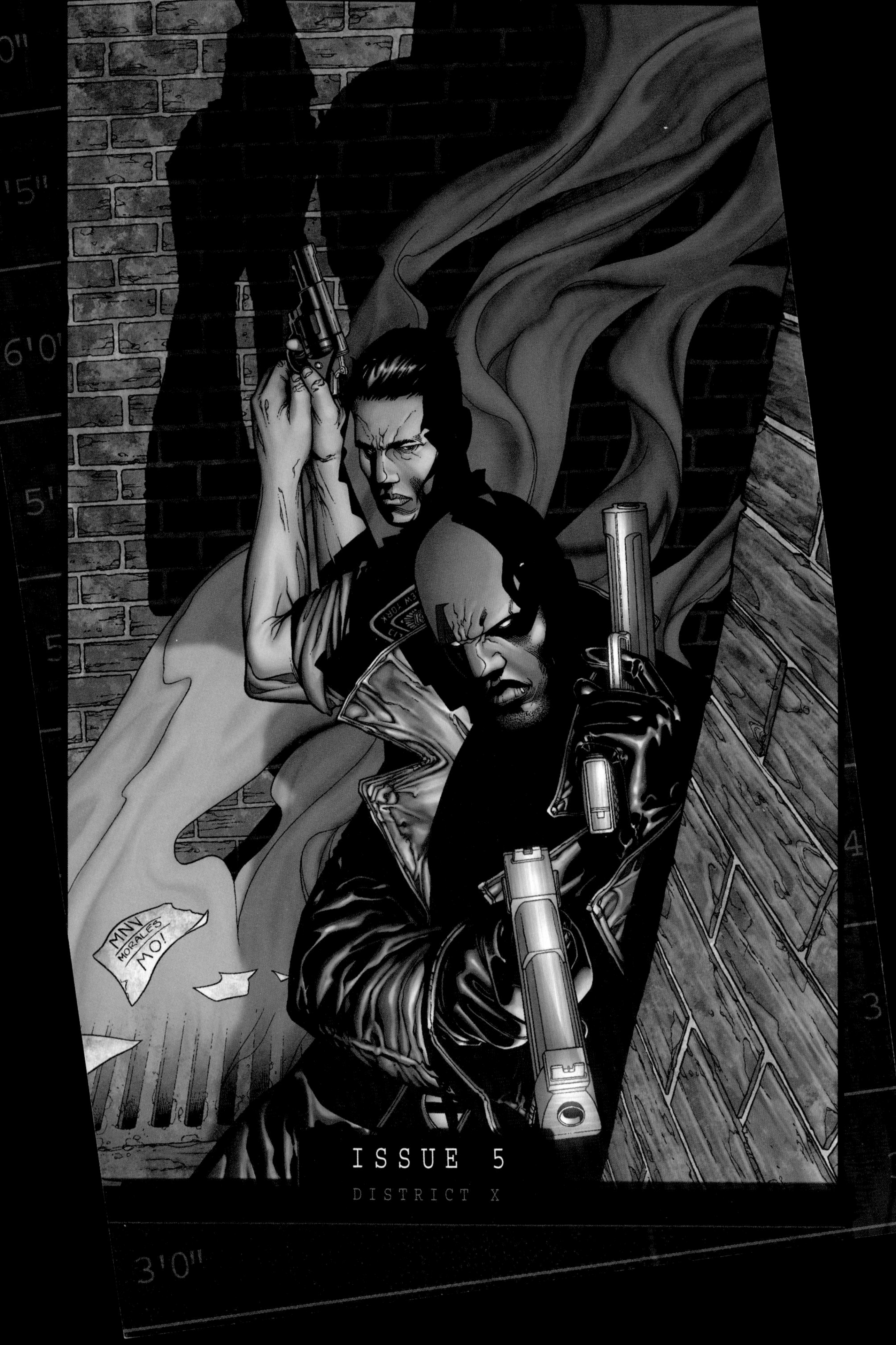
MNV
MORALES
MO!

ISSUE 5

DISTRICT X

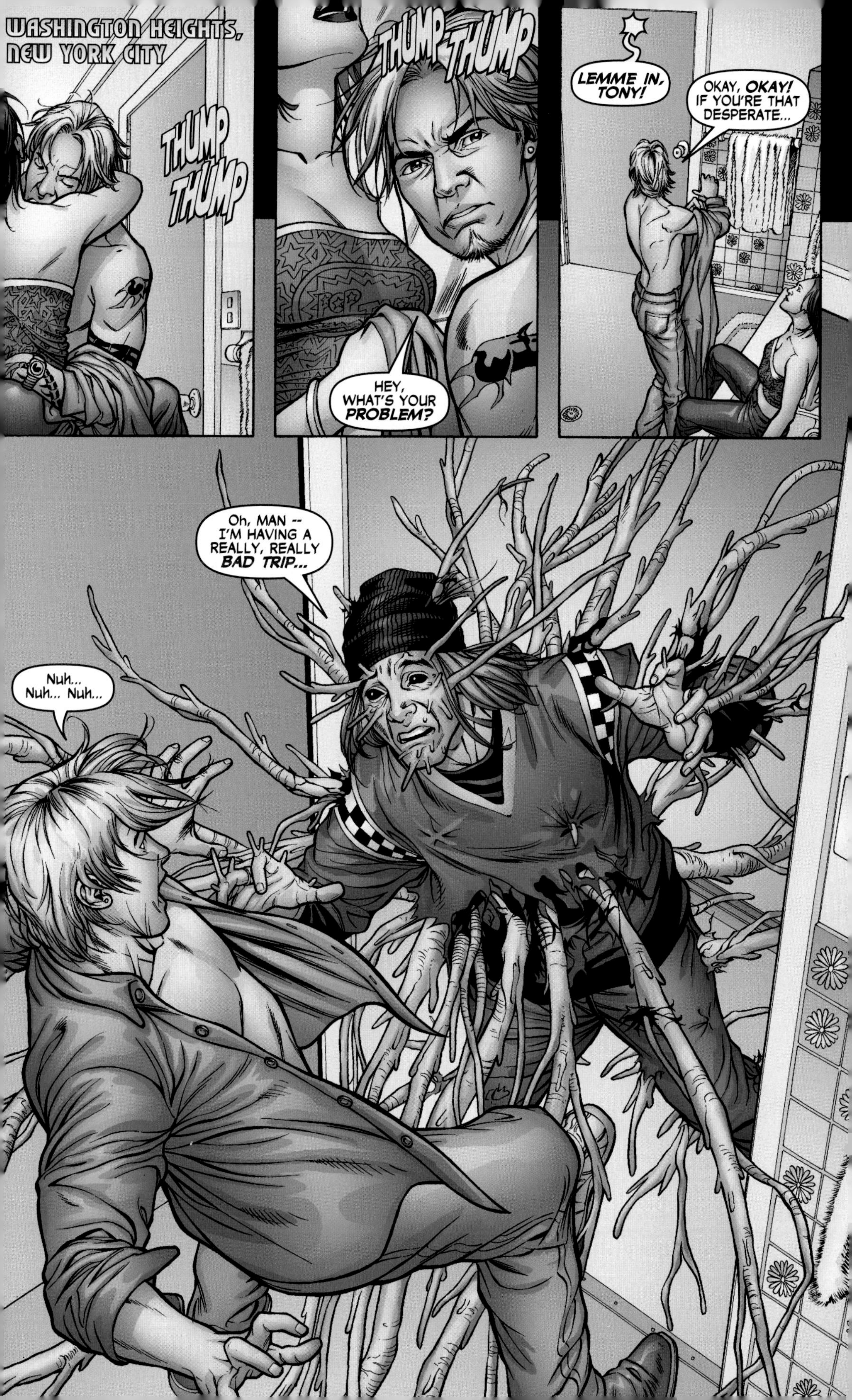
WASHINGTON HEIGHTS, NEW YORK CITY
THUMP THUMP
THUMP THUMP
HEY, WHAT'S YOUR PROBLEM?
LEMME IN, TONY!
OKAY, OKAY! IF YOU'RE THAT DESPERATE...
Oh, MAN -- I'M HAVING A REALLY, REALLY BAD TRIP...
Nuh... Nuh... Nuh...

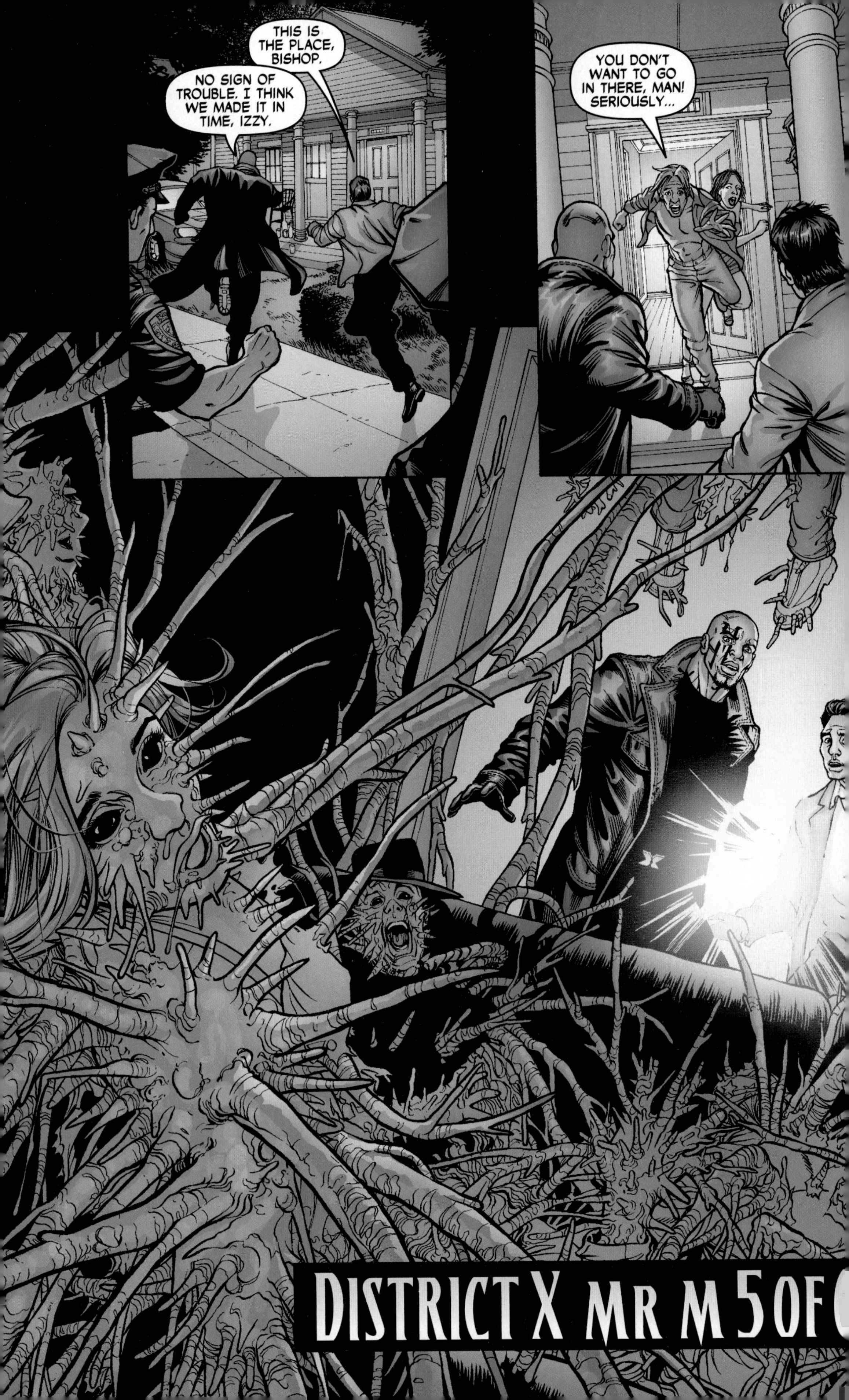
THIS IS THE PLACE, BISHOP.
NO SIGN OF TROUBLE. I THINK WE MADE IT IN TIME, IZZY.
YOU DON'T WANT TO GO IN THERE, MAN! SERIOUSLY...
DISTRICT X MR M 5 OF

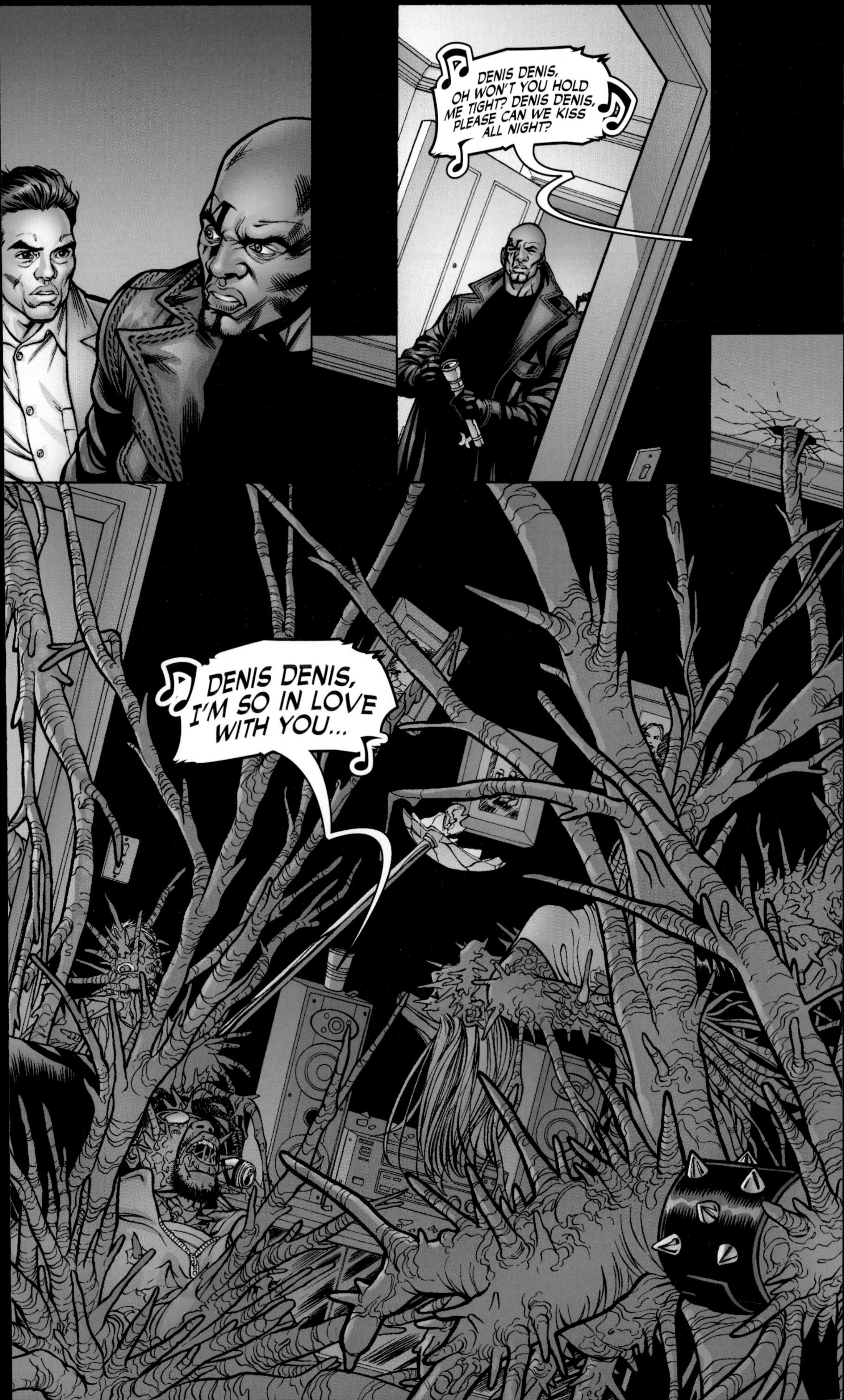

DENIS DENIS, OH WON'T YOU HOLD ME TIGHT? DENIS DENIS, PLEASE CAN WE KISS ALL NIGHT?
DENIS DENIS, I'M SO IN LOVE WITH YOU...

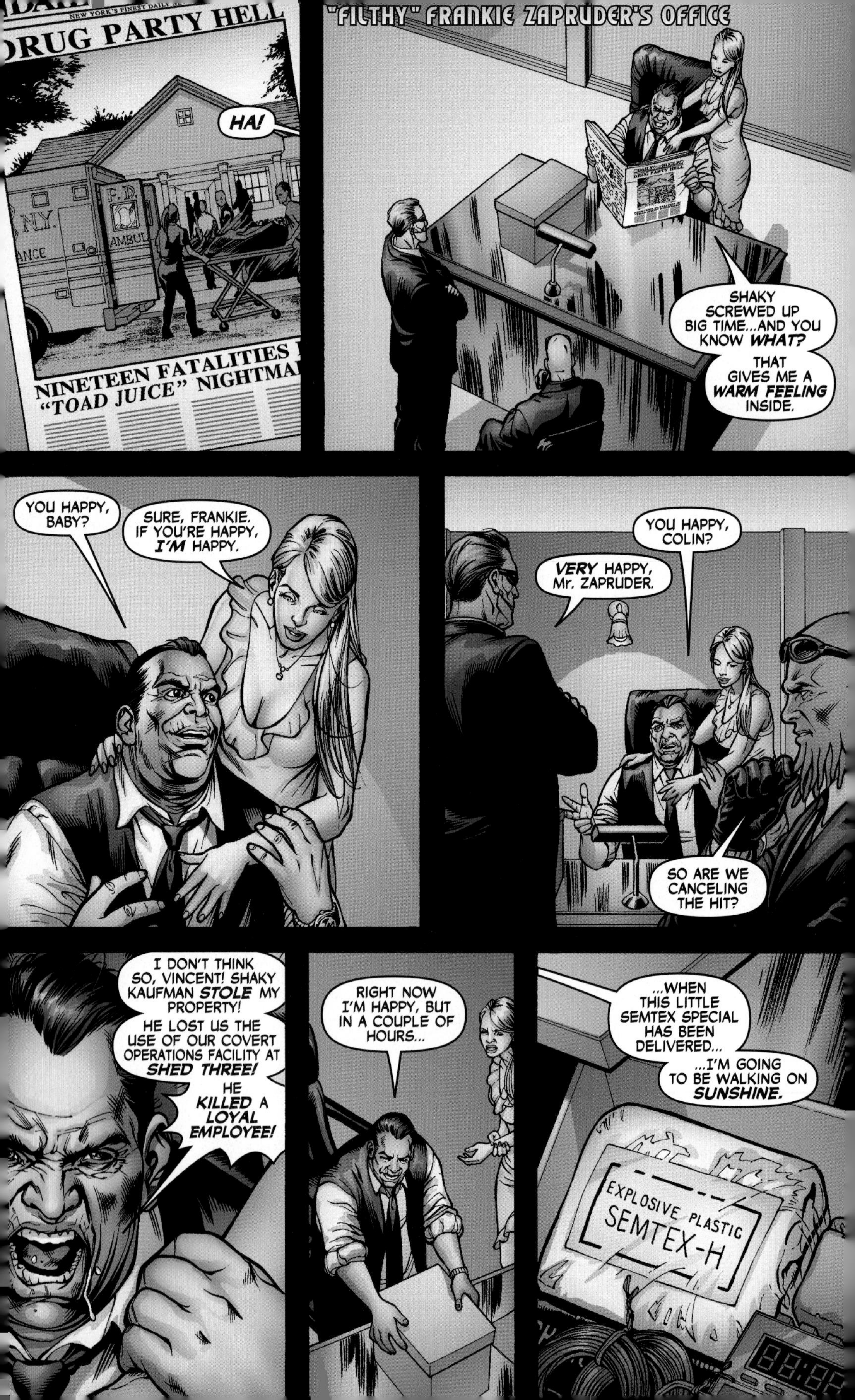
NEW YORK'S FINEST DAILY
DRUG PARTY HELL
F.D.
N.Y.
AMBUL
ANCE
NINETEEN FATALITIES
"TOAD JUICE" NIGHTMA
HA!
"FILTHY" FRANKIE ZAPRUDER'S OFFICE
SHAKY SCREWED UP BIG TIME...AND YOU KNOW WHAT?
THAT GIVES ME A WARM FEELING INSIDE.
YOU HAPPY, BABY?
SURE, FRANKIE. IF YOU'RE HAPPY, I'M HAPPY.
YOU HAPPY, COLIN?
VERY HAPPY, Mr. ZAPRUDER.
SO ARE WE CANCELING THE HIT?
I DON'T THINK SO, VINCENT! SHAKY KAUFMAN STOLE MY PROPERTY!
HE LOST US THE USE OF OUR COVERT OPERATIONS FACILITY AT SHED THREE!
HE KILLED A LOYAL EMPLOYEE!
RIGHT NOW I'M HAPPY, BUT IN A COUPLE OF HOURS...
...WHEN THIS LITTLE SEMTEX SPECIAL HAS BEEN DELIVERED...
...I'M GOING TO BE WALKING ON SUNSHINE.
EXPLOSIVE PLASTIC
SEMTEX-H

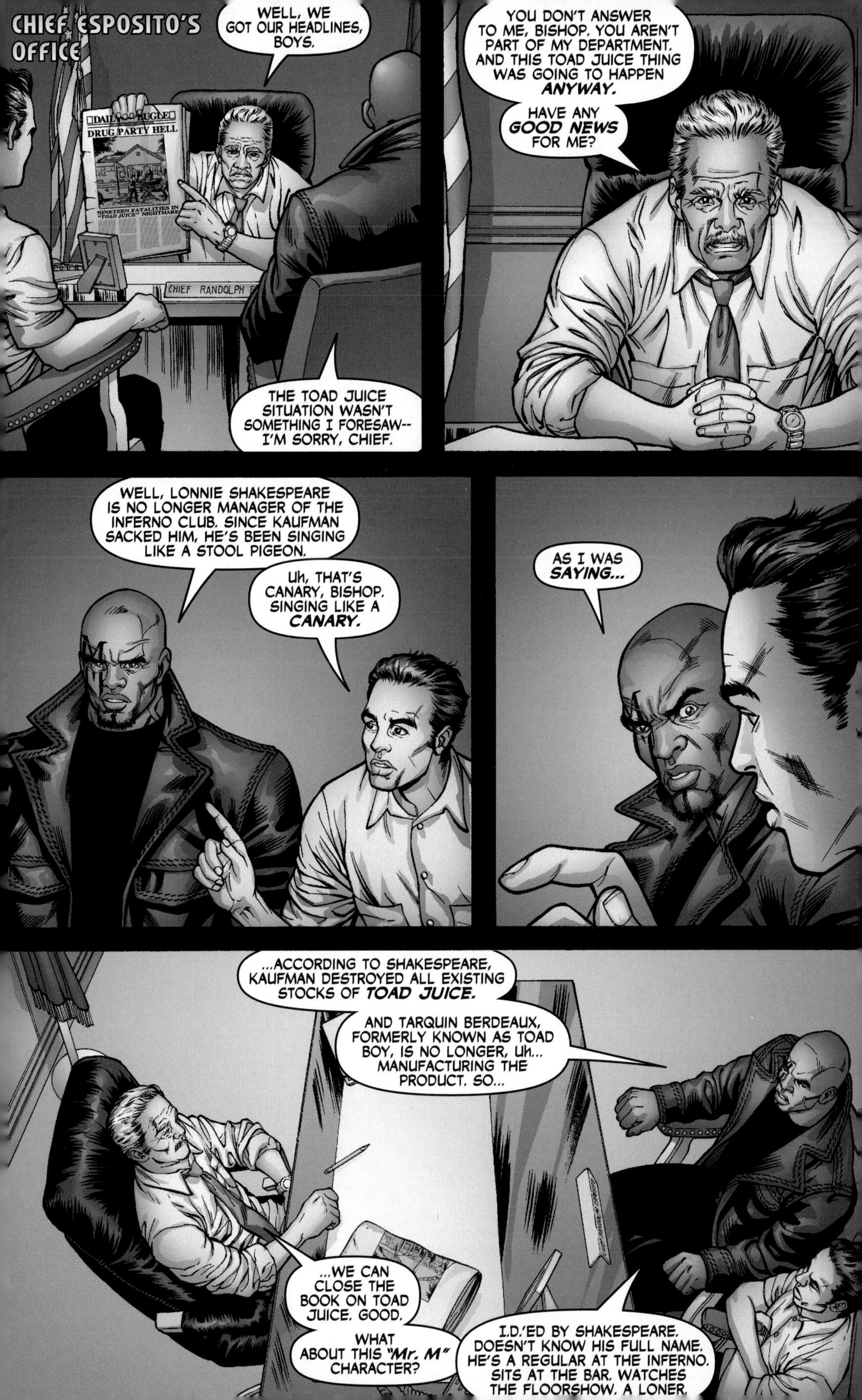
CHIEF ESPOSITO'S OFFICE
WELL, WE GOT OUR HEADLINES, BOYS.
DAILY BUGLE
DRUG PARTY HELL
NINETEEN FATALITIES IN "TOAD JUICE" NIGHTMARE
CHIEF RANDOLPH E
THE TOAD JUICE SITUATION WASN'T SOMETHING I FORESAW-- I'M SORRY, CHIEF.
YOU DON'T ANSWER TO ME, BISHOP. YOU AREN'T PART OF MY DEPARTMENT. AND THIS TOAD JUICE THING WAS GOING TO HAPPEN ANYWAY.
HAVE ANY GOOD NEWS FOR ME?
WELL, LONNIE SHAKESPEARE IS NO LONGER MANAGER OF THE INFERNO CLUB. SINCE KAUFMAN SACKED HIM, HE'S BEEN SINGING LIKE A STOOL PIGEON.
Uh, THAT'S CANARY, BISHOP. SINGING LIKE A CANARY.
AS I WAS SAYING...
...ACCORDING TO SHAKESPEARE, KAUFMAN DESTROYED ALL EXISTING STOCKS OF TOAD JUICE.
AND TARQUIN BERDEAUX, FORMERLY KNOWN AS TOAD BOY, IS NO LONGER, Uh... MANUFACTURING THE PRODUCT. SO...
...WE CAN CLOSE THE BOOK ON TOAD JUICE. GOOD.
WHAT ABOUT THIS "Mr. M" CHARACTER?
I.D.'ED BY SHAKESPEARE. DOESN'T KNOW HIS FULL NAME. HE'S A REGULAR AT THE INFERNO. SITS AT THE BAR. WATCHES THE FLOORSHOW. A LONER.

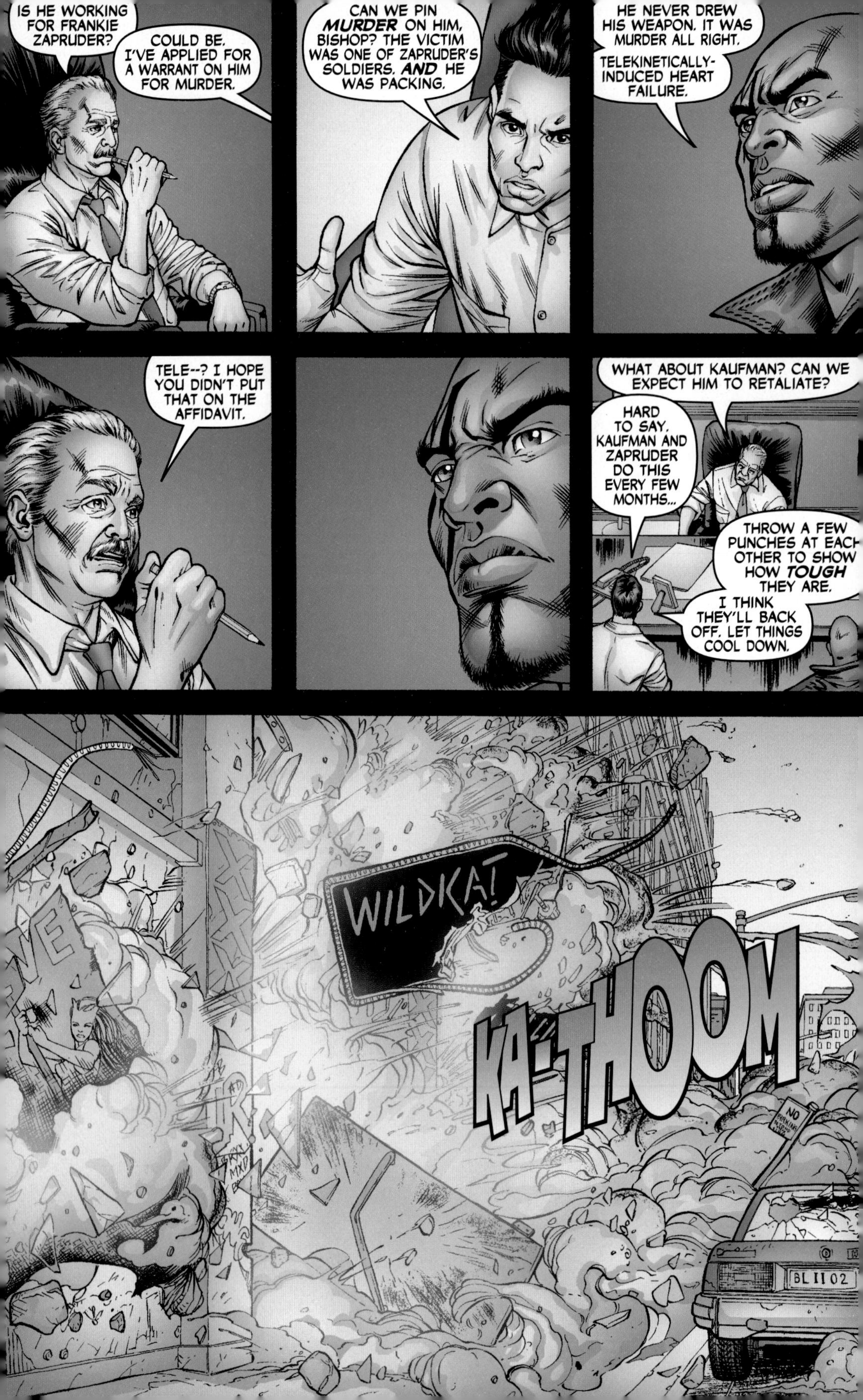
IS HE WORKING FOR FRANKIE ZAPRUDER?
COULD BE. I'VE APPLIED FOR A WARRANT ON HIM FOR MURDER.
CAN WE PIN **MURDER** ON HIM, BISHOP? THE VICTIM WAS ONE OF ZAPRUDER'S SOLDIERS. **AND** HE WAS PACKING.
HE NEVER DREW HIS WEAPON. IT WAS MURDER ALL RIGHT.
TELEKINETICALLY-INDUCED HEART FAILURE.
TELE--? I HOPE YOU DIDN'T PUT THAT ON THE AFFIDAVIT.
WHAT ABOUT KAUFMAN? CAN WE EXPECT HIM TO RETALIATE?
HARD TO SAY. KAUFMAN AND ZAPRUDER DO THIS EVERY FEW MONTHS...
THROW A FEW PUNCHES AT EACH OTHER TO SHOW HOW **TOUGH** THEY ARE.
I THINK THEY'LL BACK OFF. LET THINGS COOL DOWN.
WILDKAT
KA-THOOM
NO PARKING
BL II 02

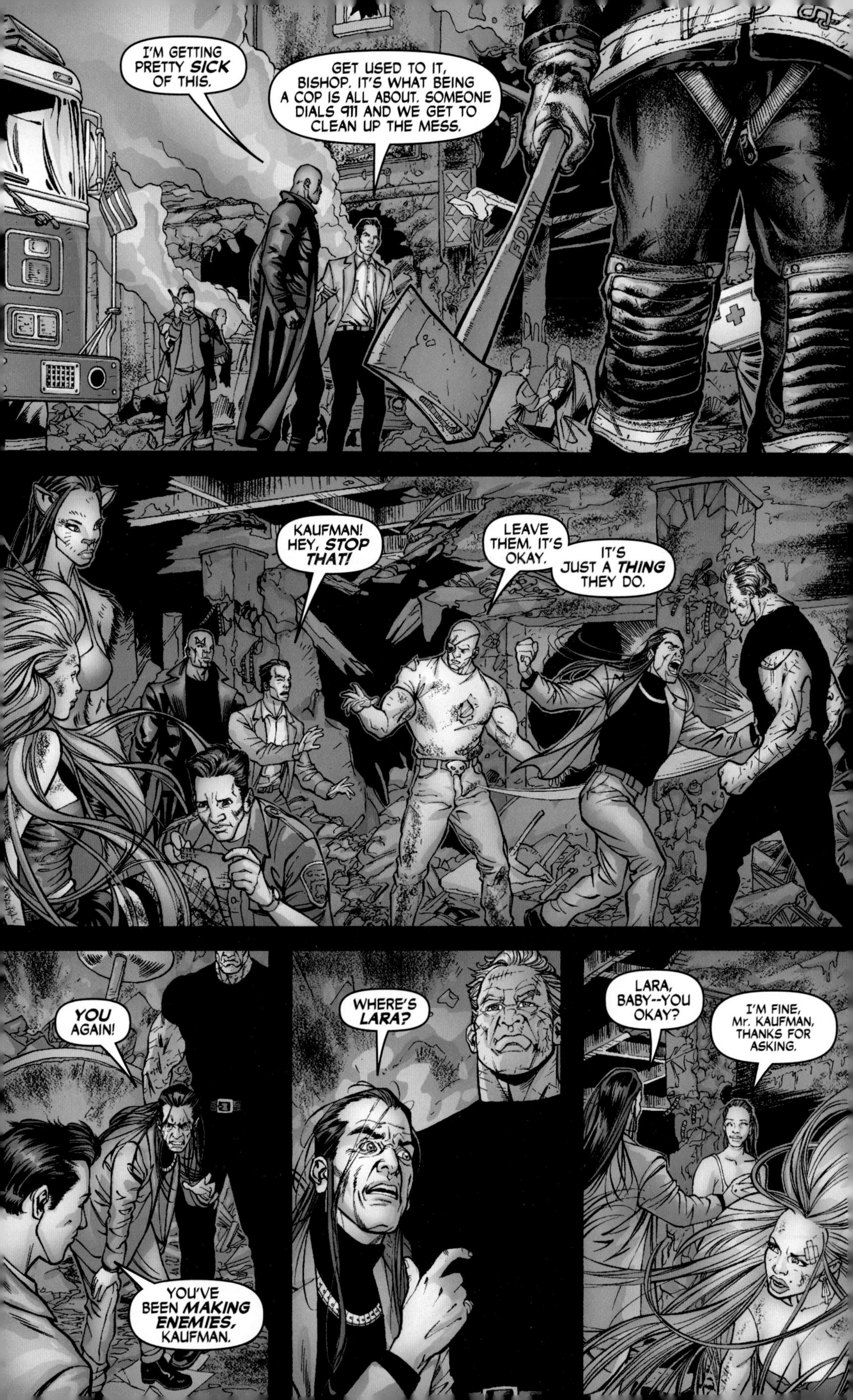

I'M GETTING PRETTY SICK OF THIS.
GET USED TO IT, BISHOP. IT'S WHAT BEING A COP IS ALL ABOUT. SOMEONE DIALS 911 AND WE GET TO CLEAN UP THE MESS.
FDNY
KAUFMAN! HEY, STOP THAT!
LEAVE THEM. IT'S OKAY.
IT'S JUST A THING THEY DO.
YOU AGAIN!
YOU'VE BEEN MAKING ENEMIES, KAUFMAN.
WHERE'S LARA?
LARA, BABY--YOU OKAY?
I'M FINE, Mr. KAUFMAN, THANKS FOR ASKING.

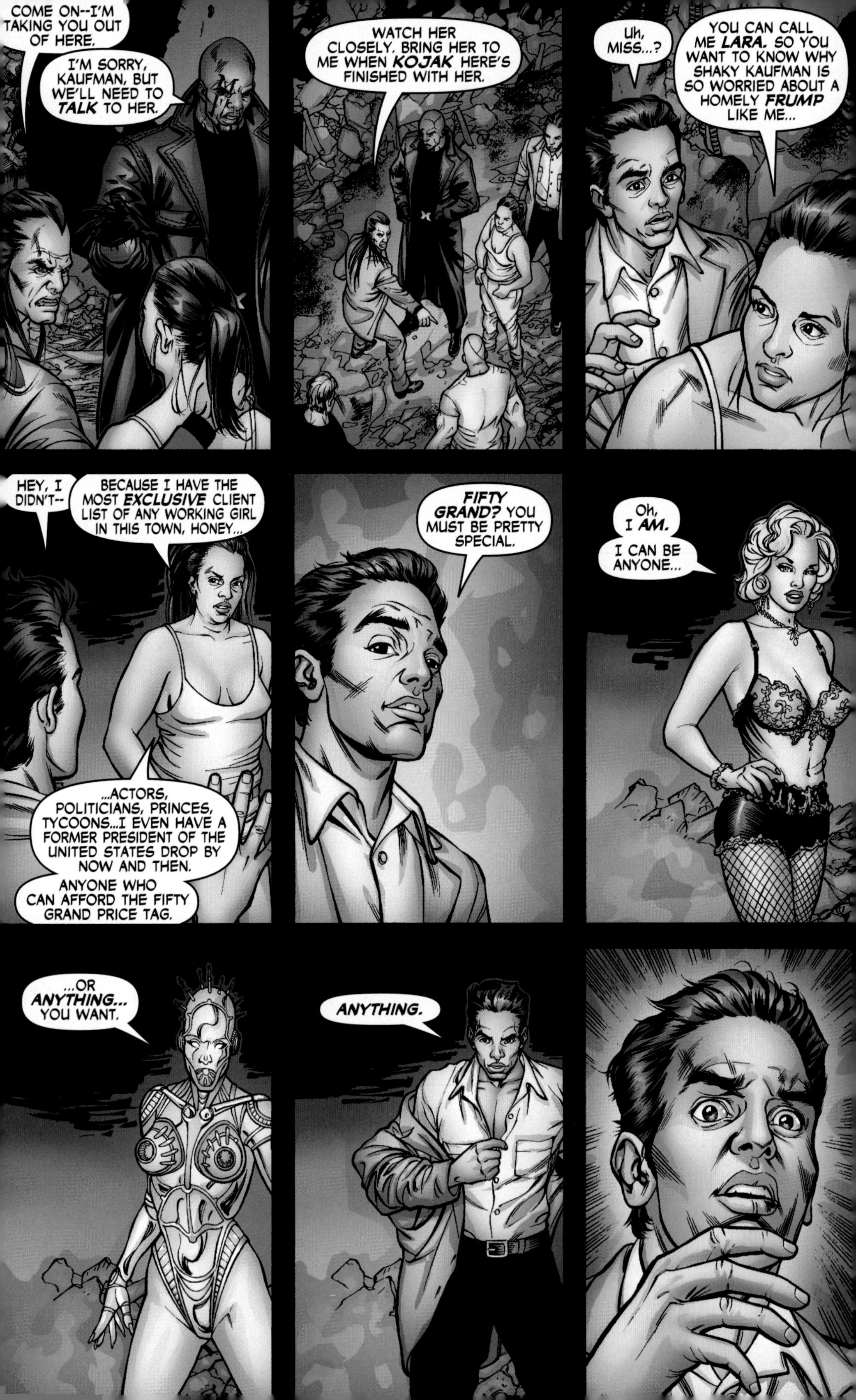
COME ON--I'M TAKING YOU OUT OF HERE.
I'M SORRY, KAUFMAN, BUT WE'LL NEED TO TALK TO HER.
WATCH HER CLOSELY. BRING HER TO ME WHEN KOJAK HERE'S FINISHED WITH HER.
UH, MISS...?
YOU CAN CALL ME LARA. SO YOU WANT TO KNOW WHY SHAKY KAUFMAN IS SO WORRIED ABOUT A HOMELY FRUMP LIKE ME...
HEY, I DIDN'T--
BECAUSE I HAVE THE MOST EXCLUSIVE CLIENT LIST OF ANY WORKING GIRL IN THIS TOWN, HONEY...
...ACTORS, POLITICIANS, PRINCES, TYCOONS...I EVEN HAVE A FORMER PRESIDENT OF THE UNITED STATES DROP BY NOW AND THEN.
ANYONE WHO CAN AFFORD THE FIFTY GRAND PRICE TAG.
FIFTY GRAND? YOU MUST BE PRETTY SPECIAL.
OH, I AM.
I CAN BE ANYONE...
...OR ANYTHING... YOU WANT.
ANYTHING.

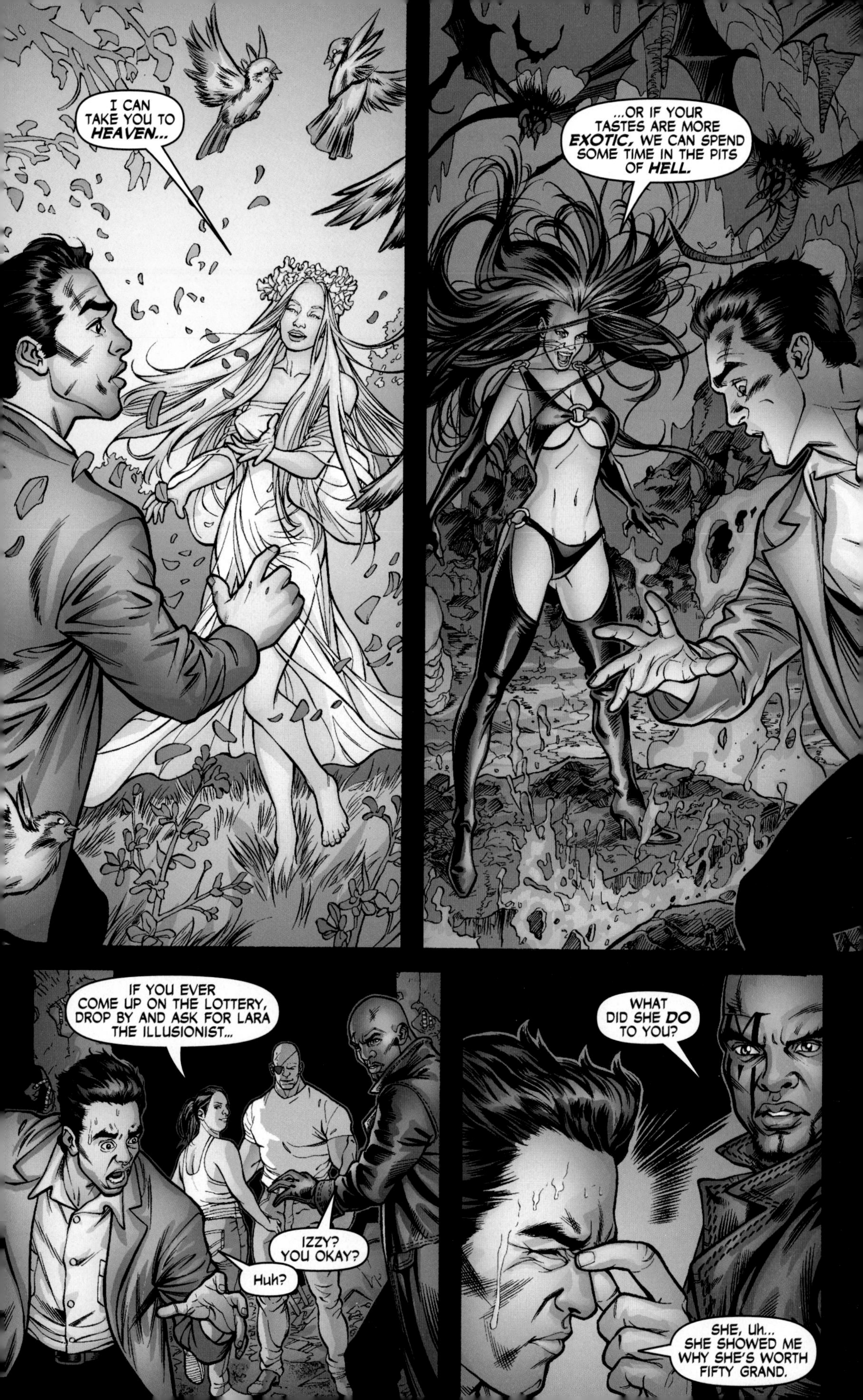
I CAN TAKE YOU TO HEAVEN...
...OR IF YOUR TASTES ARE MORE EXOTIC, WE CAN SPEND SOME TIME IN THE PITS OF HELL.
IF YOU EVER COME UP ON THE LOTTERY, DROP BY AND ASK FOR LARA THE ILLUSIONIST...
IZZY? YOU OKAY?
Huh?
WHAT DID SHE DO TO YOU?
SHE, UH... SHE SHOWED ME WHY SHE'S WORTH FIFTY GRAND.

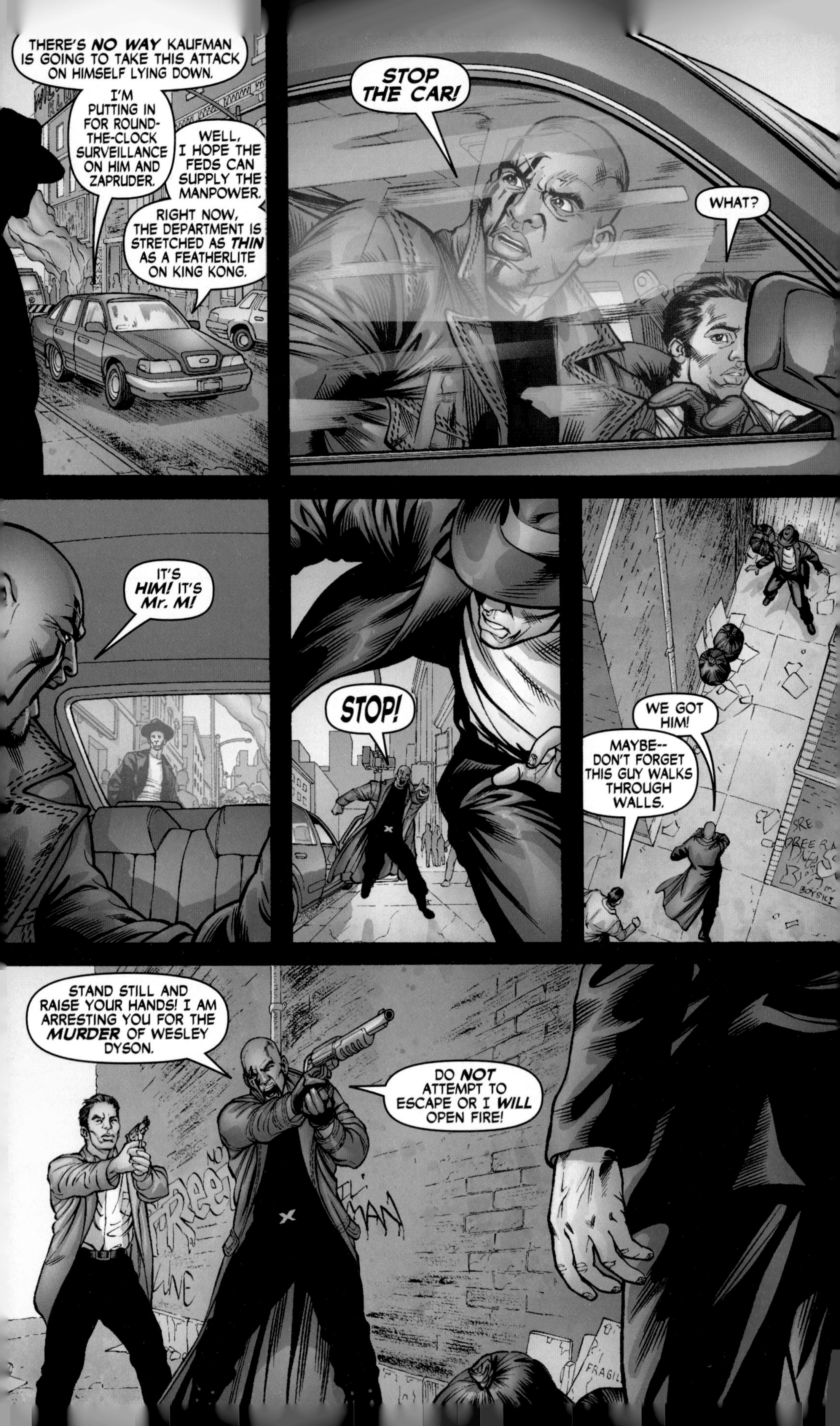
THERE'S **NO WAY** KAUFMAN IS GOING TO TAKE THIS ATTACK ON HIMSELF LYING DOWN.
I'M PUTTING IN FOR ROUND-THE-CLOCK SURVEILLANCE ON HIM AND ZAPRUDER.
WELL, I HOPE THE FEDS CAN SUPPLY THE MANPOWER.
RIGHT NOW, THE DEPARTMENT IS STRETCHED AS **THIN** AS A FEATHERLITE ON KING KONG.
STOP THE CAR!
WHAT?
IT'S **HIM!** IT'S **Mr. M!**
STOP!
WE GOT HIM!
MAYBE-- DON'T FORGET THIS GUY WALKS THROUGH WALLS.
STAND STILL AND RAISE YOUR HANDS! I AM ARRESTING YOU FOR THE **MURDER** OF WESLEY DYSON.
DO **NOT** ATTEMPT TO ESCAPE OR I **WILL** OPEN FIRE!

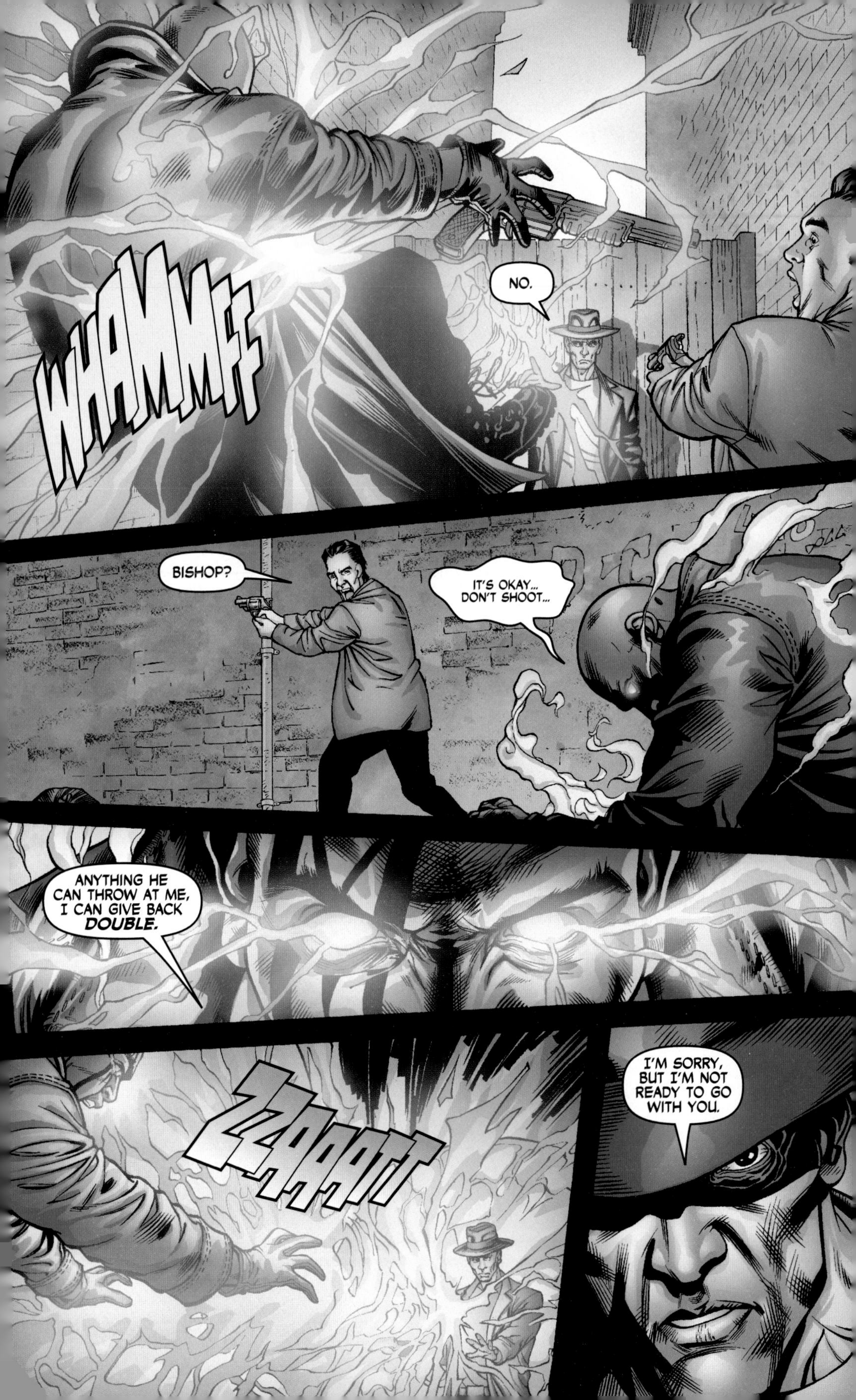
WHAMMFF
NO.
BISHOP?
IT'S OKAY... DON'T SHOOT...
ANYTHING HE CAN THROW AT ME, I CAN GIVE BACK DOUBLE.
ZZAAATTT
I'M SORRY, BUT I'M NOT READY TO GO WITH YOU.

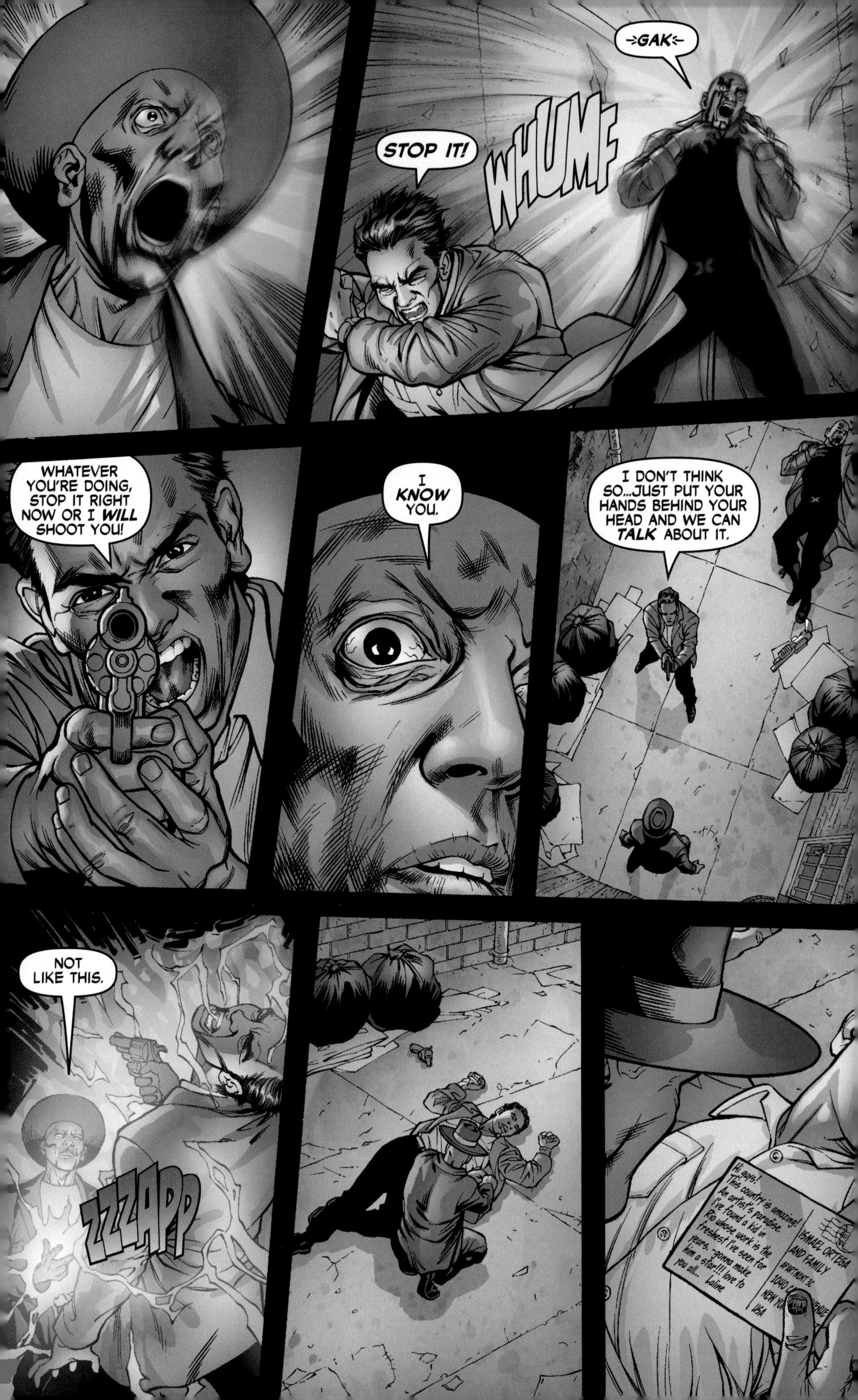

-GAK-
STOP IT!
WHUMF
WHATEVER YOU'RE DOING, STOP IT RIGHT NOW OR I WILL SHOOT YOU!
I KNOW YOU.
I DON'T THINK SO...JUST PUT YOUR HANDS BEHIND YOUR HEAD AND WE CAN TALK ABOUT IT.
NOT LIKE THIS.
ZZZAPP
Hi guys! This country is amazing! An artist's paradise. I've found a kid in Rio whose work is the freshest I've seen for years. --gonna make him a star!!! love to you all... Laline
ISMAEL ORTEGA AND FAMILY
APARTMENT 3C
USA

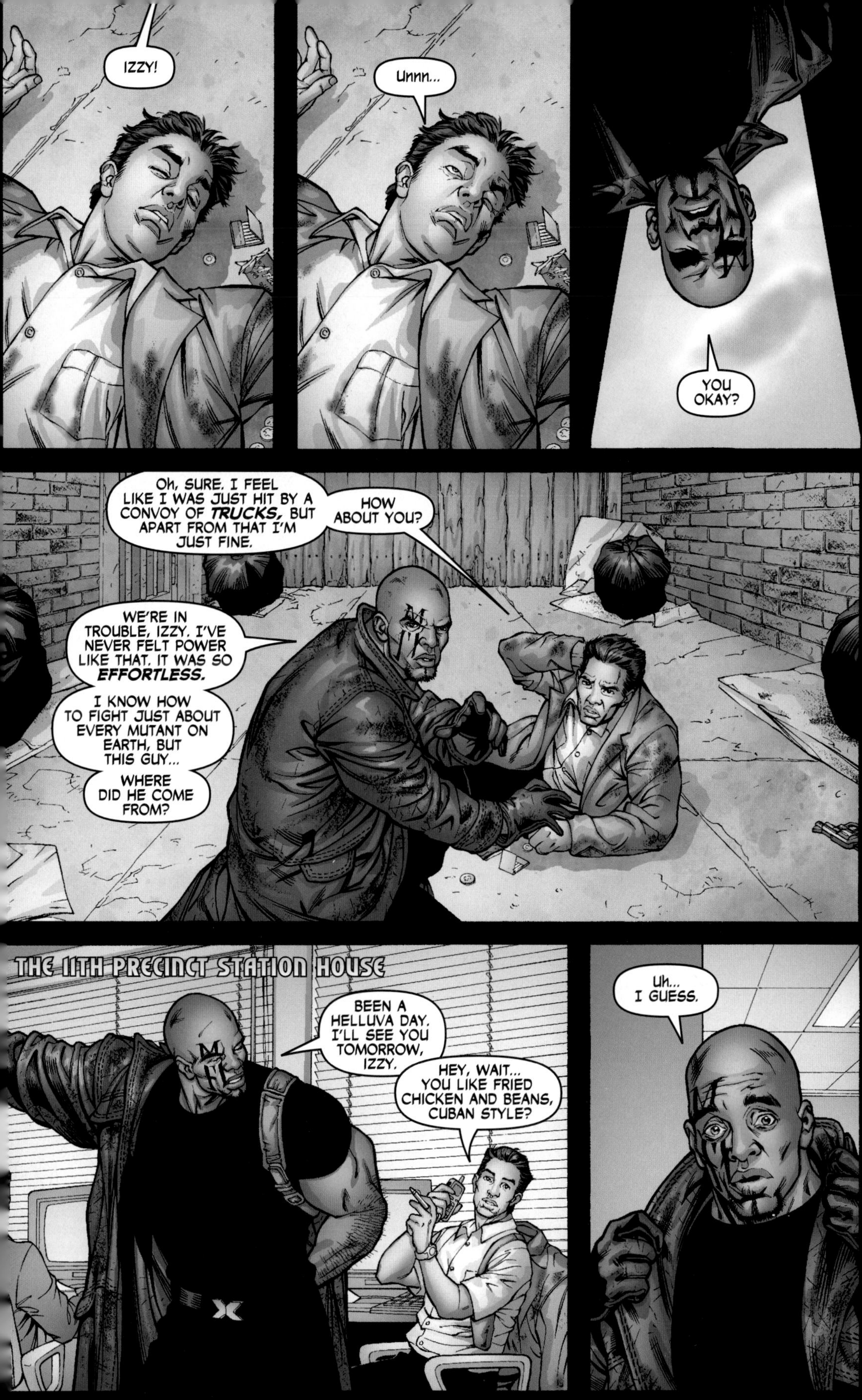
IZZY!
Unnn...
YOU OKAY?
Oh, SURE. I FEEL LIKE I WAS JUST HIT BY A CONVOY OF TRUCKS, BUT APART FROM THAT I'M JUST FINE.
HOW ABOUT YOU?
WE'RE IN TROUBLE, IZZY. I'VE NEVER FELT POWER LIKE THAT. IT WAS SO EFFORTLESS.
I KNOW HOW TO FIGHT JUST ABOUT EVERY MUTANT ON EARTH, BUT THIS GUY...
WHERE DID HE COME FROM?
THE 11TH PRECINCT STATION HOUSE
BEEN A HELLUVA DAY. I'LL SEE YOU TOMORROW, IZZY.
HEY, WAIT... YOU LIKE FRIED CHICKEN AND BEANS, CUBAN STYLE?
Uh... I GUESS.

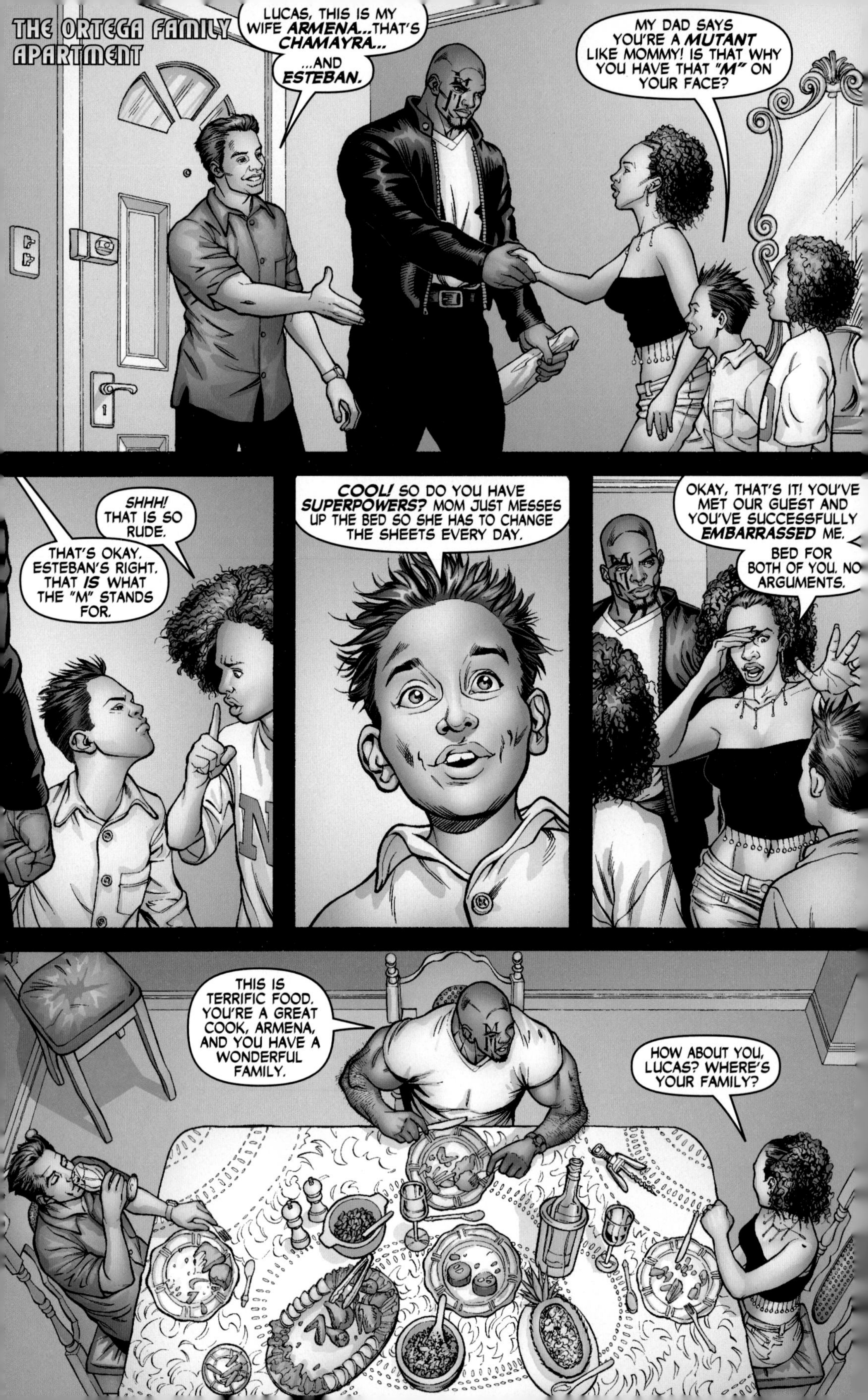
THE ORTEGA FAMILY APARTMENT
LUCAS, THIS IS MY WIFE ARMENA...THAT'S CHAMAYRA...
...AND ESTEBAN.
MY DAD SAYS YOU'RE A MUTANT LIKE MOMMY! IS THAT WHY YOU HAVE THAT "M" ON YOUR FACE?
SHHH! THAT IS SO RUDE.
THAT'S OKAY. ESTEBAN'S RIGHT. THAT IS WHAT THE "M" STANDS FOR.
COOL! SO DO YOU HAVE SUPERPOWERS? MOM JUST MESSES UP THE BED SO SHE HAS TO CHANGE THE SHEETS EVERY DAY.
OKAY, THAT'S IT! YOU'VE MET OUR GUEST AND YOU'VE SUCCESSFULLY EMBARRASSED ME.
BED FOR BOTH OF YOU. NO ARGUMENTS.
THIS IS TERRIFIC FOOD. YOU'RE A GREAT COOK, ARMENA, AND YOU HAVE A WONDERFUL FAMILY.
HOW ABOUT YOU, LUCAS? WHERE'S YOUR FAMILY?

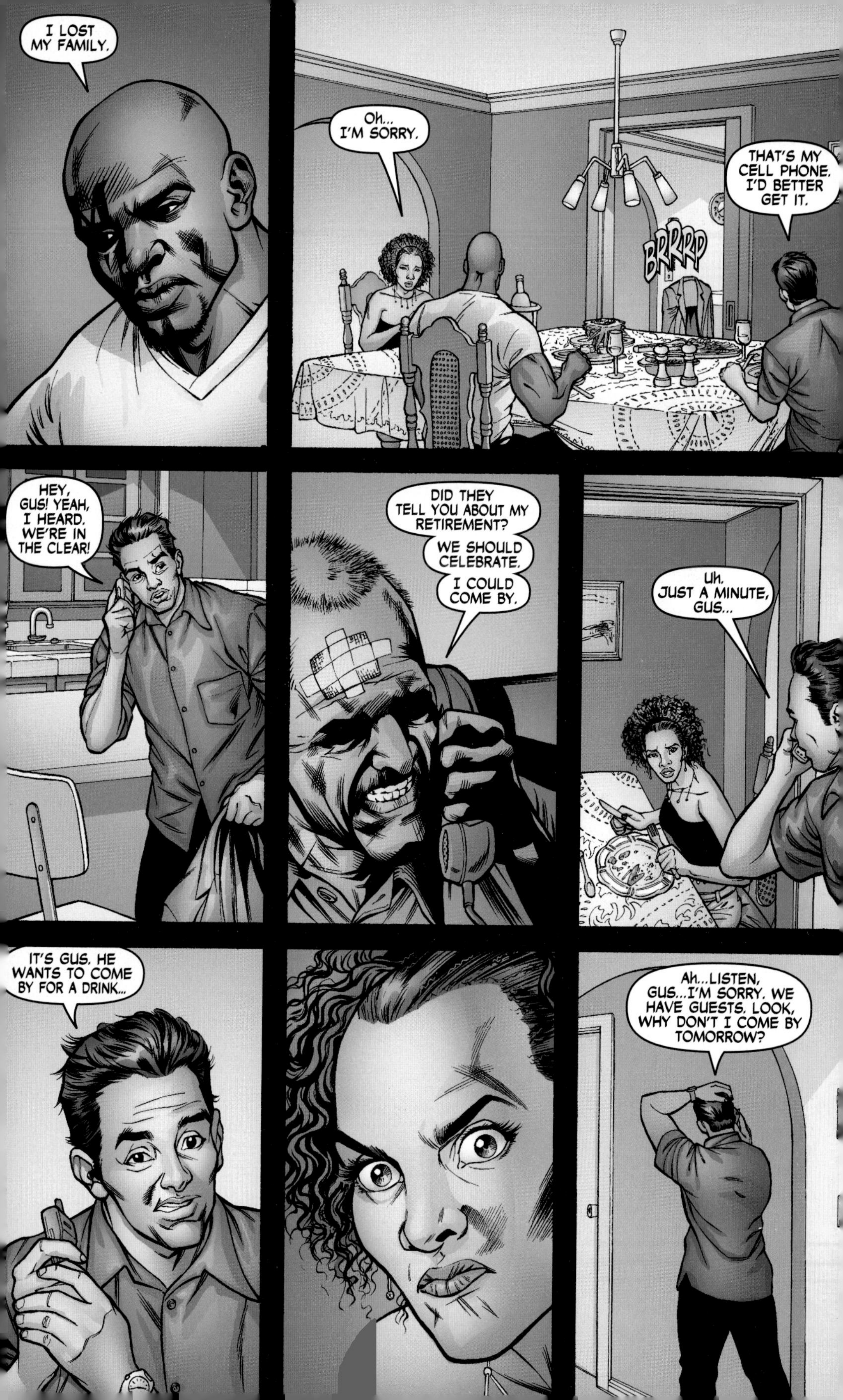
I LOST MY FAMILY.
Oh... I'M SORRY.
BRRRP
THAT'S MY CELL PHONE. I'D BETTER GET IT.
HEY, GUS! YEAH, I HEARD. WE'RE IN THE CLEAR!
DID THEY TELL YOU ABOUT MY RETIREMENT?
WE SHOULD CELEBRATE.
I COULD COME BY.
Uh. JUST A MINUTE, GUS...
IT'S GUS. HE WANTS TO COME BY FOR A DRINK...
Ah...LISTEN, GUS...I'M SORRY. WE HAVE GUESTS. LOOK, WHY DON'T I COME BY TOMORROW?

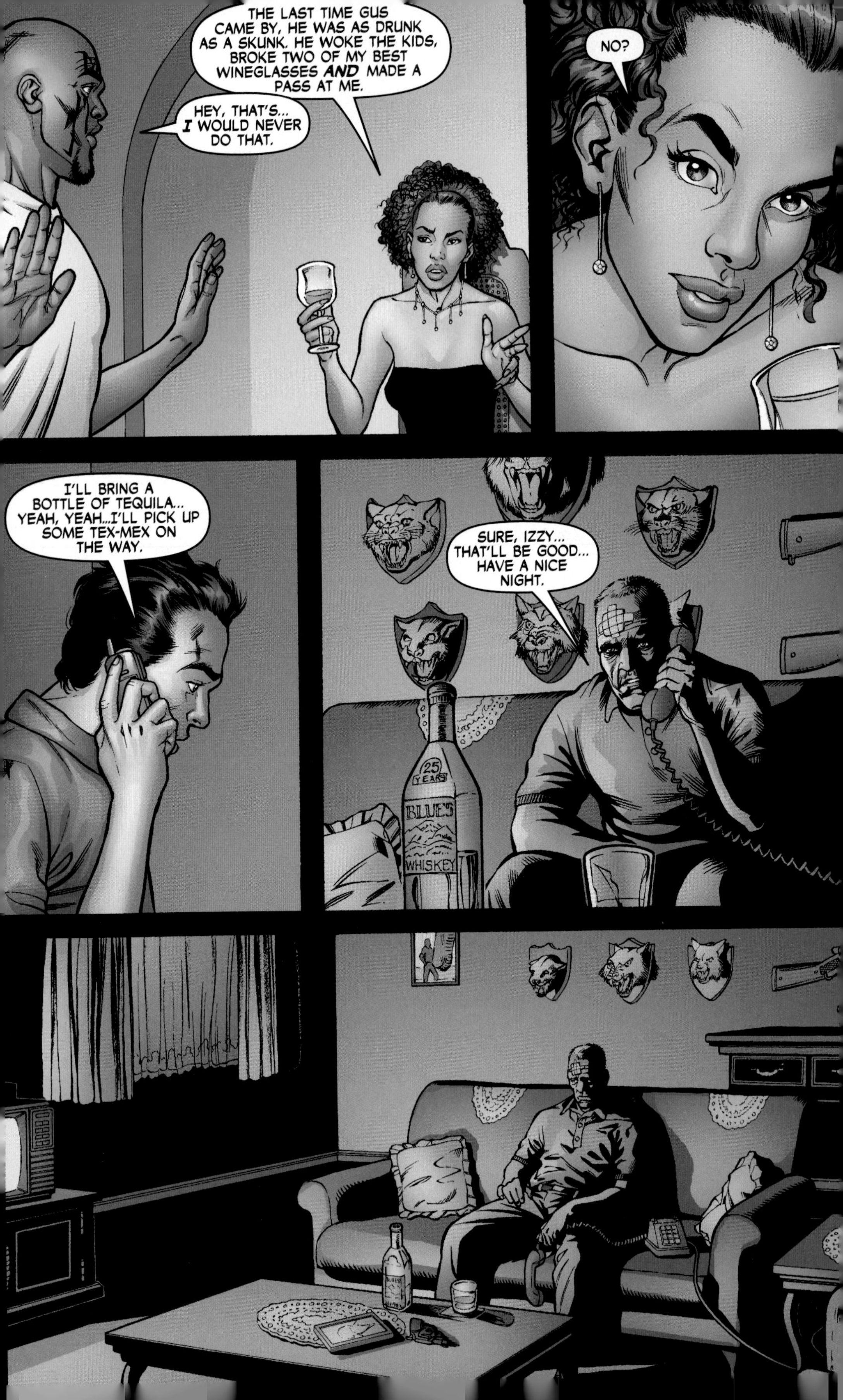
THE LAST TIME GUS CAME BY, HE WAS AS DRUNK AS A SKUNK. HE WOKE THE KIDS, BROKE TWO OF MY BEST WINEGLASSES *AND* MADE A PASS AT ME.
HEY, THAT'S... *I* WOULD NEVER DO THAT.
NO?
I'LL BRING A BOTTLE OF TEQUILA... YEAH, YEAH...I'LL PICK UP SOME TEX-MEX ON THE WAY.
SURE, IZZY... THAT'LL BE GOOD... HAVE A NICE NIGHT.
25 YEARS
BLUES
WHISKEY

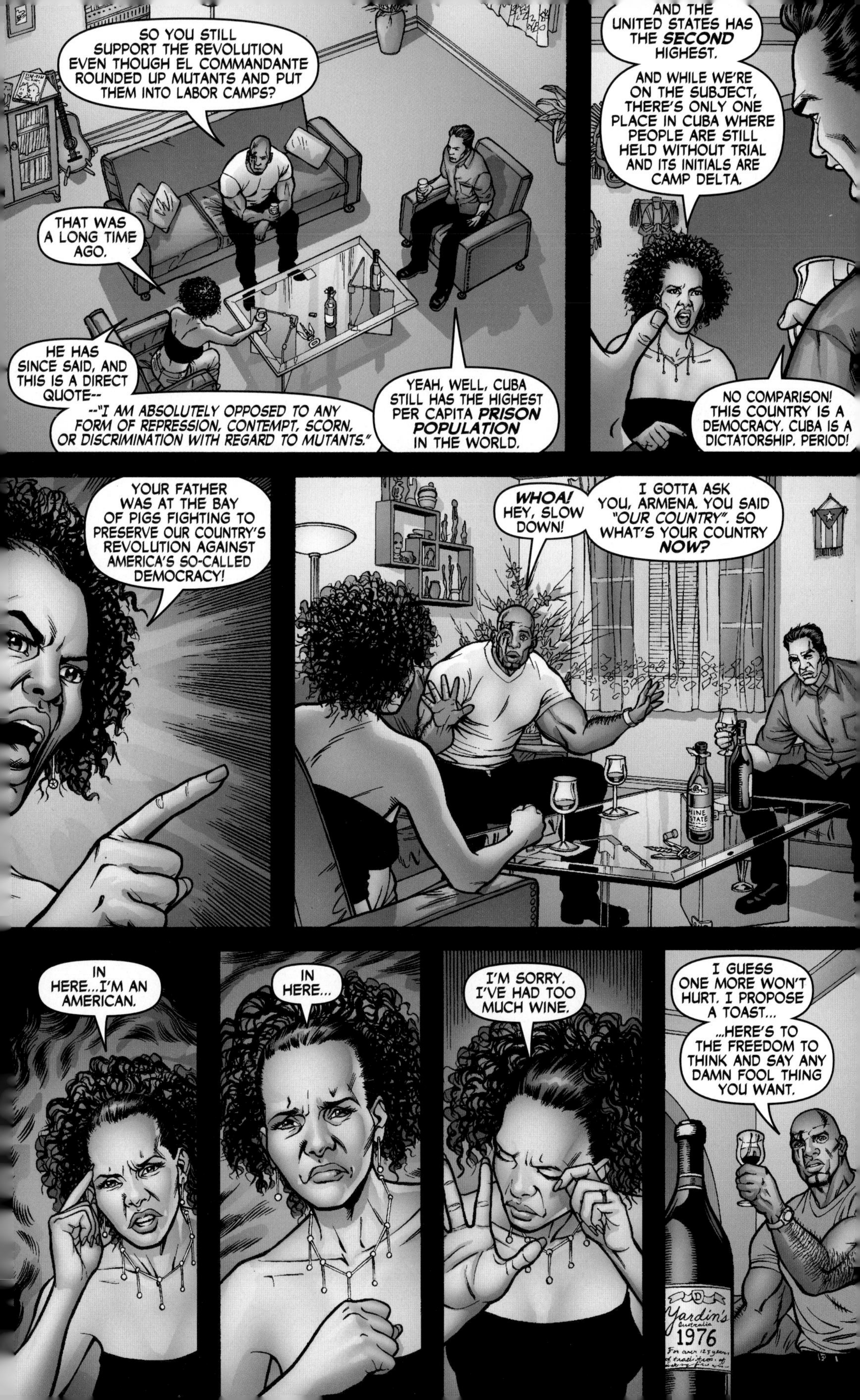
SO YOU STILL SUPPORT THE REVOLUTION EVEN THOUGH EL COMMANDANTE ROUNDED UP MUTANTS AND PUT THEM INTO LABOR CAMPS?
THAT WAS A LONG TIME AGO.
HE HAS SINCE SAID, AND THIS IS A DIRECT QUOTE--
--"I AM ABSOLUTELY OPPOSED TO ANY FORM OF REPRESSION, CONTEMPT, SCORN, OR DISCRIMINATION WITH REGARD TO MUTANTS."
YEAH, WELL, CUBA STILL HAS THE HIGHEST PER CAPITA PRISON POPULATION IN THE WORLD.
AND THE UNITED STATES HAS THE SECOND HIGHEST.
AND WHILE WE'RE ON THE SUBJECT, THERE'S ONLY ONE PLACE IN CUBA WHERE PEOPLE ARE STILL HELD WITHOUT TRIAL AND ITS INITIALS ARE CAMP DELTA.
NO COMPARISON! THIS COUNTRY IS A DEMOCRACY. CUBA IS A DICTATORSHIP. PERIOD!
YOUR FATHER WAS AT THE BAY OF PIGS FIGHTING TO PRESERVE OUR COUNTRY'S REVOLUTION AGAINST AMERICA'S SO-CALLED DEMOCRACY!
WHOA! HEY, SLOW DOWN!
I GOTTA ASK YOU, ARMENA. YOU SAID "OUR COUNTRY". SO WHAT'S YOUR COUNTRY NOW?
IN HERE...I'M AN AMERICAN.
IN HERE...
I'M SORRY. I'VE HAD TOO MUCH WINE.
I GUESS ONE MORE WON'T HURT. I PROPOSE A TOAST...
...HERE'S TO THE FREEDOM TO THINK AND SAY ANY DAMN FOOL THING YOU WANT.
Yardin's
1976

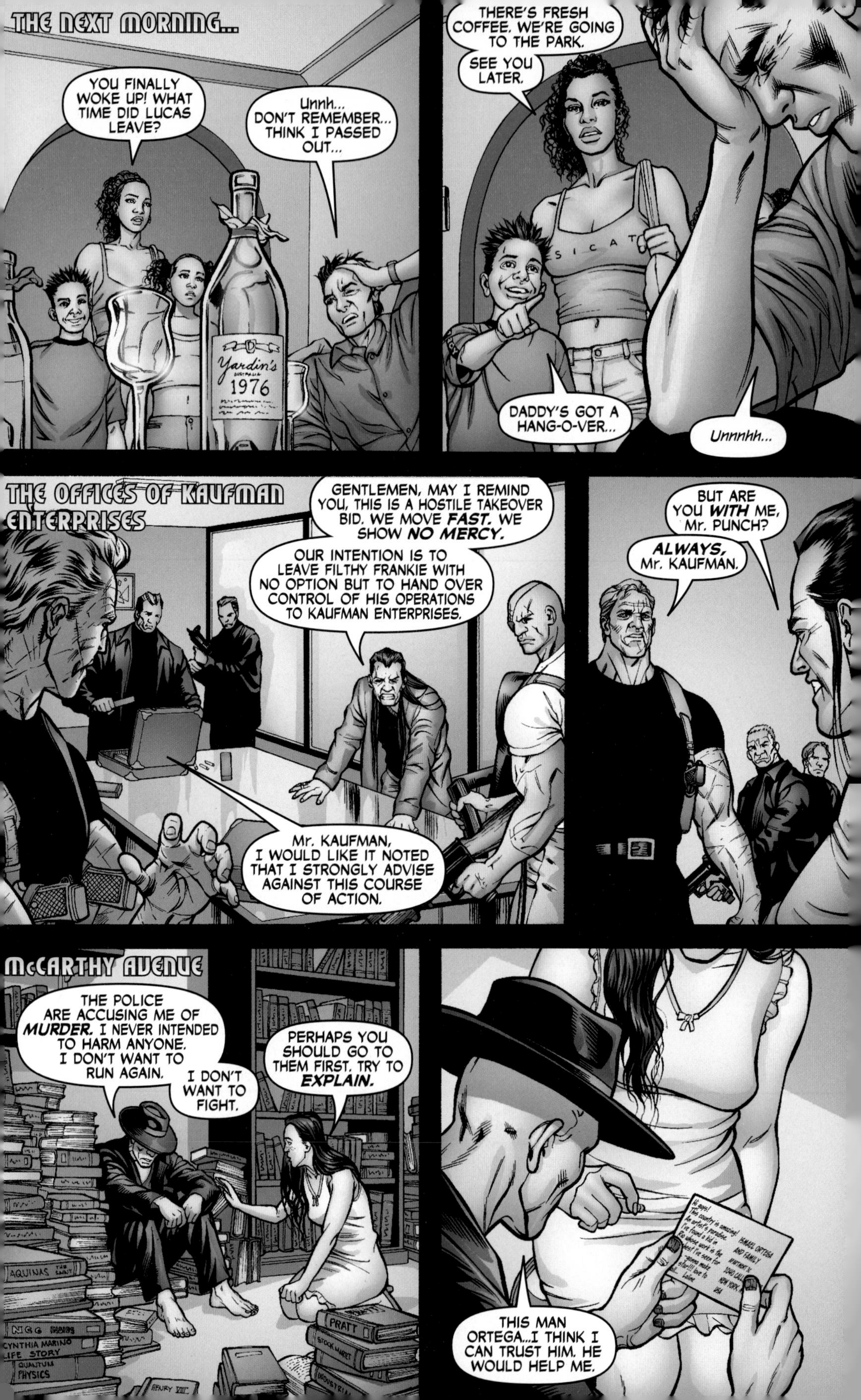
THE NEXT MORNING...
YOU FINALLY WOKE UP! WHAT TIME DID LUCAS LEAVE?
Unnh... DON'T REMEMBER... THINK I PASSED OUT...
THERE'S FRESH COFFEE. WE'RE GOING TO THE PARK.
SEE YOU LATER.
DADDY'S GOT A HANG-O-VER...
Unnnhh...
THE OFFICES OF KAUFMAN ENTERPRISES
GENTLEMEN, MAY I REMIND YOU, THIS IS A HOSTILE TAKEOVER BID. WE MOVE FAST. WE SHOW NO MERCY.
OUR INTENTION IS TO LEAVE FILTHY FRANKIE WITH NO OPTION BUT TO HAND OVER CONTROL OF HIS OPERATIONS TO KAUFMAN ENTERPRISES.
Mr. KAUFMAN, I WOULD LIKE IT NOTED THAT I STRONGLY ADVISE AGAINST THIS COURSE OF ACTION.
BUT ARE YOU WITH ME, Mr. PUNCH?
ALWAYS, Mr. KAUFMAN.
McCARTHY AVENUE
THE POLICE ARE ACCUSING ME OF MURDER. I NEVER INTENDED TO HARM ANYONE. I DON'T WANT TO RUN AGAIN.
I DON'T WANT TO FIGHT.
PERHAPS YOU SHOULD GO TO THEM FIRST. TRY TO EXPLAIN.
THIS MAN ORTEGA...I THINK I CAN TRUST HIM. HE WOULD HELP ME.

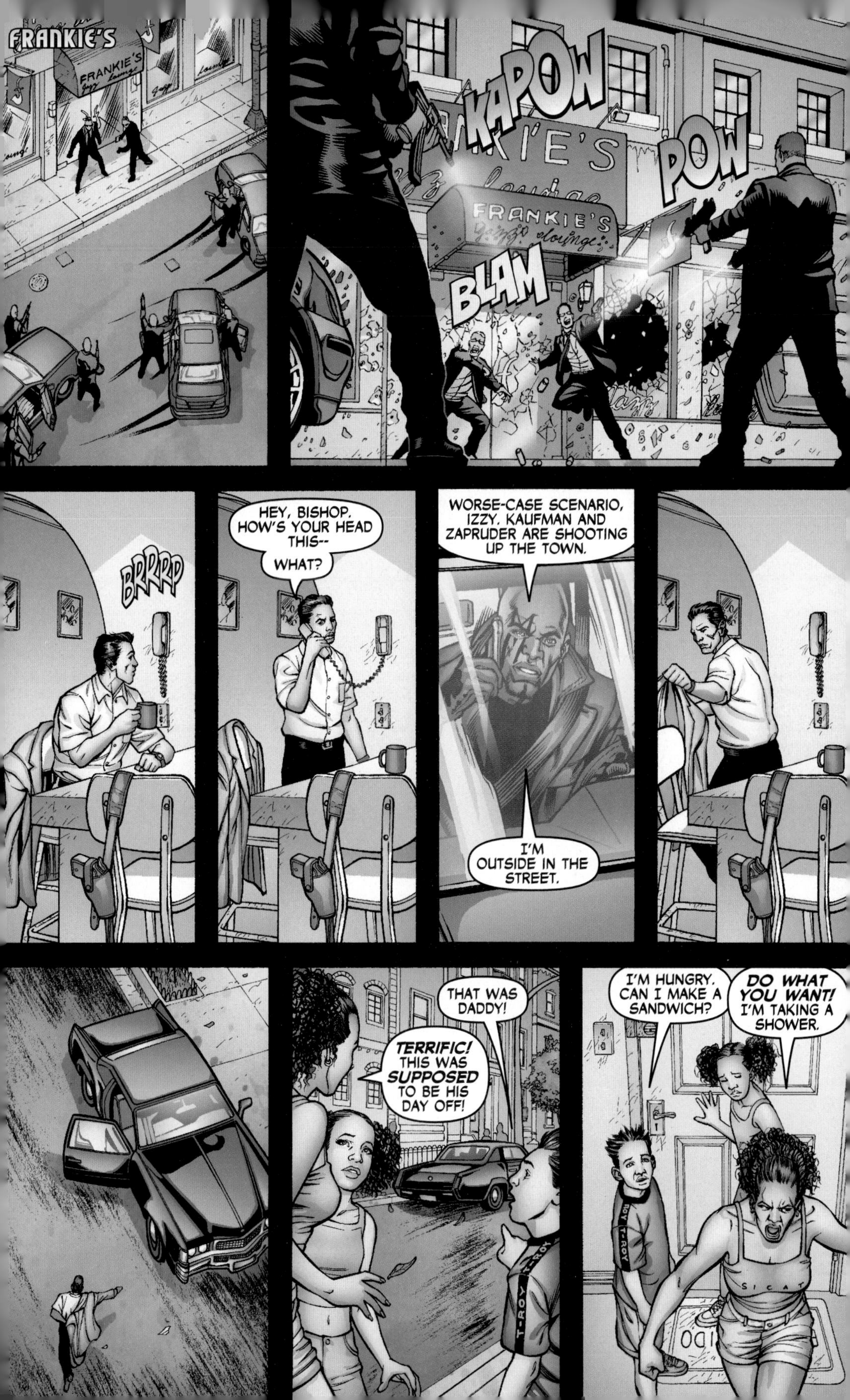
FRANKIE'S
KAPOW
POW
BLAM
BRRRAP
HEY, BISHOP. HOW'S YOUR HEAD THIS--
WHAT?
WORSE-CASE SCENARIO, IZZY. KAUFMAN AND ZAPRUDER ARE SHOOTING UP THE TOWN.
I'M OUTSIDE IN THE STREET.
THAT WAS DADDY!
TERRIFIC! THIS WAS SUPPOSED TO BE HIS DAY OFF!
I'M HUNGRY. CAN I MAKE A SANDWICH?
DO WHAT YOU WANT! I'M TAKING A SHOWER.

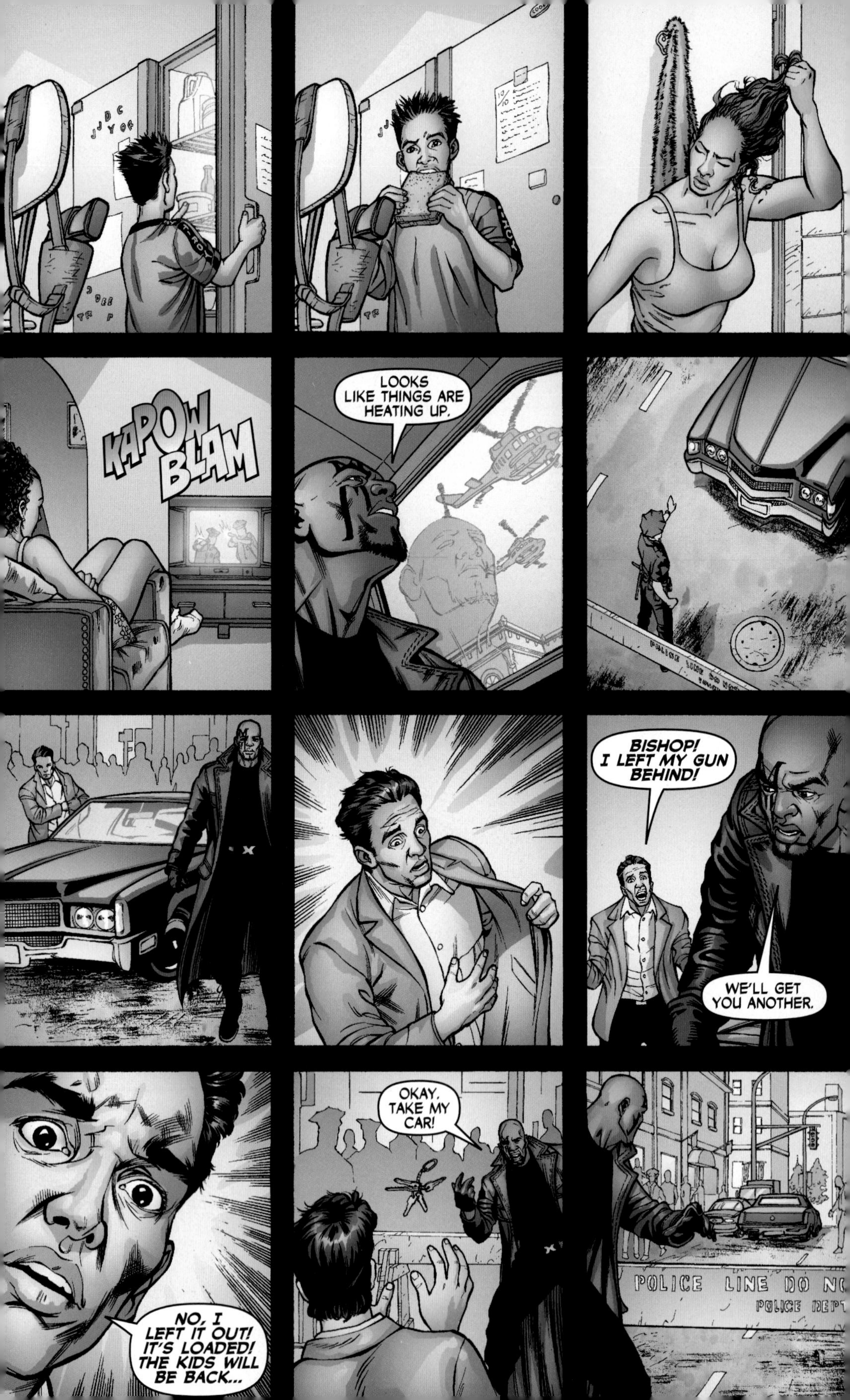
KAPOW
BLAM
LOOKS LIKE THINGS ARE HEATING UP.
POLICE LINE DO NOT
BISHOP! I LEFT MY GUN BEHIND!
WE'LL GET YOU ANOTHER.
NO, I LEFT IT OUT! IT'S LOADED! THE KIDS WILL BE BACK...
OKAY, TAKE MY CAR!
POLICE LINE DO N
POLICE DEPT

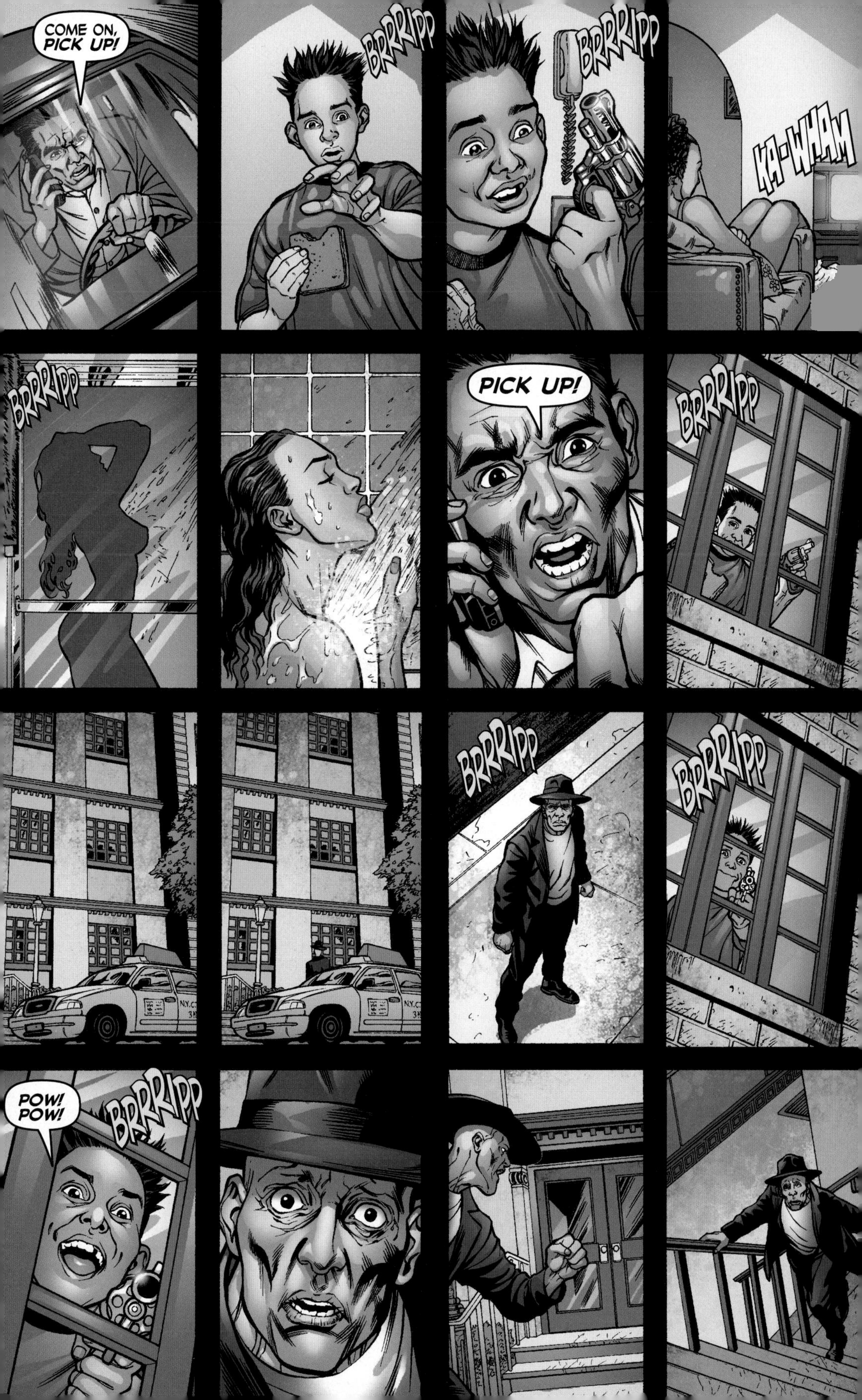
COME ON, PICK UP!
BRRRIPP
BRRRIPP
KA-WHAM
BRRRIPP
PICK UP!
BRRRIPP
BRRRIPP
BRRRIPP
POW! POW!
BRRRIPP

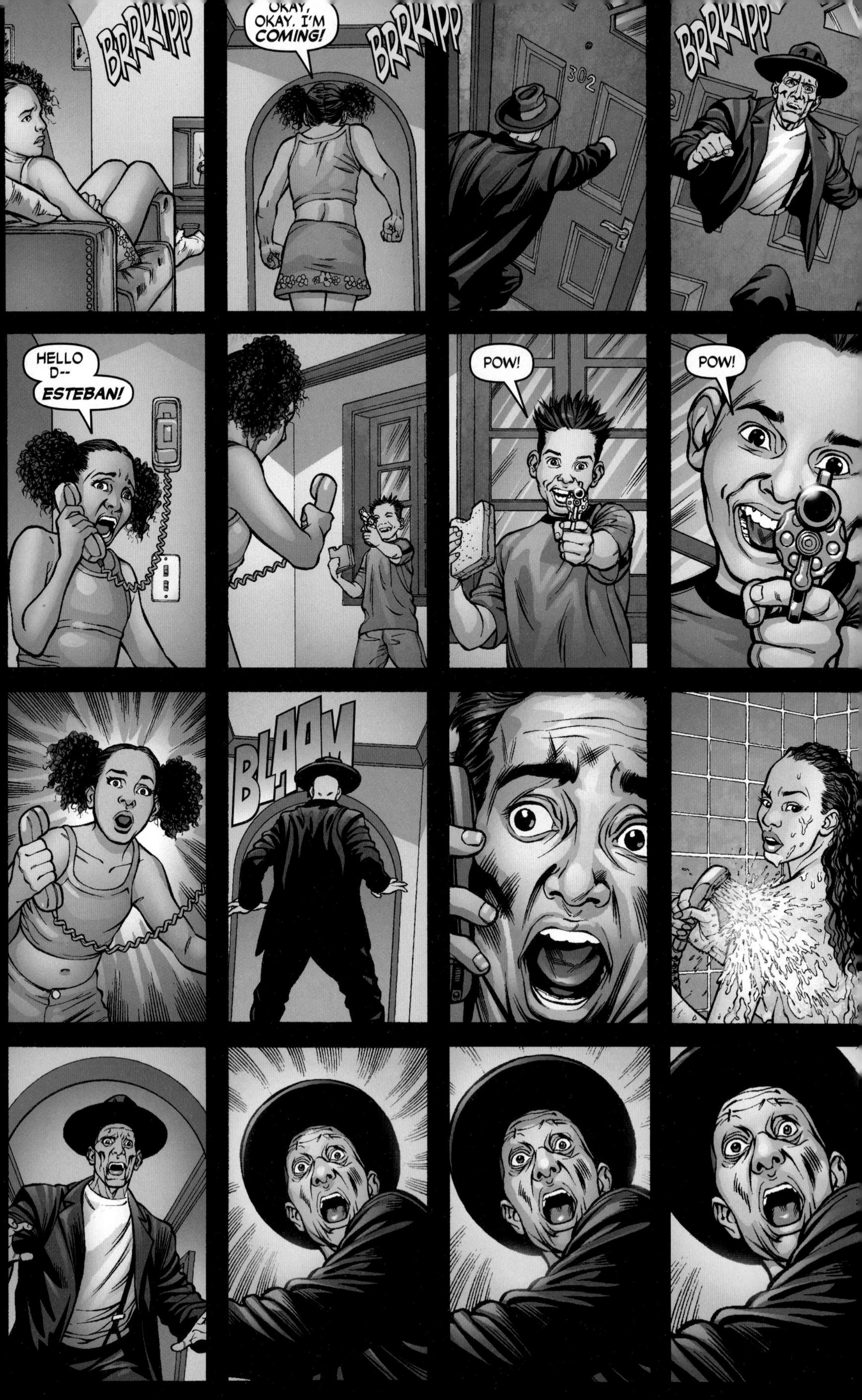
BRRRIPP
OKAY, OKAY. I'M COMING!
BRRRIPP
302
BRRRIPP
HELLO D-- ESTEBAN!
POW!
POW!
BLAAM

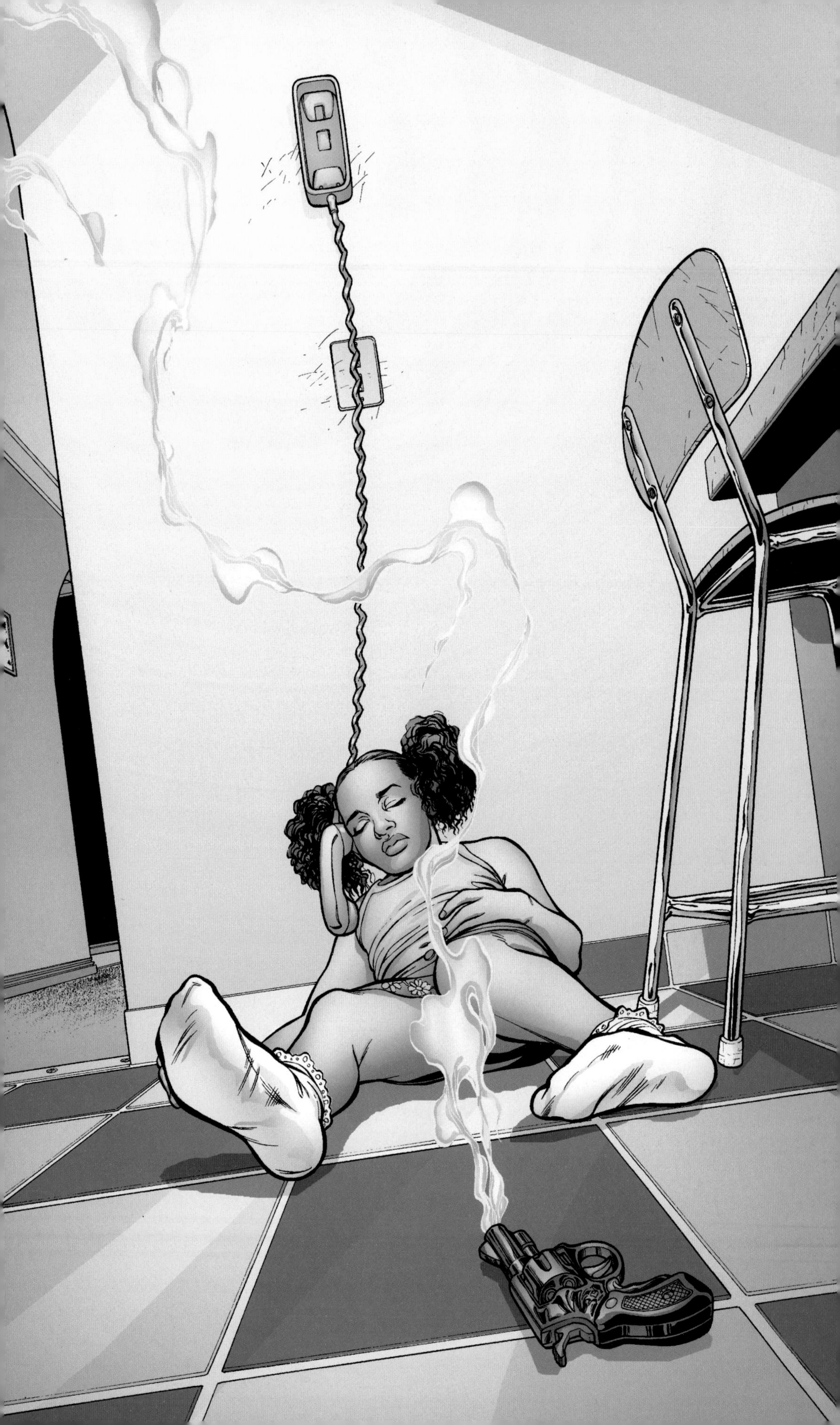

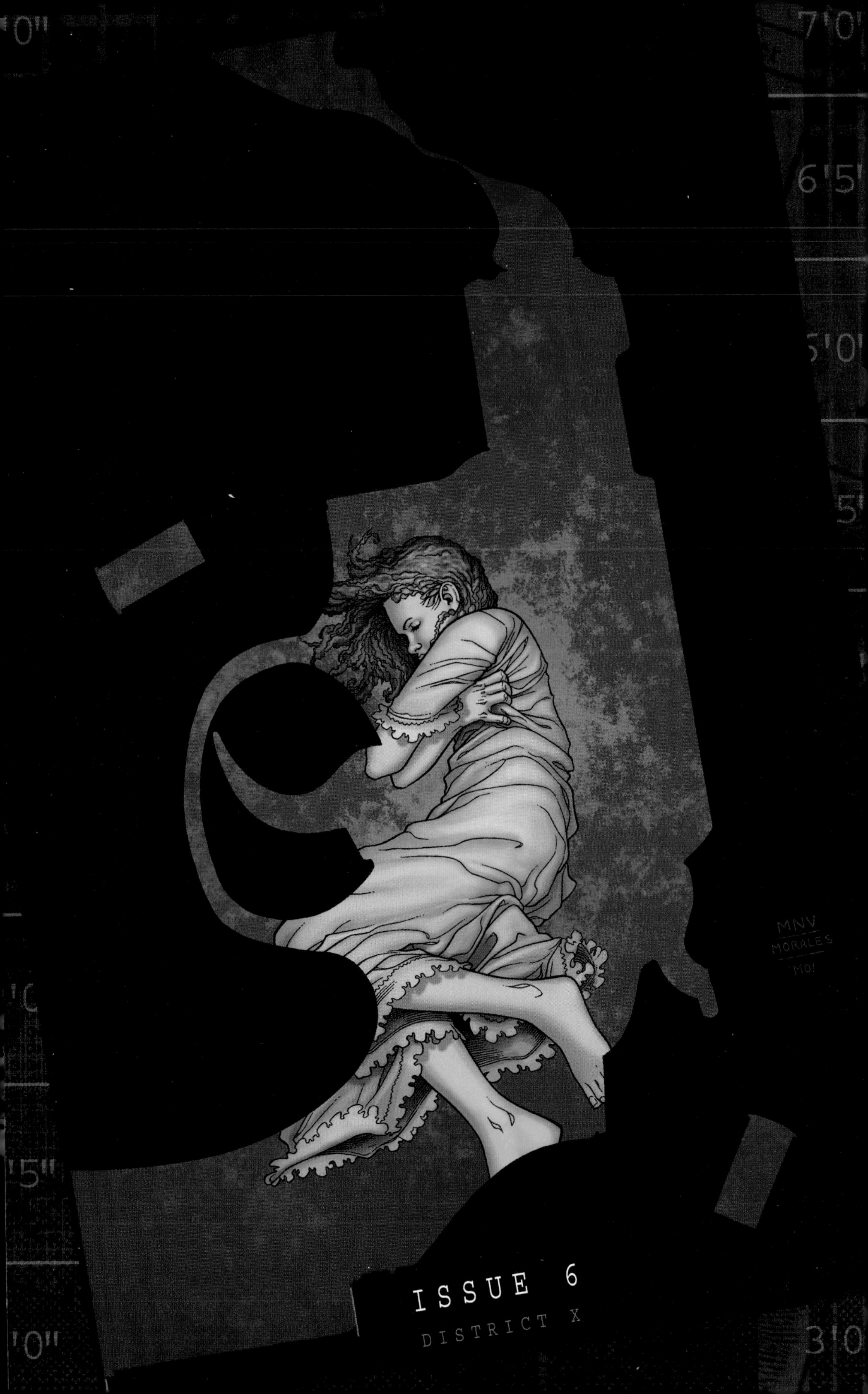
ISSUE 6
DISTRICT X

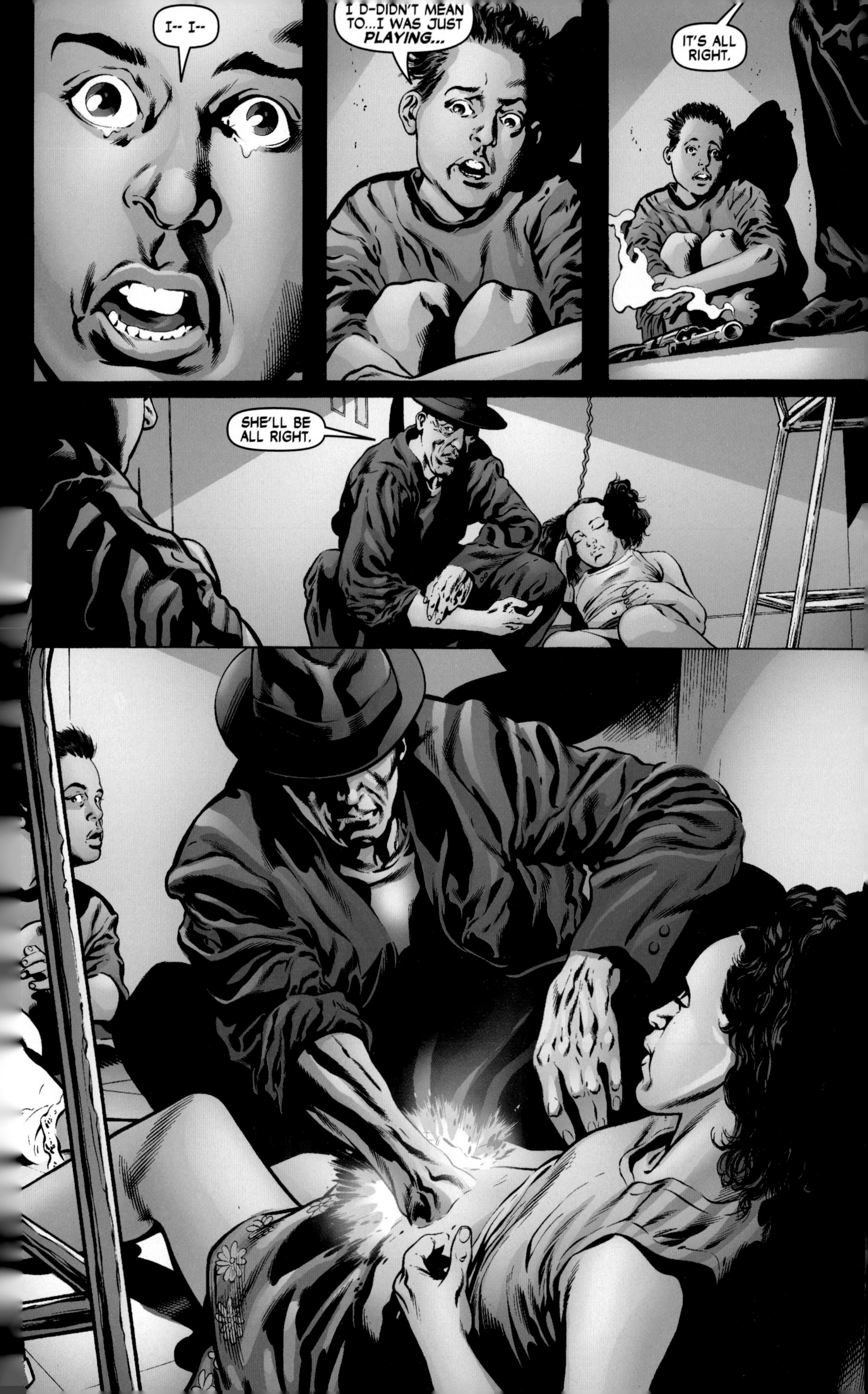
I-- I--
I D-DIDN'T MEAN TO...I WAS JUST *PLAYING...*
IT'S ALL RIGHT.
SHE'LL BE ALL RIGHT.

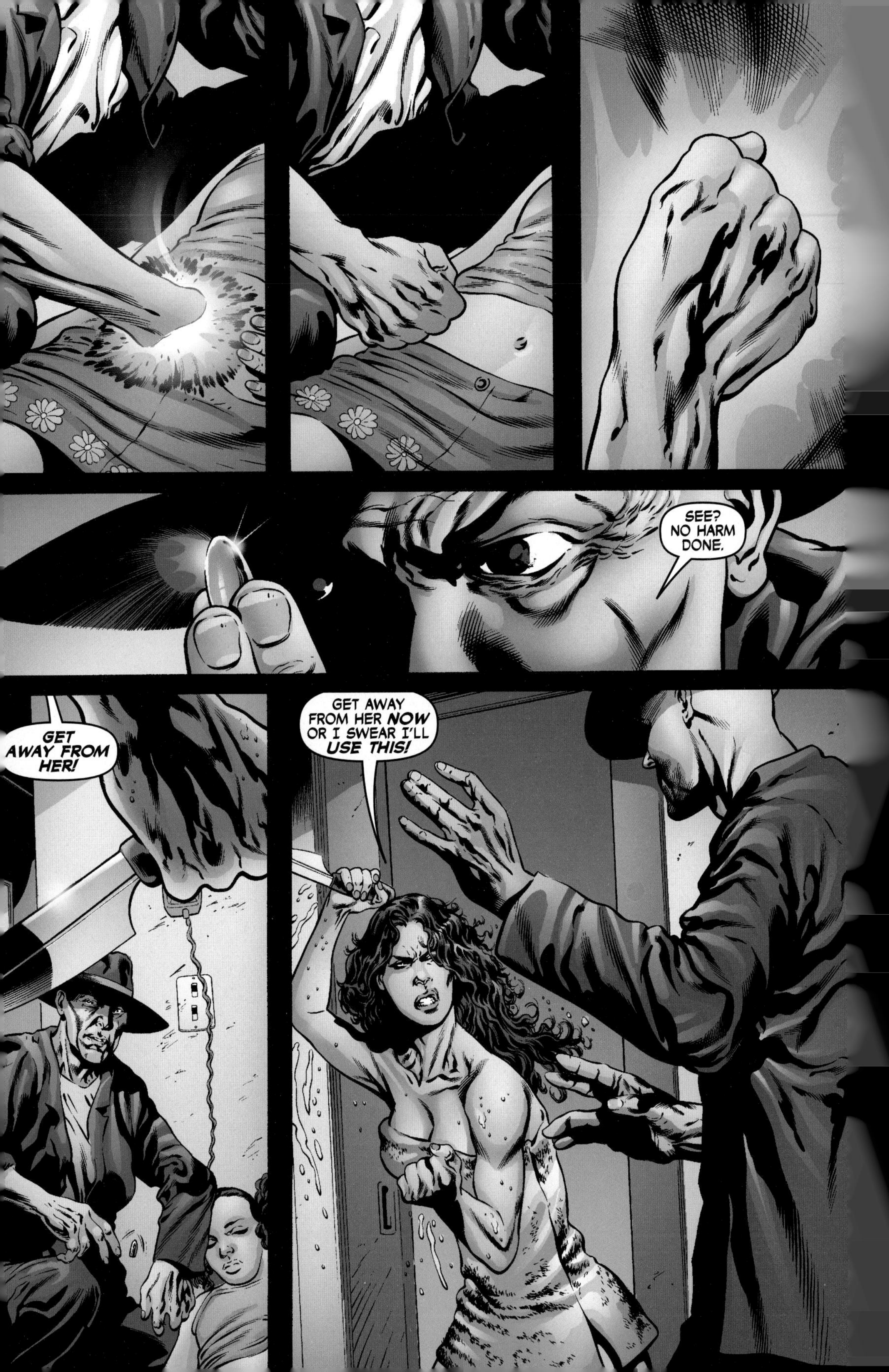
SEE? NO HARM DONE.
GET AWAY FROM HER!
GET AWAY FROM HER *NOW* OR I SWEAR I'LL *USE THIS!*

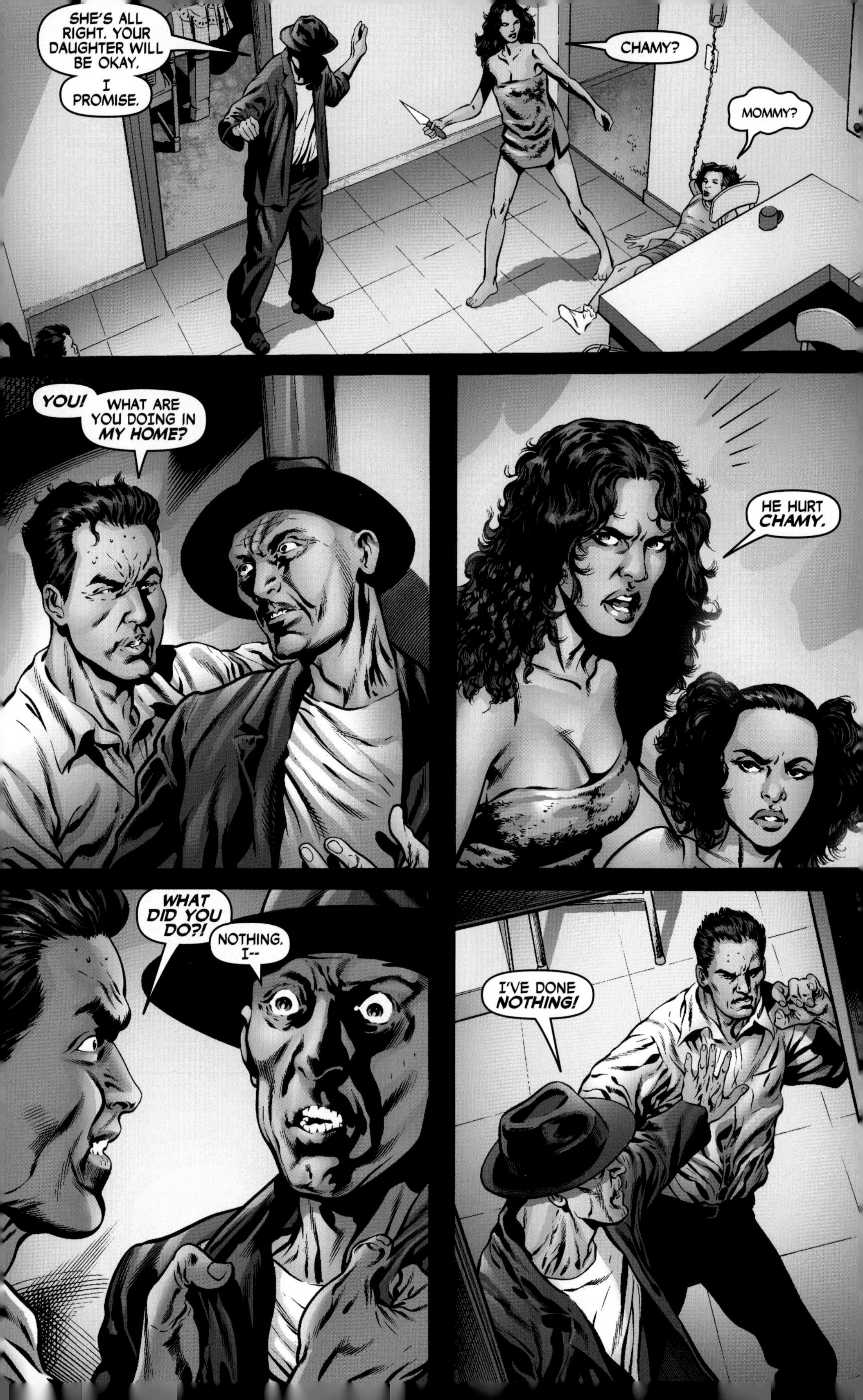
SHE'S ALL RIGHT. YOUR DAUGHTER WILL BE OKAY.
I PROMISE.
CHAMY?
MOMMY?
YOU! WHAT ARE YOU DOING IN MY HOME?
HE HURT CHAMY.
WHAT DID YOU DO?!
NOTHING. I--
I'VE DONE NOTHING!

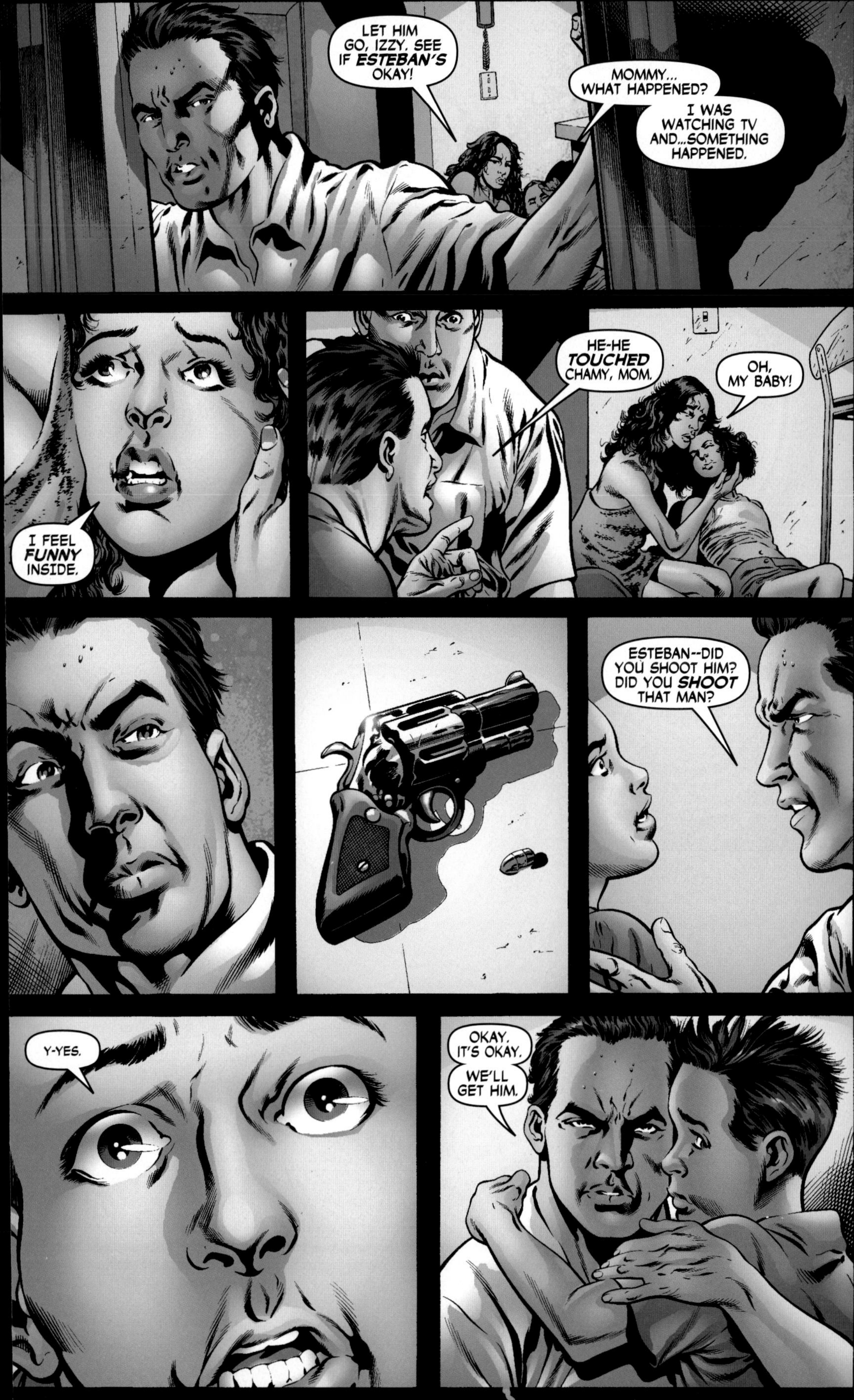
LET HIM GO, IZZY. SEE IF ESTEBAN'S OKAY!
MOMMY... WHAT HAPPENED?
I WAS WATCHING TV AND...SOMETHING HAPPENED.
I FEEL FUNNY INSIDE.
HE-HE TOUCHED CHAMY, MOM.
OH, MY BABY!
ESTEBAN--DID YOU SHOOT HIM? DID YOU SHOOT THAT MAN?
Y-YES.
OKAY. IT'S OKAY.
WE'LL GET HIM.

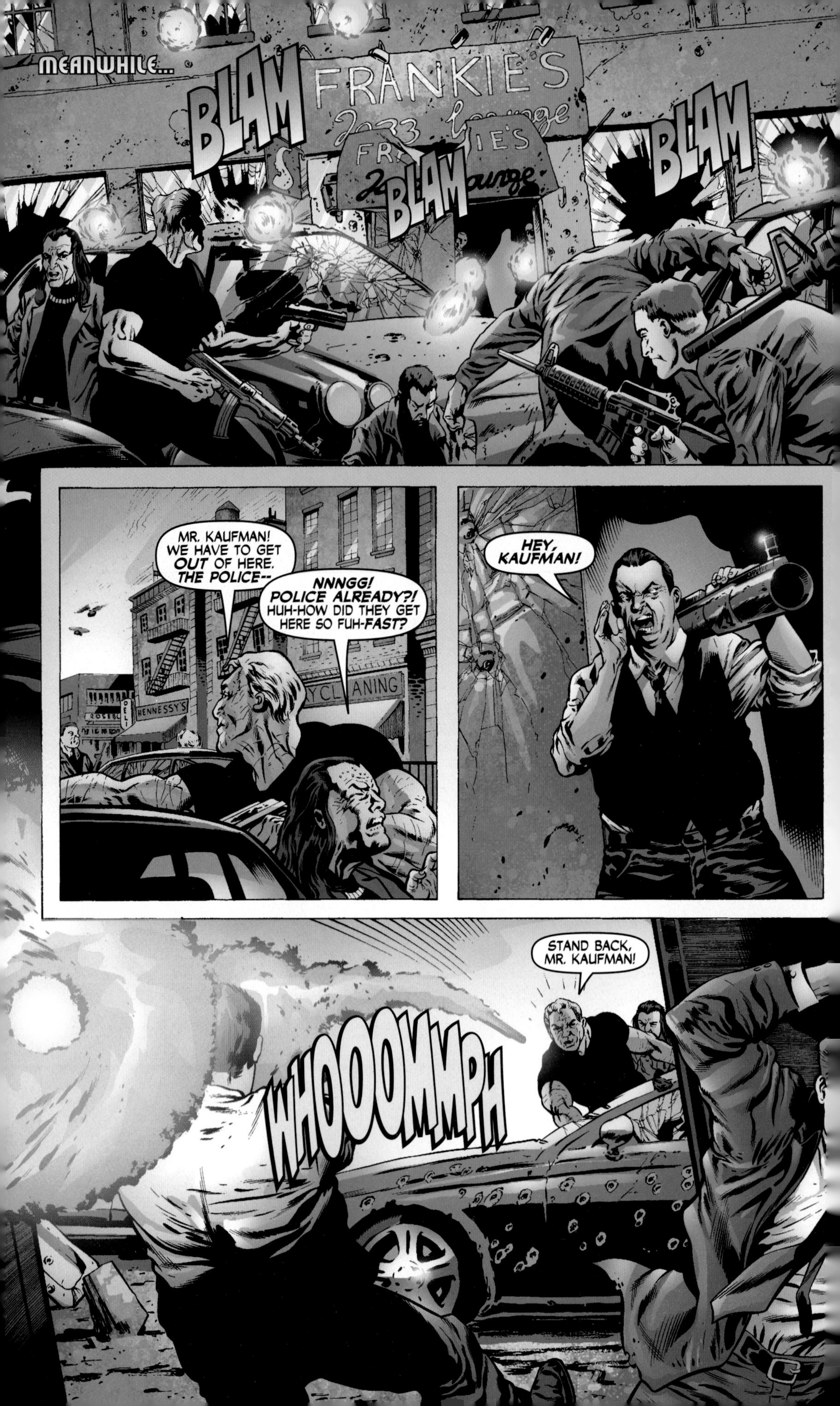
MEANWHILE...
BLAM
FRANKIE'S
Jazz Lounge
BLAM
BLAM
MR. KAUFMAN! WE HAVE TO GET OUT OF HERE. THE POLICE--
NNNGG! POLICE ALREADY?! HUH-HOW DID THEY GET HERE SO FUH-FAST?
HENNESSY'S
DELI
CLEANING
HEY, KAUFMAN!
STAND BACK, MR. KAUFMAN!
WHOOOMMPH

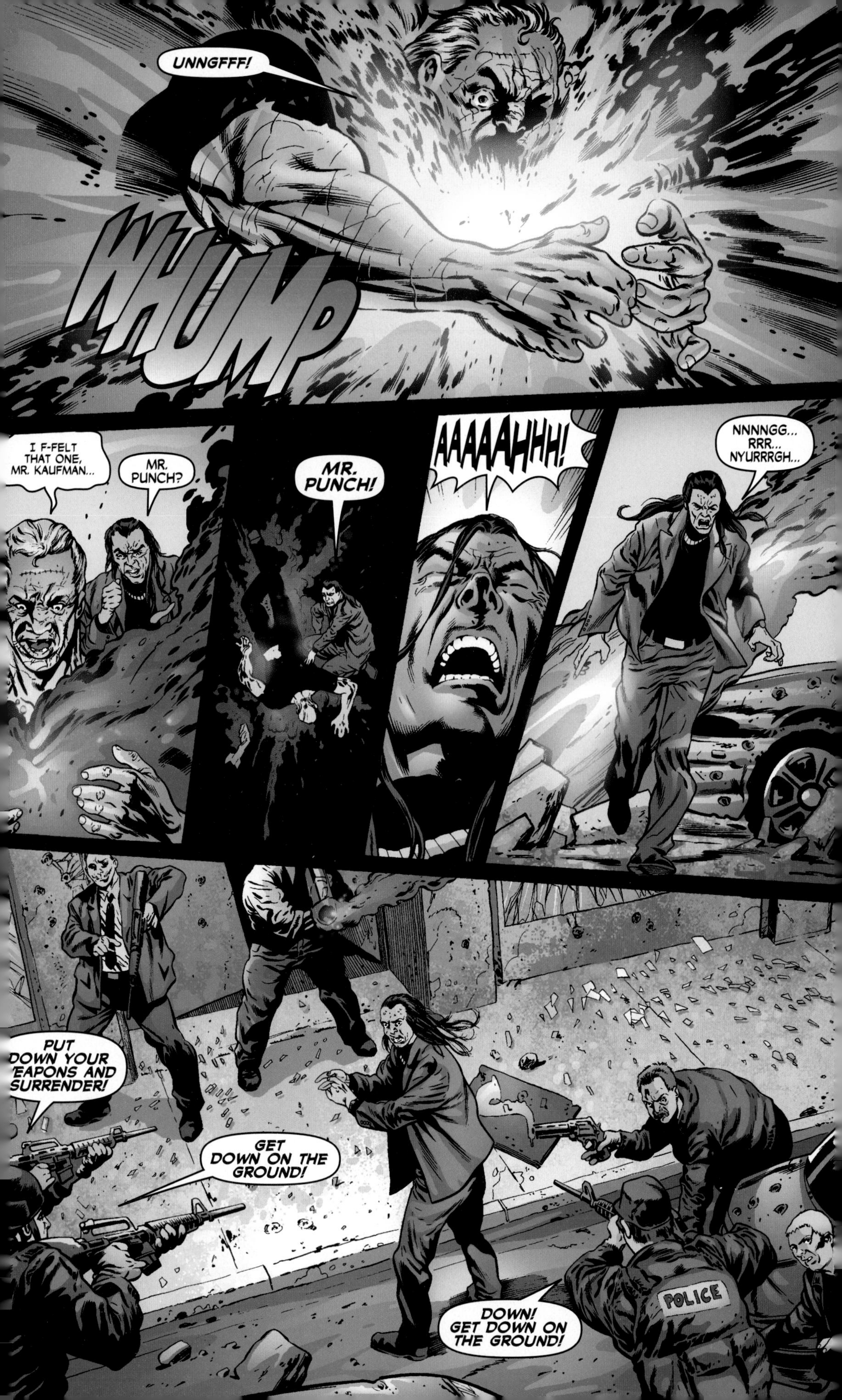
UNNGFFF!
WHUMP
I F-FELT THAT ONE, MR. KAUFMAN...
MR. PUNCH?
MR. PUNCH!
AAAAAHHH!
NNNNGG... RRR... NYURRRGH...
PUT DOWN YOUR WEAPONS AND SURRENDER!
GET DOWN ON THE GROUND!
DOWN! GET DOWN ON THE GROUND!
POLICE

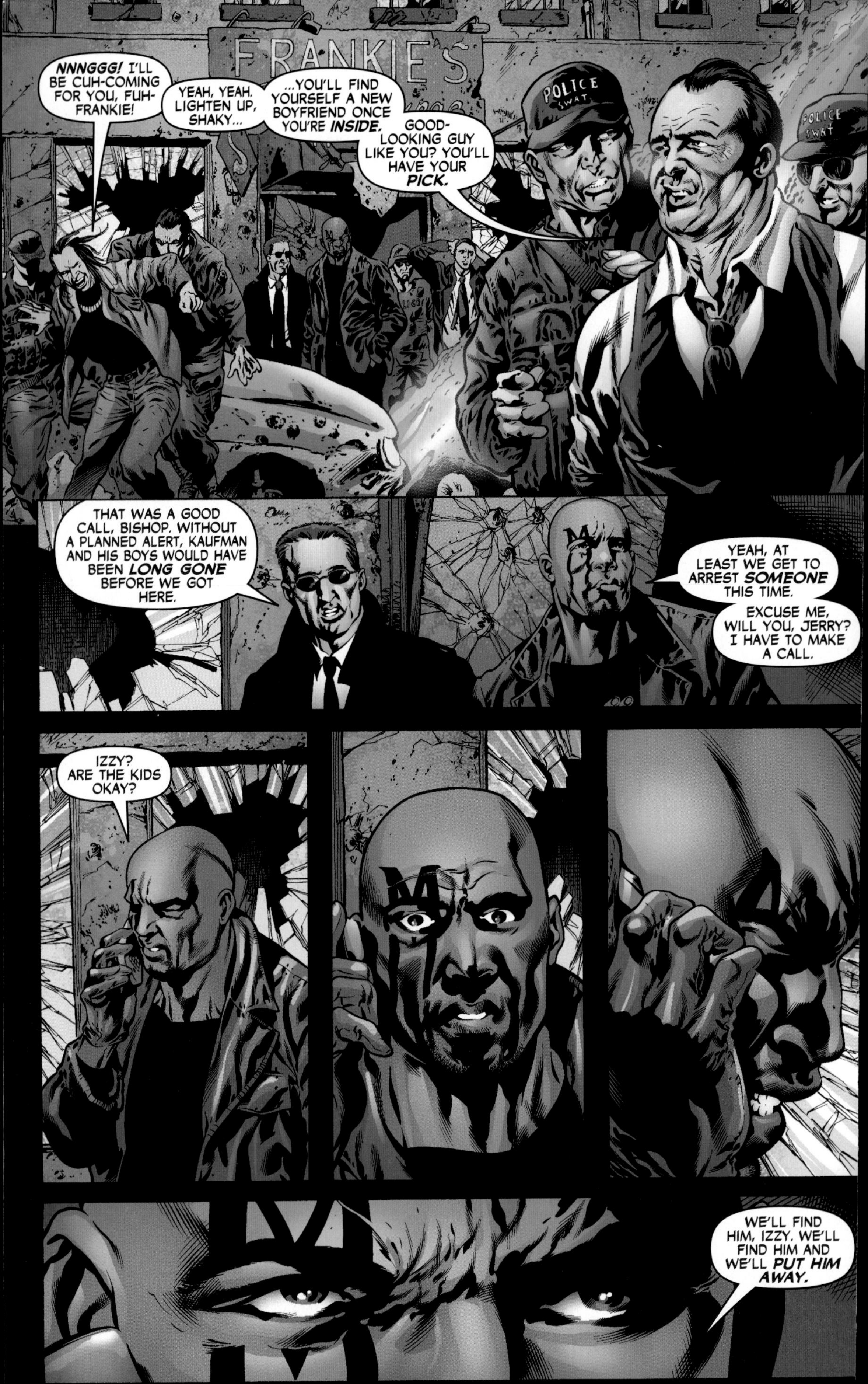
FRANKIES
NNNGGG! I'LL BE CUH-COMING FOR YOU, FUH-FRANKIE!
YEAH, YEAH. LIGHTEN UP, SHAKY...
...YOU'LL FIND YOURSELF A NEW BOYFRIEND ONCE YOU'RE INSIDE.
GOOD-LOOKING GUY LIKE YOU? YOU'LL HAVE YOUR PICK.
POLICE SWAT
THAT WAS A GOOD CALL, BISHOP. WITHOUT A PLANNED ALERT, KAUFMAN AND HIS BOYS WOULD HAVE BEEN LONG GONE BEFORE WE GOT HERE.
YEAH, AT LEAST WE GET TO ARREST SOMEONE THIS TIME.
EXCUSE ME, WILL YOU, JERRY? I HAVE TO MAKE A CALL.
IZZY? ARE THE KIDS OKAY?
WE'LL FIND HIM, IZZY. WE'LL FIND HIM AND WE'LL PUT HIM AWAY.

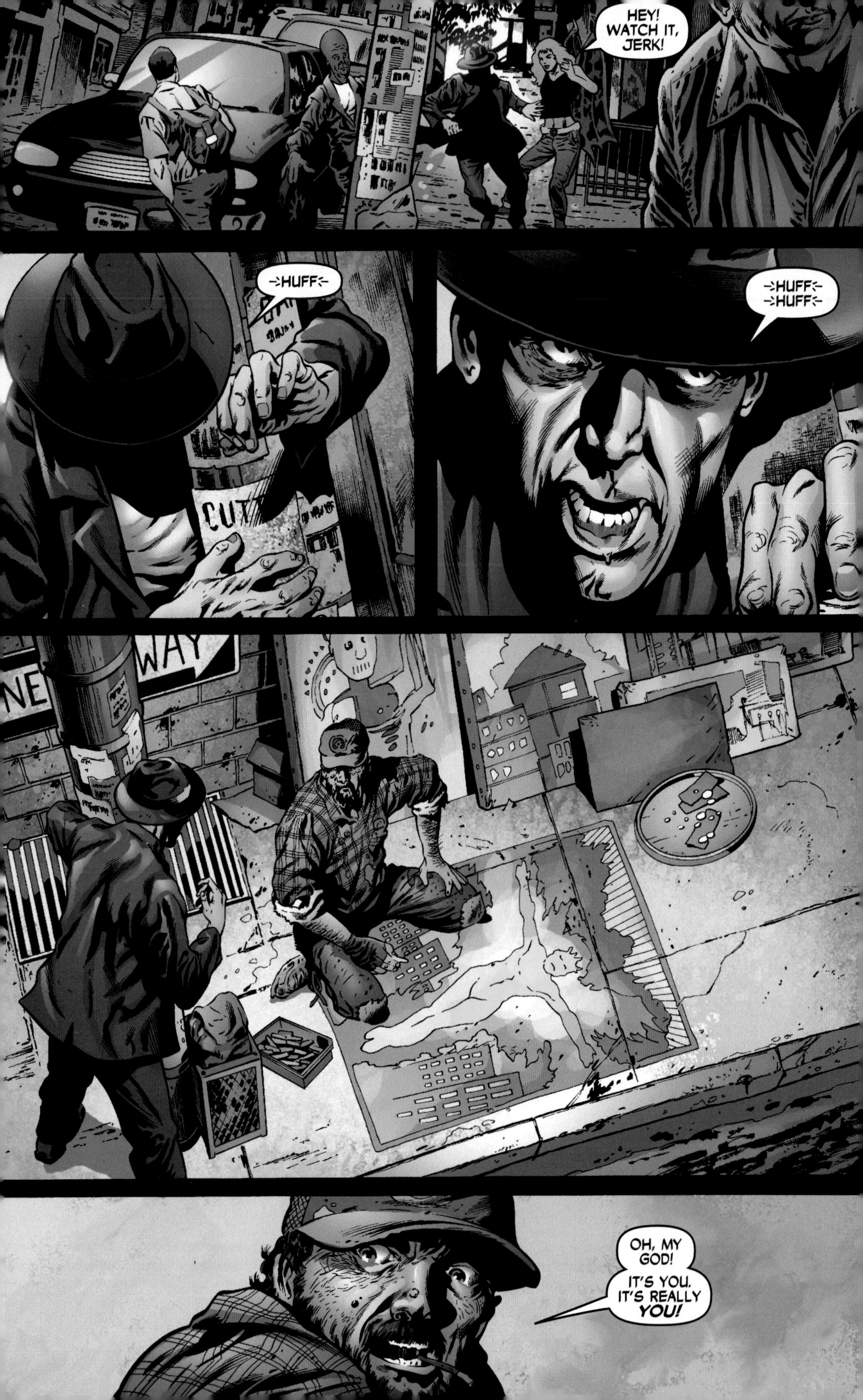
HEY! WATCH IT, JERK!
-HUFF-
-HUFF- -HUFF-
OH, MY GOD!
IT'S YOU. IT'S REALLY *YOU!*

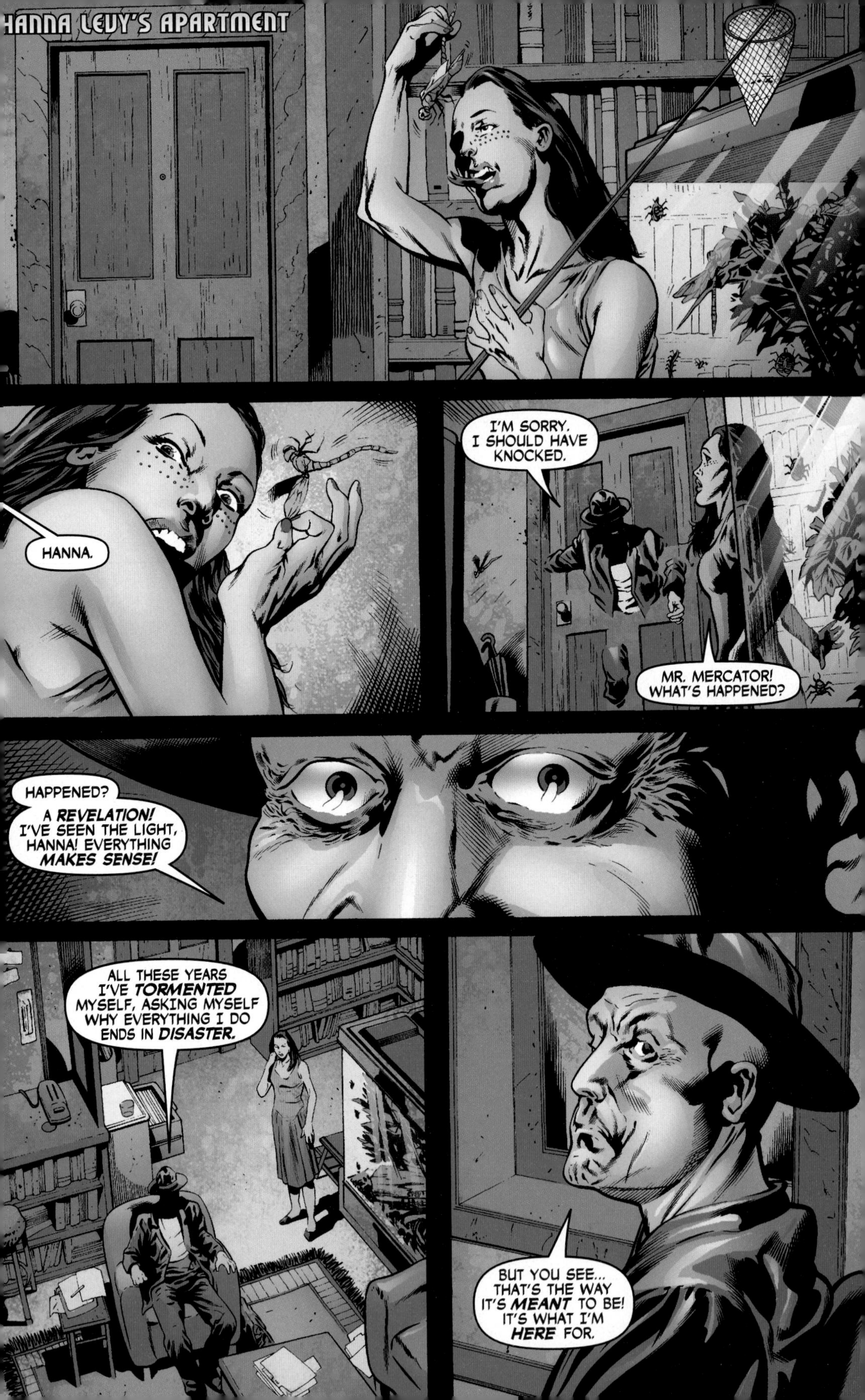
HANNA LEVY'S APARTMENT
HANNA.
I'M SORRY. I SHOULD HAVE KNOCKED.
MR. MERCATOR! WHAT'S HAPPENED?
HAPPENED? A REVELATION! I'VE SEEN THE LIGHT, HANNA! EVERYTHING MAKES SENSE!
ALL THESE YEARS I'VE TORMENTED MYSELF, ASKING MYSELF WHY EVERYTHING I DO ENDS IN DISASTER.
BUT YOU SEE... THAT'S THE WAY IT'S MEANT TO BE! IT'S WHAT I'M HERE FOR.

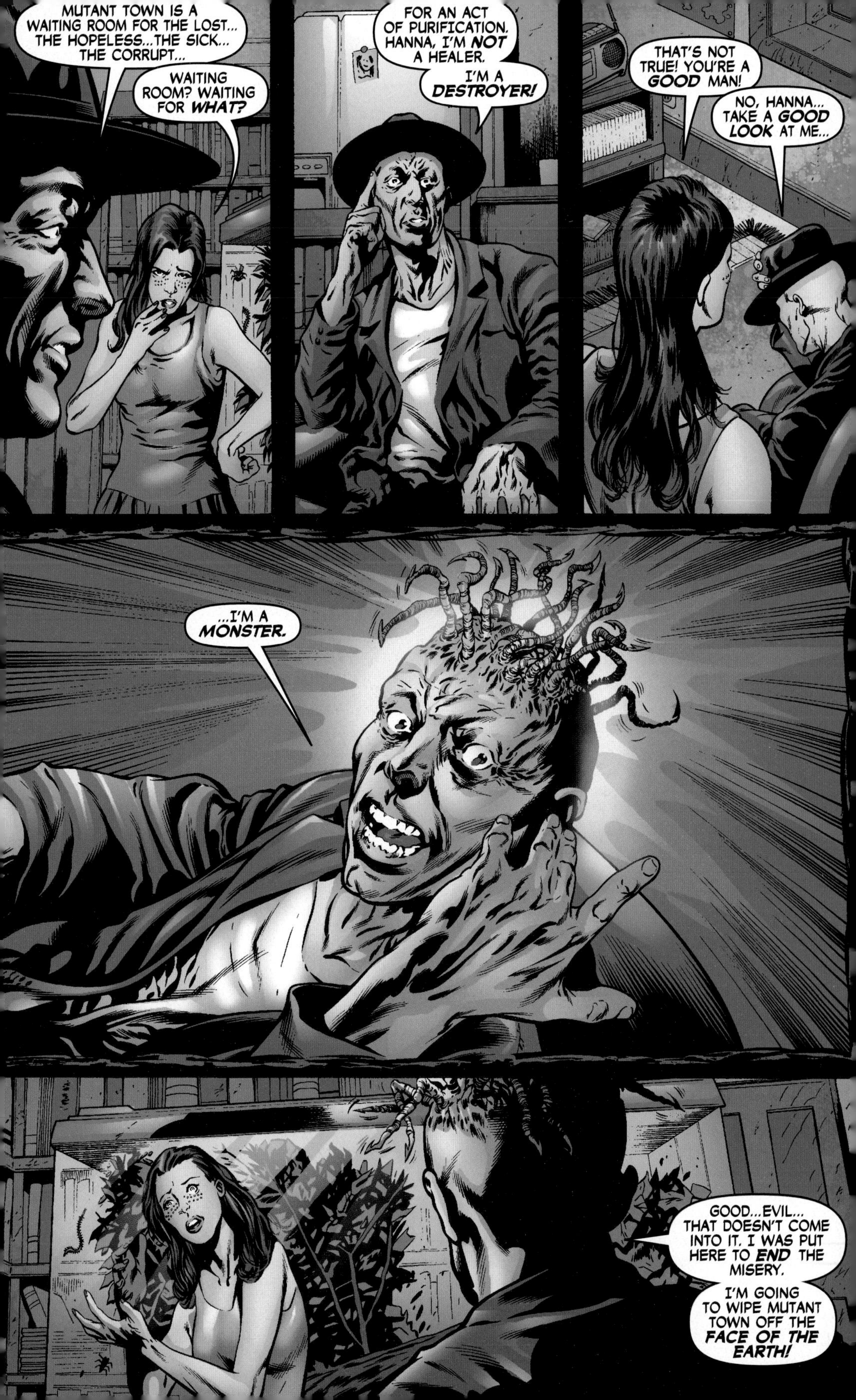
MUTANT TOWN IS A WAITING ROOM FOR THE LOST... THE HOPELESS...THE SICK... THE CORRUPT...
WAITING ROOM? WAITING FOR *WHAT?*
FOR AN ACT OF PURIFICATION. HANNA, I'M *NOT* A HEALER.
I'M A *DESTROYER!*
THAT'S NOT TRUE! YOU'RE A *GOOD* MAN!
NO, HANNA... TAKE A *GOOD LOOK* AT ME...
...I'M A *MONSTER.*
GOOD...EVIL... THAT DOESN'T COME INTO IT. I WAS PUT HERE TO *END* THE MISERY.
I'M GOING TO WIPE MUTANT TOWN OFF THE *FACE OF THE EARTH!*

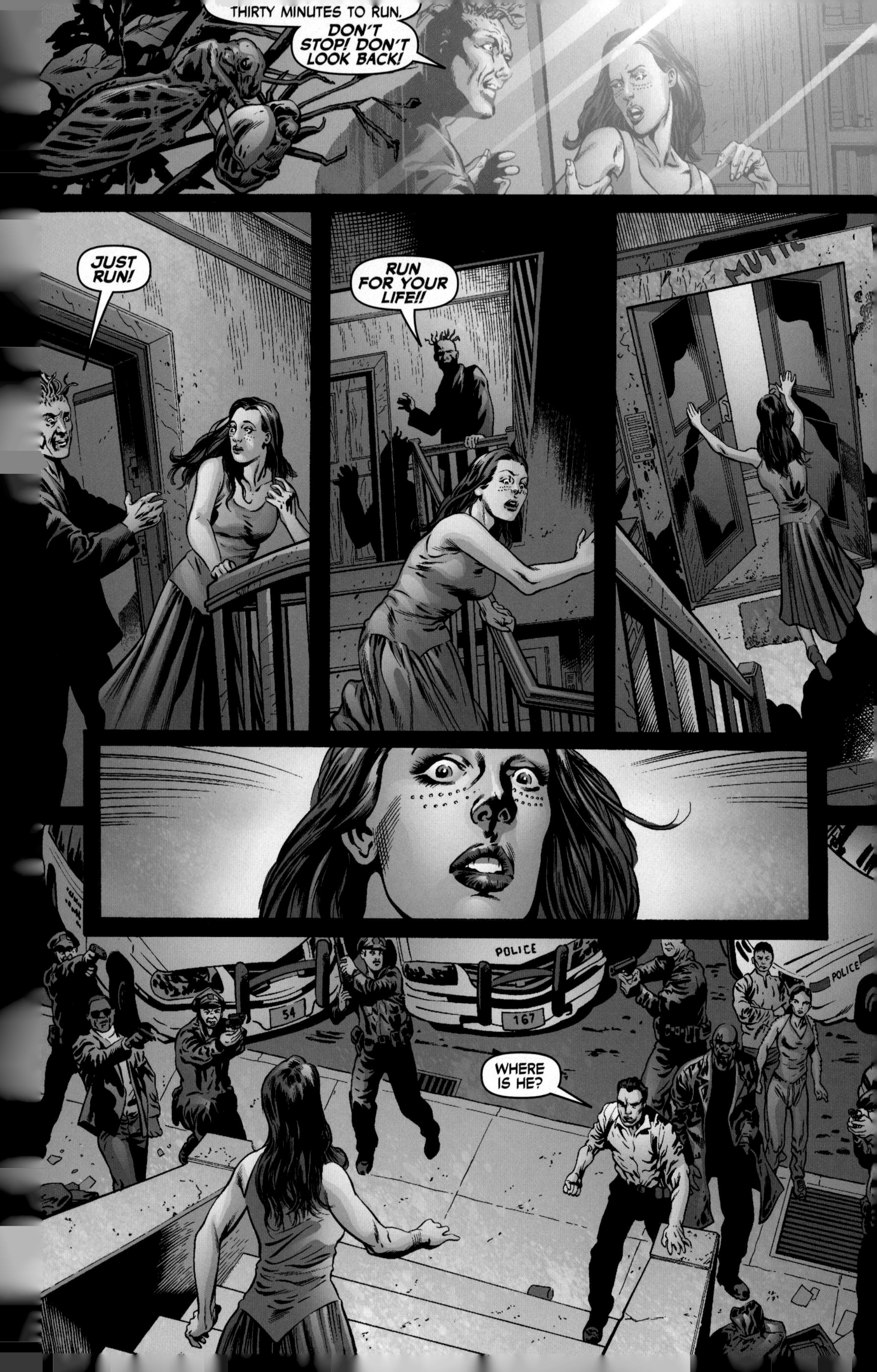
THIRTY MINUTES TO RUN. DON'T STOP! DON'T LOOK BACK!
JUST RUN!
RUN FOR YOUR LIFE!!
MUTIE
POLICE
54
167
POLICE
WHERE IS HE?

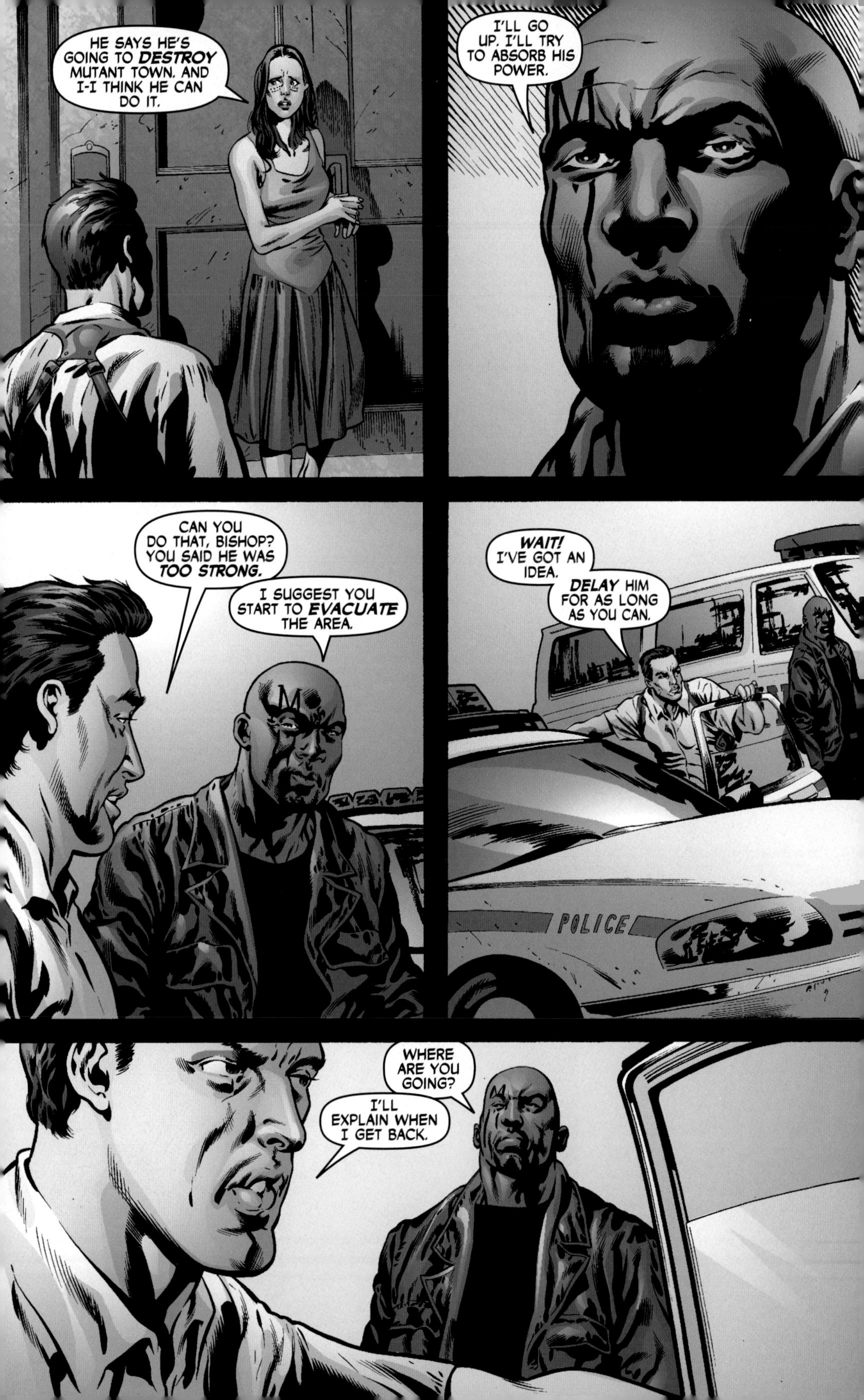
HE SAYS HE'S GOING TO **DESTROY** MUTANT TOWN. AND I-I THINK HE CAN DO IT.
I'LL GO UP. I'LL TRY TO ABSORB HIS POWER.
CAN YOU DO THAT, BISHOP? YOU SAID HE WAS **TOO STRONG.**
I SUGGEST YOU START TO **EVACUATE** THE AREA.
WAIT! I'VE GOT AN IDEA.
DELAY HIM FOR AS LONG AS YOU CAN.
POLICE
WHERE ARE YOU GOING?
I'LL EXPLAIN WHEN I GET BACK.

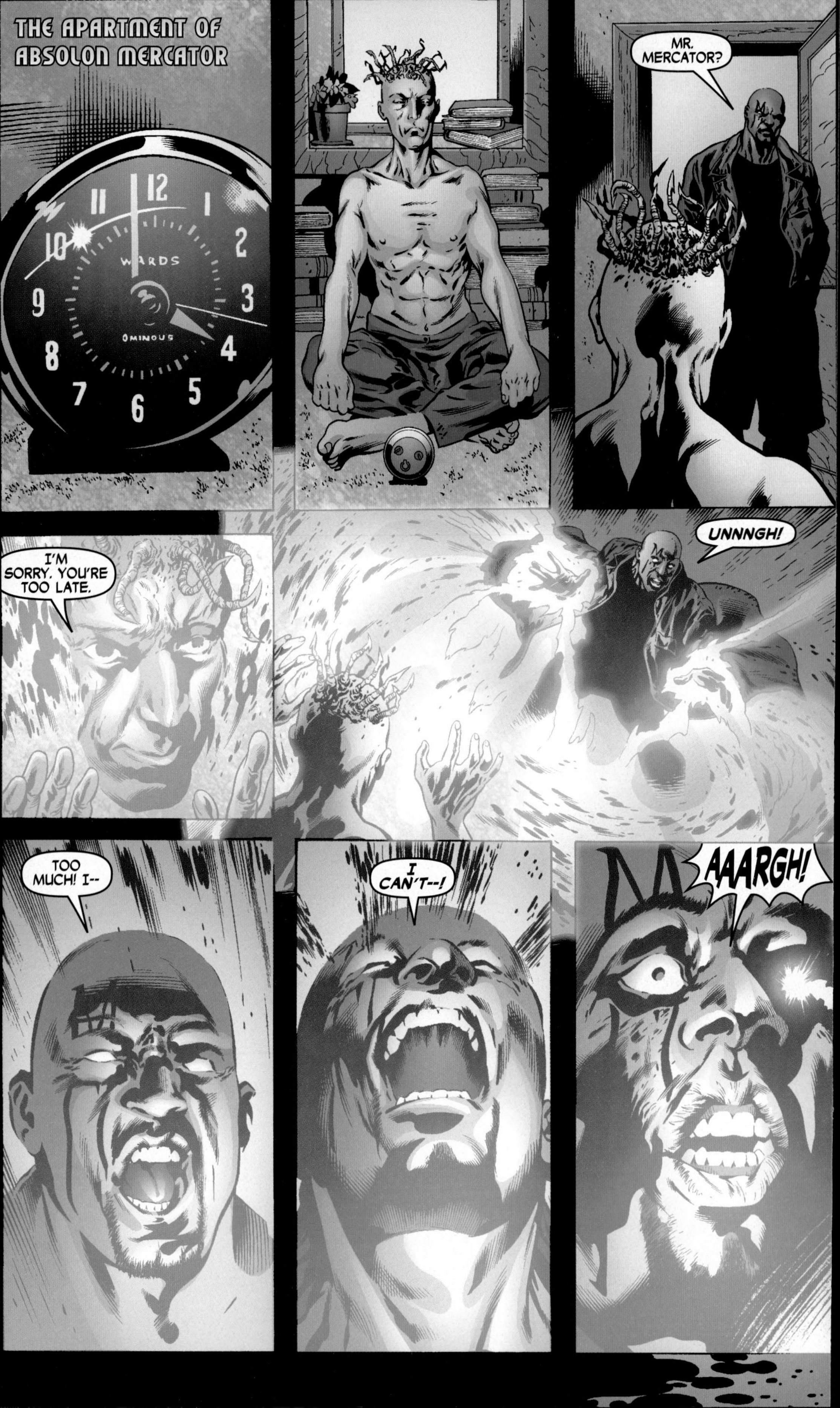
THE APARTMENT OF ABSOLON MERCATOR
WARDS
OMINOUS
MR. MERCATOR?
I'M SORRY. YOU'RE TOO LATE.
UNNNGH!
TOO MUCH! I--
I CAN'T--!
AAARGH!

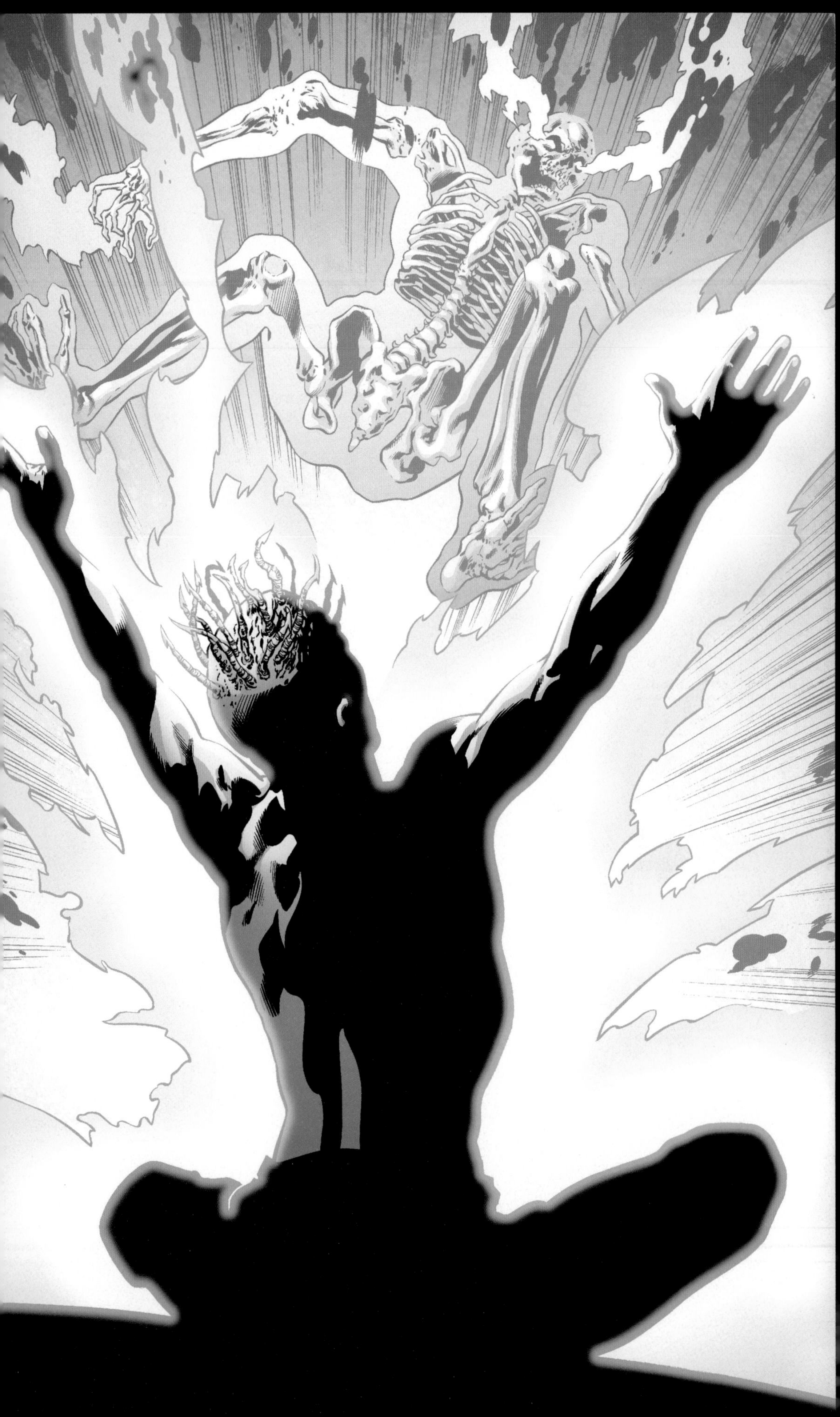

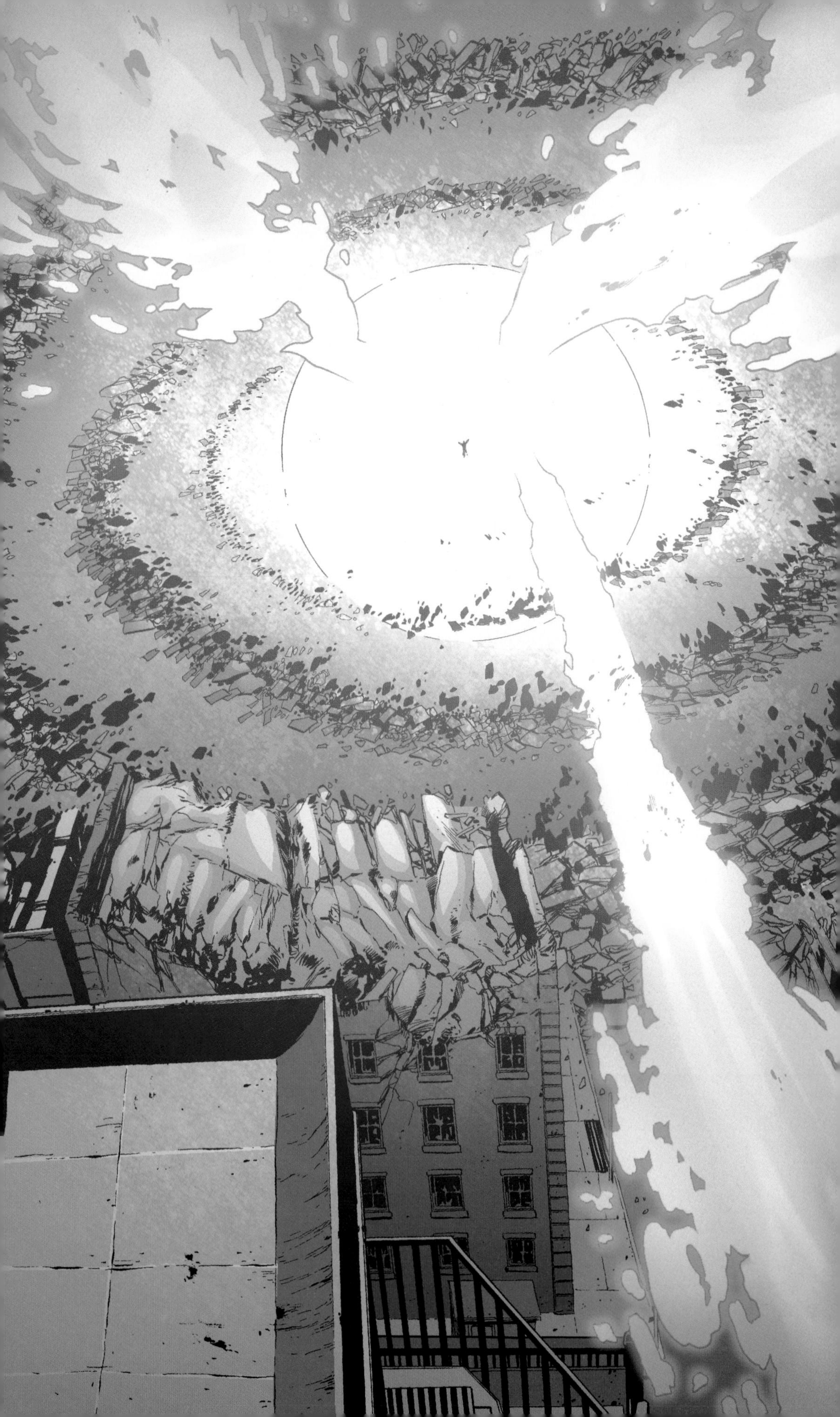

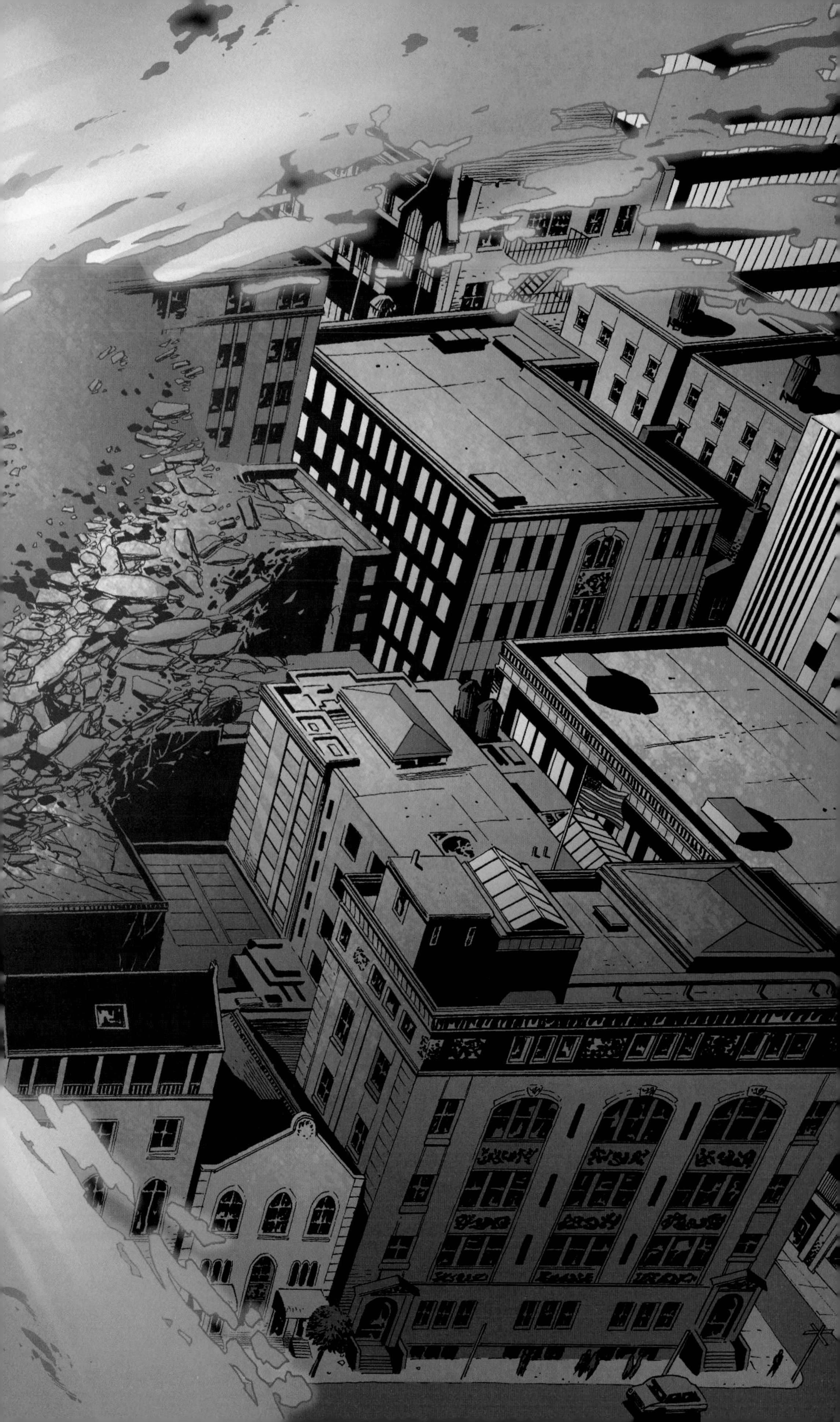

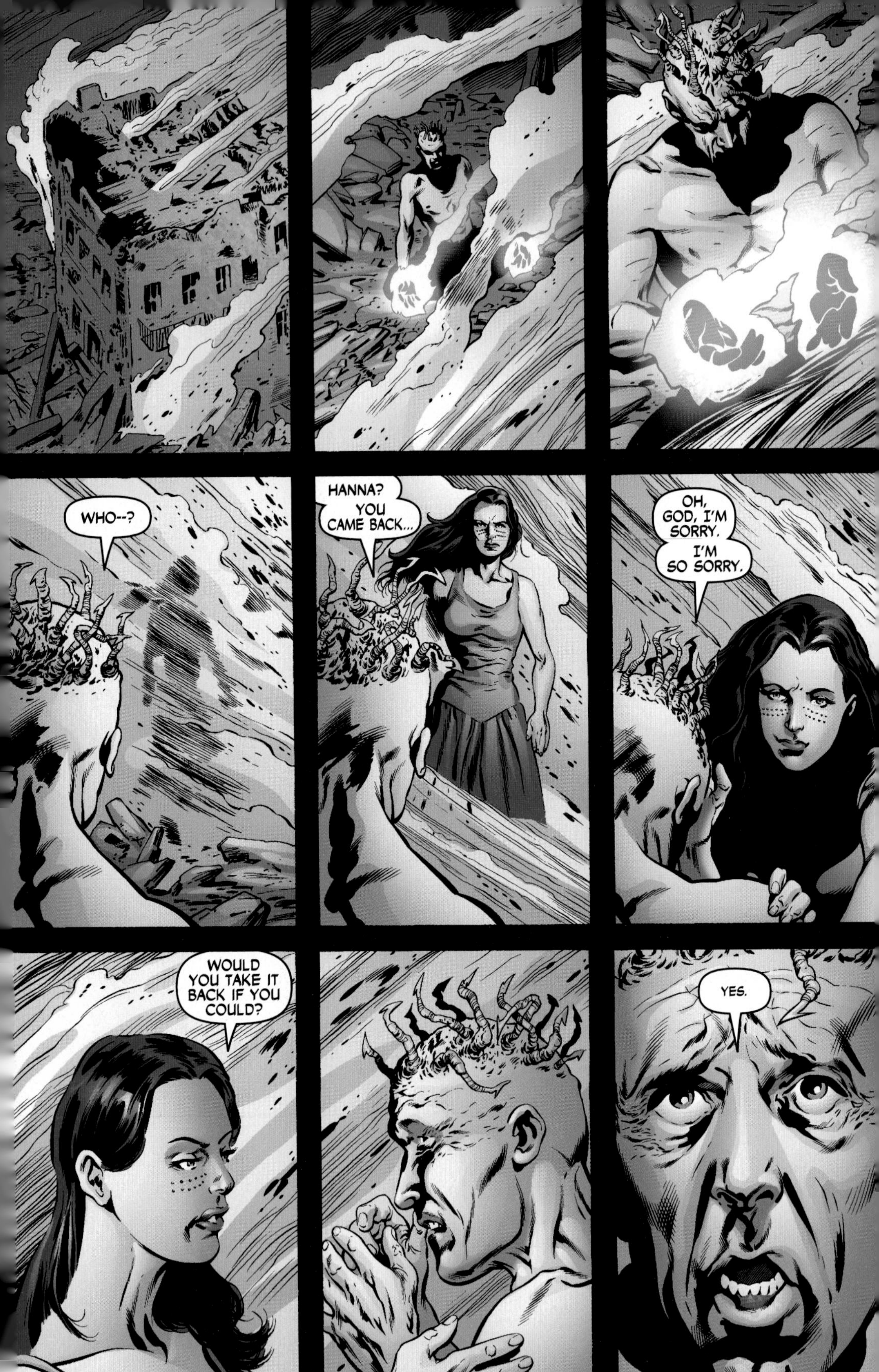
WHO--?
HANNA? YOU CAME BACK...
OH, GOD, I'M SORRY.
I'M SO SORRY.
WOULD YOU TAKE IT BACK IF YOU COULD?
YES.

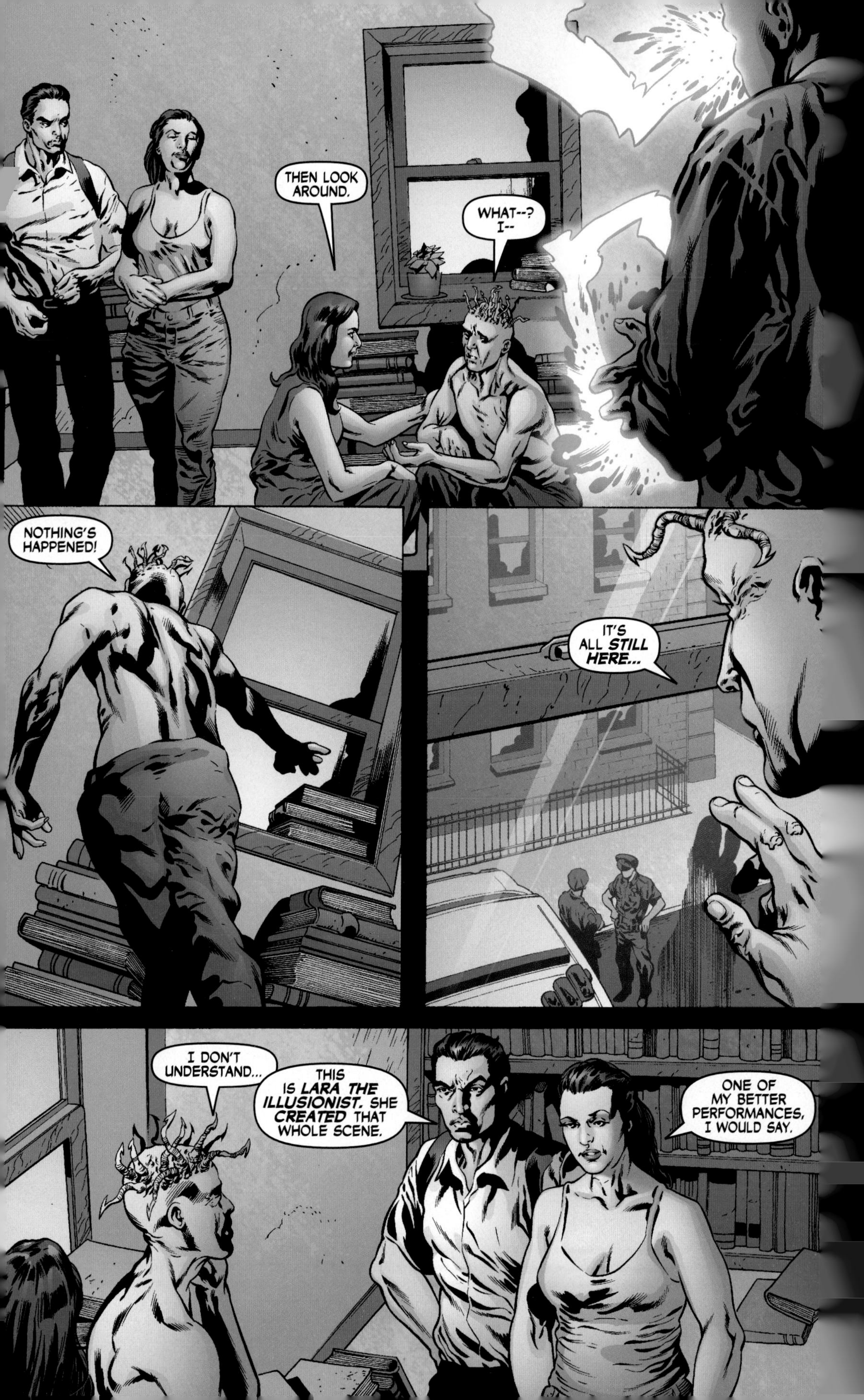
THEN LOOK AROUND.
WHAT--? I--
NOTHING'S HAPPENED!
IT'S ALL STILL HERE...
I DON'T UNDERSTAND...
THIS IS LARA THE ILLUSIONIST. SHE CREATED THAT WHOLE SCENE.
ONE OF MY BETTER PERFORMANCES, I WOULD SAY.

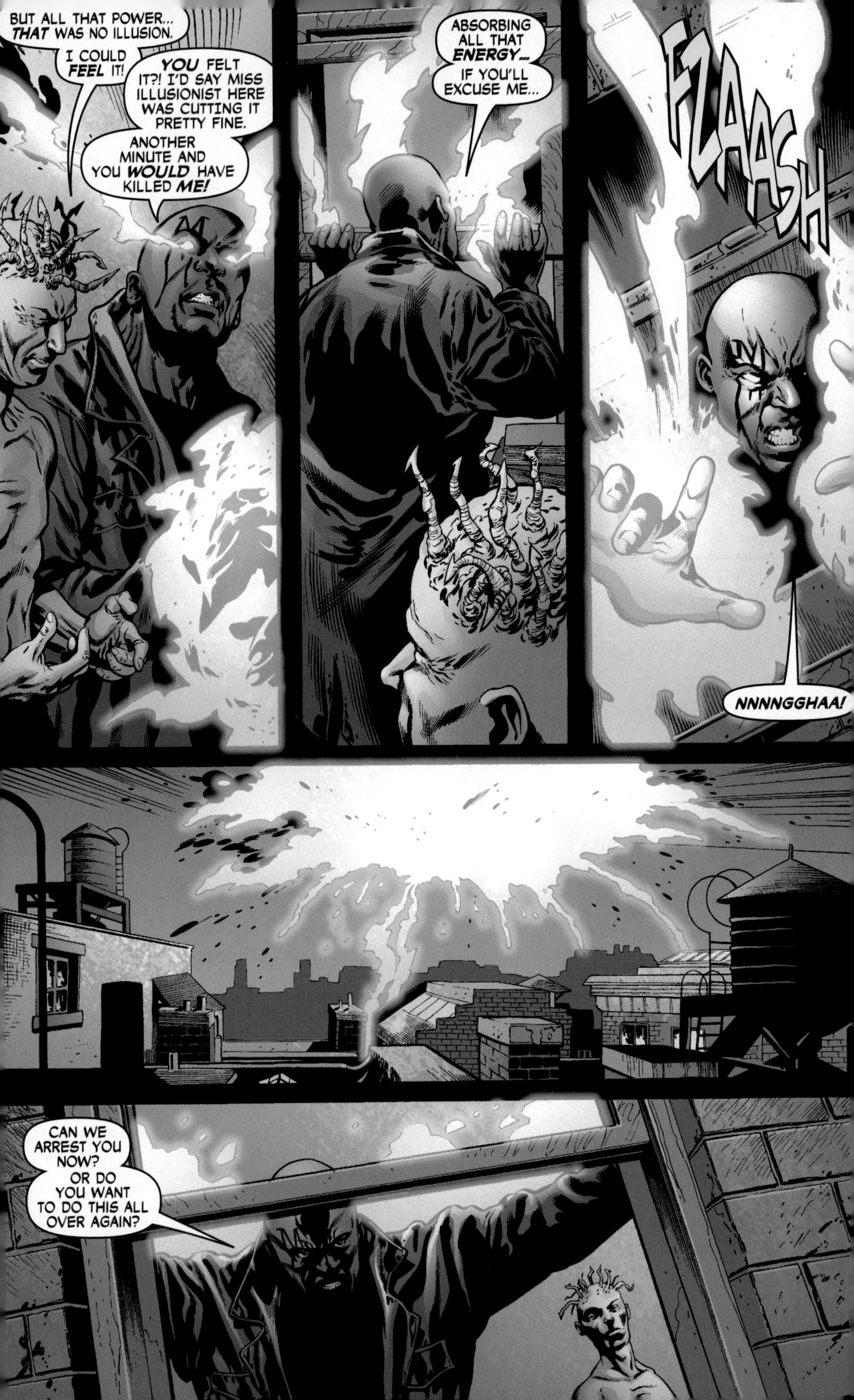
BUT ALL THAT POWER... THAT WAS NO ILLUSION.
I COULD FEEL IT!
YOU FELT IT?! I'D SAY MISS ILLUSIONIST HERE WAS CUTTING IT PRETTY FINE.
ANOTHER MINUTE AND YOU WOULD HAVE KILLED ME!
ABSORBING ALL THAT ENERGY... IF YOU'LL EXCUSE ME...
FZAASH
NNNNGGHAA!
CAN WE ARREST YOU NOW? OR DO YOU WANT TO DO THIS ALL OVER AGAIN?

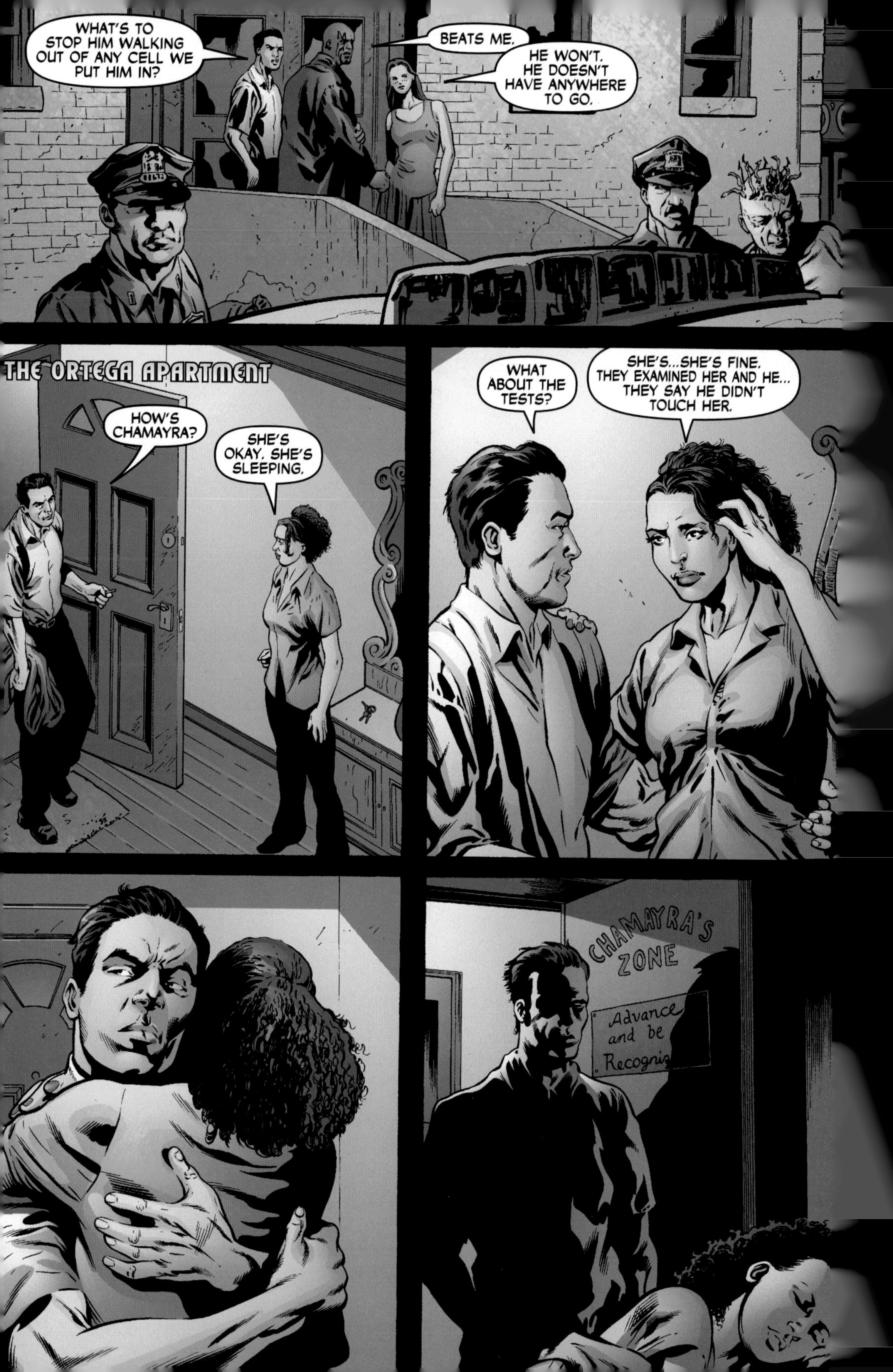
WHAT'S TO STOP HIM WALKING OUT OF ANY CELL WE PUT HIM IN?
BEATS ME.
HE WON'T. HE DOESN'T HAVE ANYWHERE TO GO.
THE ORTEGA APARTMENT
HOW'S CHAMAYRA?
SHE'S OKAY. SHE'S SLEEPING.
WHAT ABOUT THE TESTS?
SHE'S...SHE'S FINE. THEY EXAMINED HER AND HE... THEY SAY HE DIDN'T TOUCH HER.
CHAMAYRA'S ZONE
Advance and be Recogni

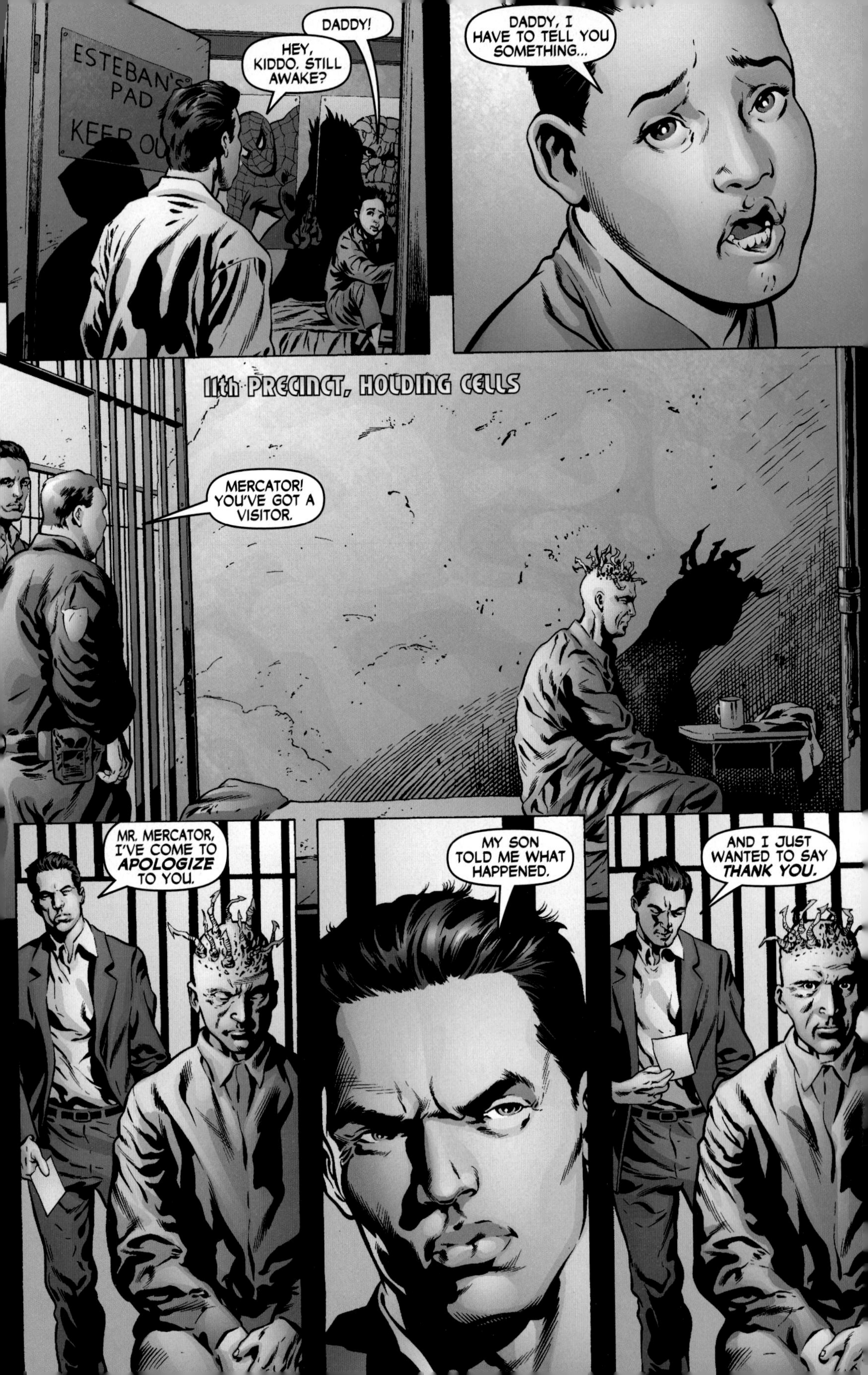
ESTEBAN'S PAD
KEEP OU
DADDY!
HEY, KIDDO. STILL AWAKE?
DADDY, I HAVE TO TELL YOU SOMETHING...
11th PRECINCT, HOLDING CELLS
MERCATOR! YOU'VE GOT A VISITOR.
MR. MERCATOR, I'VE COME TO *APOLOGIZE* TO YOU.
MY SON TOLD ME WHAT HAPPENED.
AND I JUST WANTED TO SAY *THANK YOU.*

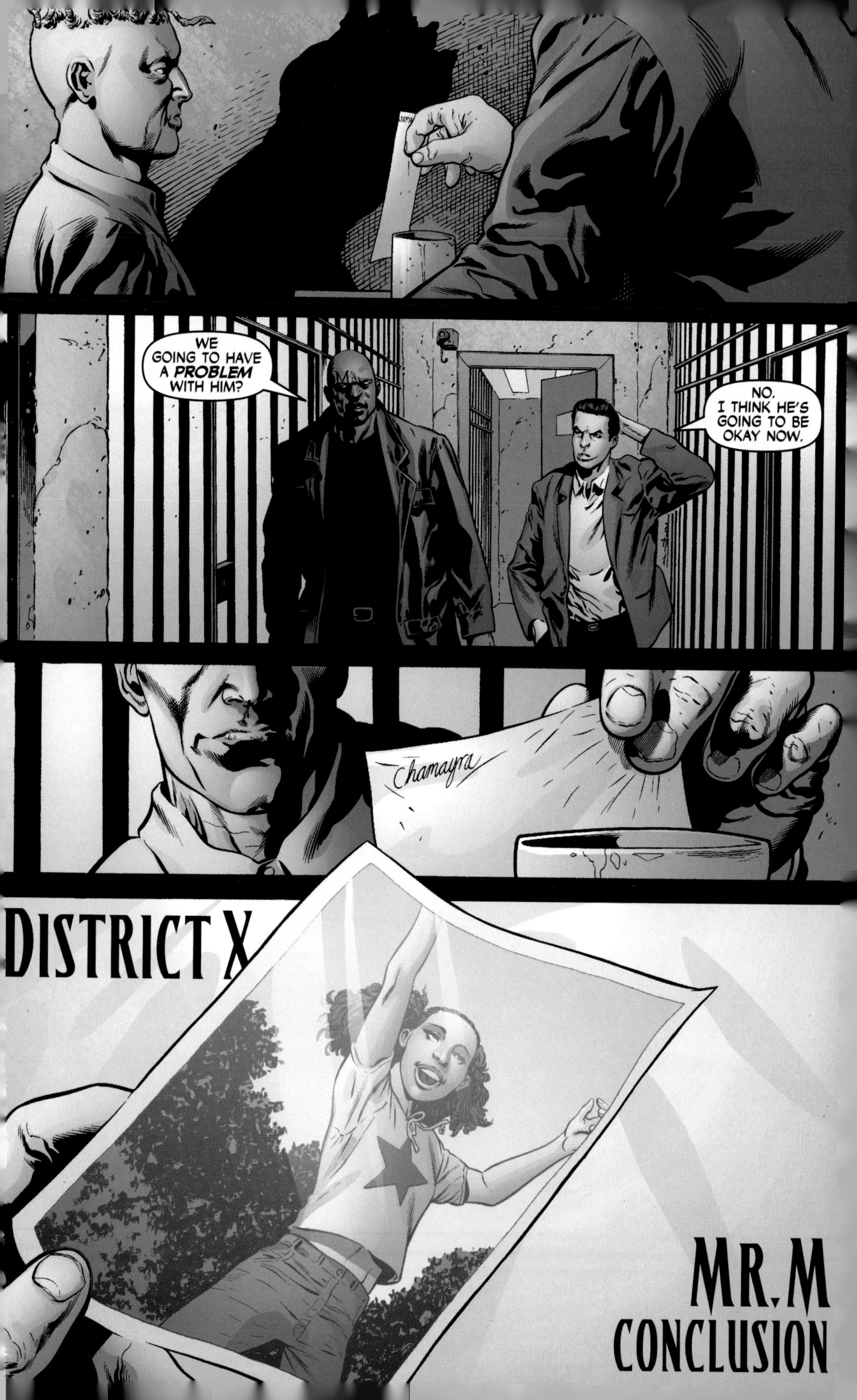
WE GOING TO HAVE A PROBLEM WITH HIM?
NO, I THINK HE'S GOING TO BE OKAY NOW.
Chamayra
DISTRICT X
MR. M
CONCLUSION

Character Sketches
By David Yardi

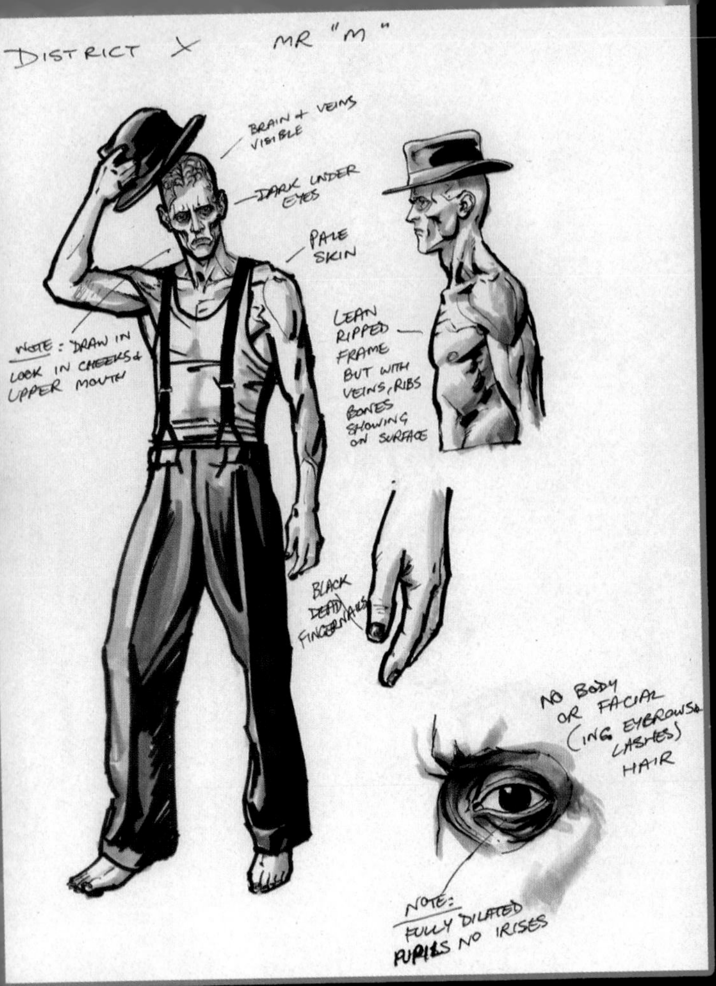
DISTRICT X MR "M"
BRAIN + VEINS VISIBLE
DARK UNDER EYES
PALE SKIN
NOTE: DRAW IN LOOK IN CHEEKS & UPPER MOUTH
LEAN RIPPED FRAME BUT WITH VEINS, RIBS BONES SHOWING ON SURFACE
BLACK DEAD FINGERNAILS
NO BODY OR FACIAL (ING EYEBROWS & LASHES) HAIR
NOTE: FULLY DILATED PUPILS NO IRISES

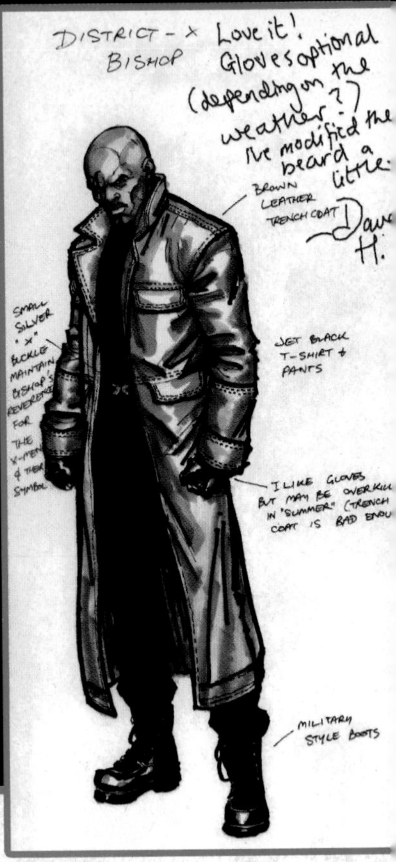
DISTRICT - X BISHOP
Love it! Gloves optional (depending on the weather?) I've modified the beard a little.
BROWN LEATHER TRENCH COAT
SMALL SILVER "X" BUCKLE MAINTAIN BISHOP'S REVERENCE FOR THE X-MEN & THEIR SYMBOL
JET BLACK T-SHIRT & PANTS
I LIKE GLOVES BUT MAY BE OVERKILL IN "SUMMER" (TRENCH COAT IS BAD ENOU
MILITARY STYLE BOOTS

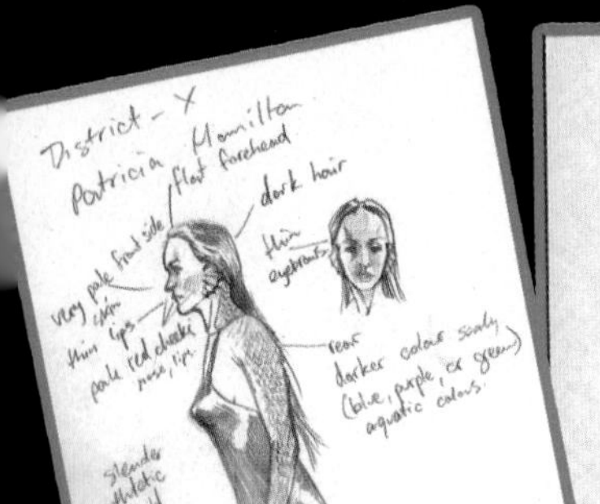
District - X
Patricia Hamilton
flat forehead
dark hair
thin eyebrows
very pale fund side
thin lips
pale red cheeks nose, lips
darker colour scaly (blue, purple, or green) aquatic colours
slender athletic build

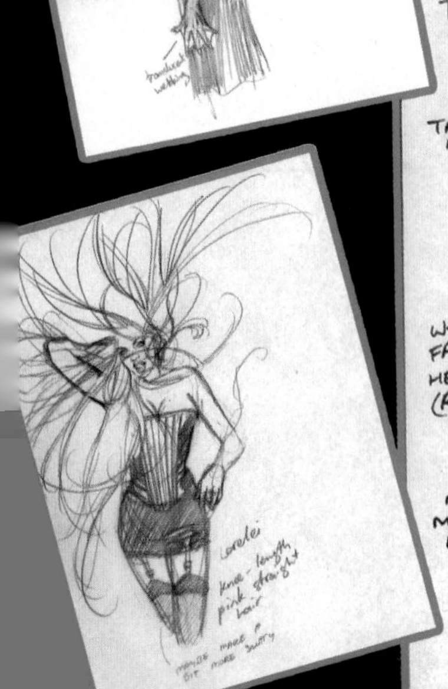
Lorelei
knee-length pink straight hair

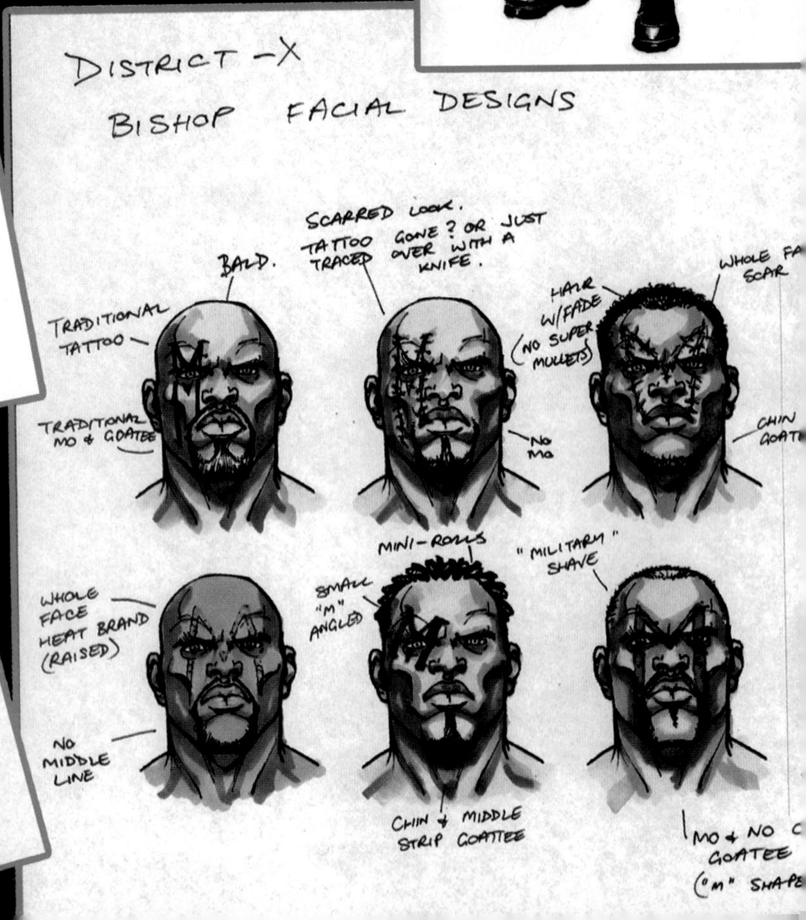
DISTRICT -X
BISHOP FACIAL DESIGNS
BALD.
TRADITIONAL TATTOO
TRADITIONAL MO & GOATEE
SCARRED LOOK. TATTOO GONE? OR JUST TRACED OVER WITH A KNIFE.
NO MO
HAIR W/FADE (NO SUPER MULLETS)
WHOLE FA SCAR
CHIN GOATE
WHOLE FACE HEAT BRAND (RAISED)
NO MIDDLE LINE
MINI-ROLLS
SMALL "M" ANGLED
CHIN & MIDDLE STRIP GOATEE
"MILITARY" SHAVE
MO & NO C GOATEE ("M" SHAPE